Separated and Divorced Women in India

Separated and Divorced Women in India

Economic Rights and Entitlements

Kirti Singh

International Development Research Centre
Ottawa • Cairo • Montevideo • Nairobi • New Delhi

SAGE www.sagepublications.com
Los Angeles • London • New Delhi • Singapore • Washington DC

Jointly published in 2013 by

SAGE Publications India Pvt Ltd
B1/I-1 Mohan Cooperative Industrial Area
Mathura Road, New Delhi 110 044, India
www.sagepub.in

SAGE Publications Inc
2455 Teller Road
Thousand Oaks, California 91320, USA

SAGE Publications Ltd
1 Oliver's Yard, 55 City Road
London EC1Y 1SP, United Kingdom

SAGE Publications Asia-Pacific Pte Ltd
33 Pekin Street
#02-01 Far East Square
Singapore 048763

International Development Research Centre
P.O. Box 8500
Ottawa, ON
Canada K1G 3H9
www.idrc.ca
info@idrc.ca
ISBN (e-book) 978-1-55250-551-9

Published by Vivek Mehra for SAGE Publications India Pvt Ltd, typeset in 10/12pt Adobe Garamond by RECTO Graphics, Delhi and printed at De-Unique, New Delhi.

Library of Congress Cataloging-in-Publication Data

Singh, Kirti.

Separated and divorced women in India: economic rights and entitlements/Kirti Singh.

pages cm

Includes bibliographical references and index.

1. Divorced women—India—Economic conditions. 2. Separated women—India—Economic conditions. 3. Separated maintenance—India. 4. Divorced women—Legal status, laws, etc.—India. I. Title.

HQ928.S56 306.89'30954—dc23 2013 2012046755

ISBN: 978-81-321-0952-5 (HB)

The SAGE Team: Rudra Narayan, Aniruddha De, Anju Saxena and Rajinder Kaur

To my parents, Vir Bala Singh and Mahendra Pratap Singh.

Contents

Tables

Graphs

Foreword

I must congratulate the compilers of the survey report on 'Economic Rights and Entitlements of Women'. I am really honoured to have been asked to write the foreword to this report. 'The history of women's work needs to be retold ... as part of the story of the creation of a gendered workforce.'[1]

This report demonstrates that marriage, parenting, divorce, separation, etc., fall unequally on women. The surveyors have met women from the north, east, south and west. One sentence in the report gives the clue to the ills that afflict women's entitlement to economic resources:

> Women's economic position is adverse as neither Indian law nor Government policy views the work at home as productive work with economic value.

Two judgments recently have spoken on the importance of giving an economic worth to the homemaker's work. First, in *National Insurance Co. v Minor Deepika and Ors*, the Madras High Court dealt with it, and then in *Arun Kumar Agarwal v National Insurance Co.*, the Supreme Court has laid down the law by approving of the Madras High Court's decision.

The survey has been made of women belonging to the four regions of India—north, east, south and west. It has looked at women and recorded the differences on the basis of caste and religion; it has also viewed them from various perspectives, like lifestyle, family support, educational qualification, work status, etc. It has looked at women's conditions before marriage, during marriage and after the dissolution of the marriage. It is very interesting to read the comparison between the four regions of our country as regards percentage of arranged marriages, percentage of men who help at home with household chores, the drop in the number of working women after marriage, etc.

The report shows that women do suffer an economic loss after death of the spouse or divorce or desertion. The study is divided into several chapters: (*a*) work status and earning capacity; (*b*) family status and lifestyle; (*c*) spousal

---

[1] Joan W. Scott, 'Deconstructing Equality versus Difference: Or the uses of Post Structuralist Theory for Feminism', in *Applications of Feminist Legal Theory: Sex, Violence, Work & Reproduction*, ed. D. Kelly Weisberg (Temple University Press, Philadelphia USA, 1996), 611–623.

and child support and the dowry system; and (*d*) social status, mobility, skills and decision making. These chapter headings are self-explanatory. In each chapter, in addition to the survey results, real life cases are given; e.g., 'Fighting for her share', 'No maintenance for a working woman', 'A hostile natal family', 'From plentiful to restricted means and lifestyle', etc. These case studies bring to life the problems that the survey records.

The report quotes from Justice Claire L'Heureux-Dube's 'Economic Consequences of Divorce: A View from Canada', 'To recognize that each spouse is an equal and social partner in marriage regardless of function is a monumental revision of assumptions.'[2] It shows us that no simple solutions are possible. The right to maintenance is limited and many women do not even know how much their husbands earn. In order to get money for minimum financial security from her spouse, she often gets assistance only from her natal family. In the courts too she faces many difficulties. The difficulties may take many forms—delay in courts, court's attitude, procrastination and harassment. Maintenance is a substantive relief and this must be understood by the players in the justice delivery system.

The truth is that a woman faces many hurdles by the time she gets, what she claims, if at all she does. The property, movable or immovable is not going to fall on her lap—that is not to say that the judges dismiss all the petitions filed by the women—but going to courts is really an ordeal for women. Women are not equally positioned in the political, economical or social space. The report shows that even after several years of marriage, when a marriage breaks down, the woman becomes asset-less. Thus, the report recommends that the right to divorce without a right to equal division of marital property violates her right to equality.

The equality right of any person is indivisibly linked with her right to material resources and her access to them. How does a woman view the court, if she is separated or divorced and needs to establish her right to equality? Does she view it with suspicion, or with trepidation, without hope or with the confidence that she will get what she rightly deserves under the Constitution? Will her answer be different, depending on who she is or where she comes from? The report provides an insight to these questions.

I must admit here that sometimes, when I was a judge of the high court, while hearing a matrimonial dispute in my chambers, I have wondered why the woman does not accept what is given, and I have felt a slight impatience. Then I have made the conscious effort to neutralise the impatience, to

---

[2] Justice Claire L' Heureux-Dube, 'Economic Consequences of Divorce: A View from Canada', *31 Hous. L. Rev. 451.*

remember that it is not dole which she asks for but a right which she asserts. That is the real issue, that what she claims is her right to equality, her right to dignity, and she is not seeking a favour done out of benevolence.

Law's gender-neutrality is a fiction. In fact, we need gender-affirming laws. Courts, too, have really not set right the imbalance. In the chapter 'Re-orienting the Mirror of Justice: Gender, Economics and the Illusion of the "natural"',[3] the writer asks while discussing a case, 'Did it reflect an unwillingness to confront the systemic character of the oppression of women in American Society, and an inclination to treat any given discrimination, so far as, possible as an isolated aberrant event?' This is true of our society too which includes judges. We are unable to see that the particular instance of discrimination is part of a whole map where women are excluded.

Tribe observes that the persistence of women's legal disabilities is part of 'a subtle mosaic of oppression'. It is a common judicial failing. He writes so tellingly:

> The image of justice ... in which pervasive inequalities in the distribution of power and status, are overlooked-one in which the evils to be extirpated are seen to lie in the law's occasional and irrational deviations from the 'natural' rather than in the omnipresent realities that the legal order simultaneously reflects and re-creates with relentless rationality.[4]

There can be no doubt that unless women have equal economic rights there can be no equality for women. I will take up the Hindu law as an example. In 1956, when Hindu law was codified, the Hindu Succession Act was seen as the most crucial of reforms. The original draft which attempted to do away with the concept of coparcenary property was vehemently resisted. And Sita Ram Jajjoo of Madhya Bharat said, 'Here we feel the pinch because it touches our pockets. We, male members of this House are in a huge majority. I do not wish that the tyranny of the majority may be imposed on the minority, the female members of this House.'[5] This, then, is the key; this is why economic equality is so difficult. The woman's right to dignity and right to life demands that she has the right of residence in her natal and marital home.

The report gives the statistics on facts like which ground for divorce is more often used by men, and which by women, what is the percentage of men seeking divorce, in contrast to women, the variations on the basis of

---

[3] Laurence H. Tribe, *Constitutional Choices* (Harvard University Press, 1986).

[4] Laurence H.Tribe, *Gender Economics* (Harvard University Press, 1985), 241–242.

[5] The Constituent Assembly of India (Legislative) Debates Vol. VI 1949 Part II.

age, caste or religion, etc., which will be very useful for understanding the dynamics of marital law.

The report will be useful in formulating the law on equal division of marital property, and government policies and social security/welfare schemes. It underscores the need for affirmative action for single women and their families. The report makes many useful recommendations like reforming law and procedures regarding maintenance, like shifting the onus of proof on the man to prove his income, new enforcement mechanisms, etc., so that the economic rights do not remain merely on paper.

I once again congratulate Ms Kirti Singh and the Economic Research Foundation team for preparing this very useful report. I hope this report is used by the stakeholders and the law-makers, law-enforcers and the justice deliverers, so that the right to equality of women is truly affirmed.

Prabha Sridevan
Former Judge, Madras High Court
Chairman, Intellectual Property Appellate Board

Acknowledgements

There are many individuals and institutions whom I need to thank for making this study possible. To begin with, I would like to thank the International Development Research Centre (IDRC) for agreeing to support this study. I would particularly like to thank Dr Navsharan Singh, Senior Programme Specialist, IDRC, for her encouragement and support through various stages of the study.

The research team for the project, which included Sandhya Kumari, Renu Sahgal, Sugandha Anand and Jayashree Bora, all lawyers, worked ceaselessly and with great enthusiasm. Renu, Sugandha and Jayashree all helped with the background legal research. Sugandha and Jayashree and later Sandhya travelled throughout the country, often with me, to painstakingly interview each separated woman for hours. They also, together with Renu, did the painful job of transcribing interviews. I was fortunate that Sandhya Kumari joined the team in August 2009 after Jayashree left. Sandhya provided me invaluable help with the study till the end. She helped with the research and discussed, in minute detail, the tables and charts with me. I thank her for her valuable inputs and for being there. I am also extremely grateful to Sujata Madhok for all her editorial and other inputs particularly on welfare schemes. I would also like to thank advocate Bulbul Das and Sunita Gupta for carrying out the interviews in Orissa. Bulbul Das also helped with the interviews in Thiruvananthapuram and Jaipur. I was fortunate that Professor Gangotri Chakraborty and her team conducted the interviews in the district of Darjeeling and I thank them for this.

The West Bengal Commission for Women and its Chairperson, Dr Malini Bhattacharya, along with others including Bharti Mutusuddi very kindly allowed us to conduct interviews of the women who came to their counseling cell. I am also grateful to the Human Rights Law Network in Kolkata for generously letting us interview the separated women who came to their legal cell. I am very grateful to Dr L.K. Jain for cooperating with us and allowing us to interview women in the shelter home run by the Rajasthan University Women's Association. I would also like to thank Ms Renuka Pamecha and Vividha in Jaipur for very kindly organising our interviews with women who came to them for help. Sabina Martins from Bailancho Saad, Goa, greatly helped us by discussing the issue of separated women in Goa and getting us in touch with women who had come to Bailancho Saad for help. I thank advocate Geeta Ramalingam from Tamil Nadu for generously helping us in conducting some of the interviews in Chennai.

Without the help and unstinted support of the various state units of the All India Democratic Women's Association (AIDWA) this survey would not have been possible. AIDWA members throughout India helped me and the research team in every way possible. They facilitated our survey by contacting separated women who had come to their legal cells and arranging for the interviews. They were always present when we needed them and helped us in interpreting surveyees who did not speak either English or Hindi. They found us places to stay and generously supported us throughout the survey. For them it was important that the survey was taking place as they had been working with separated/deserted women for several years. It is impossible to thank all the AIDWA members who helped with the survey. However, to begin with, I would like to thank Brinda Karat, Subhashini Ali, S. Sudha and Shyamali Gupta for their encouragement and support. I would also like to thank the office bearers and other members of the Delhi Janwadi Mahila Samiti including Sehba Taban, Sonia, Asha Lata and Asha Sharma for organising surveyees for our pilot survey. In Kanpur, the researchers and I enjoyed the generous hospitality of Subhashini Ali, who also along with others including Zarina Khursheed arranged for interviews with separated women who had visited the AIDWA legal cell (Uttar Pradesh branch). In Lucknow, Madhu Garg helped us with our interviews with women who had come to the AIDWA legal cell in Lucknow. I would also like to thank Sumitra and Kusum in Rajasthan for locating surveyees. I thank Sandhya Shaily for housing us, and both her and Aarti Pandey for helping us to locate separated women whom we could interview from both their legal cell and from the *bastis* in which AIDWA (Madhya Pradesh) works. I thank advocate Nalini Jadeja, and Bharti Parmar and Kiran Goswami from AIDWA Gujarat who helped us with the survey and went out of their way to arrange for our stay. In Maharashtra, Kiran Moghe, Sonya Gill, Mariam Dhawale and Hemlata Patil greatly helped us along with other members of AIDWA (Maharashtra). Advocate Milind Sahasrabhudhe and advocates Shamir Shaikh and Vaishali Waghmare who take up the legal aid cases from AIDWA helped us in Pune. In Goa, Divya Kapur helped us with the interviews and very generously drove us across the length and breadth of Goa to conduct some of these. I am also very grateful to U. Vasuki and the entire team of AIDWA (Tamil Nadu) including D. Saraswathi for not only helping us with the large number of interviews but also for allowing so many members to participate. In Andhra Pradesh, we were again greatly helped by the office bearers and the members of AIDWA (Andhra Pradesh) including Swarupa Rani, T. Jyothi and advocates Lakshmi, Indira and others. In Bangalore, K.S. Vimala of AIDWA (Karnataka) along with other members of the organisation again made it possible for us to conduct the survey there and helped us in interpreting the responses of the separated women who were surveyed.

All the tables and charts in the study have been prepared under the supervision of Mr Khursheed Anwar Siddiqui. He and Ms Rachna Sharma are largely responsible for the manner in which we have been able to depict the data in the study. Both of them were very patient and accommodating and spent a huge amount of their valuable time in making and remaking the tables.

I am grateful to Dr Kamala Shankaran for agreeing to go through the manuscript despite her busy schedule and for making various suggestions to improve it. I am also grateful to Professor Indu Agnihotri and Professor Rajni Palriwal for taking time out to go through the Introduction and for suggesting various changes to it.

Y.P. greatly helped me by encouraging me to complete the study and caring for me throughout this period. Tara's confidence that I was doing valuable work and Namrata's happy, carefree and non demanding nature all made it possible for me to write. I am also indebted to my friends Sunanda and Omita for coaxing me to write a book and to other members of my family and friends who have always encouraged me.

Kirti Singh
16 October 2012

1

Introduction

Though separations, desertions and divorces are increasing in India today,[1] not much attention has been paid to the manner in which these deserted and separated women live, often with their children, and what their rights and entitlements are in/from the marital home. Very few empirical legal studies exist on the economic status of divorced and separated women in India. In the recent past, some studies by social scientists on single women, particularly widows, highlight their general social and economic condition. In some of these studies, the condition of separated/deserted women has been described as even worse than that of a widow.[2] They are described as women 'even more despised ... in a twilight zone of neither being respectably married nor widowed—especially those who have themselves left their partners'.[3]

Under the Indian laws, a wife's economic entitlements on separation/divorce from her marital home are extremely limited. Basically, the only

[1] Bina Agarwal, 'The Idea of Gender Equality: From Legislative Vision to Everyday Family Practice', in Romila Thapar (ed.), *India: Another Millennium?* (New Delhi: Penguin Books, 2001), 48. Also see, Government of India, *Report: A Handbook of Statistical Indicators on Indian Women* (New Delhi: Ministry of Women and Child Development, 2007).

However, the Census of India 2001 had put the figure of the widowed/divorced/separated women as 7.38 per cent of the all-India female population in which the category of deserted and separated women was 0.47 per cent. Though as per National Family Health Scheme (NFHS) III (2005–2006) data, separated, deserted and divorced women formed 1.4 per cent of the total women population, wherein 3.2 per cent of the total women population were widowed. Further, as per the Sample Registration System Statistical Report 2010, the percentage of widowed/separated/divorced women is 8 per cent of the total female population. Report available at http://censusindia.gov.in/2011-Common/srs.html (last accessed on 4 May 2012).

[2] SOPPECOM, Hindola, *Assessing the Extent and Nature of Desertion in Daund Taluka and Ghole Road Ward of Pune City* (Pune: SOPPECOM, December 2008).

[3] Harsh Mander and Archana Rai, 'Living with Hunger' in V. Manikandan (ed.), *Chronic Food Deprivation among Aged People, Single Women and People with Disability: A Study of Rural Destitution and Hunger* (New Delhi: CES, 2008), 13. Available at http://sccommissioners.org/Starvation/Articles/livingwithhunger.pdf (last accessed on 15 July 2010).

legal right that an Indian woman has is a right to maintenance[4] from her spouse[5]. As is well known, Indians are governed by different personal laws, according to the religious community they belong to, in the area of family law. These laws govern marriage and divorce and specify the rights/entitlements of women and children in petitions filed under the various personal laws. Two Indians can also opt to marry under the civil law, known as the Special Marriage Act, 1954 (hereafter termed as the SMA), even if they belong to different religions. A wife is entitled to ask for maintenance (financial support) as an ancillary relief under most of these laws in a petition for divorce or judicial separation or restitution of conjugal rights.[6] Both Muslim and Hindu women can also file for maintenance under their respective personal laws during the period of marriage.[7] There are also general laws under which maintenance can be claimed by women of all communities. Under Section 125 of the Code of Criminal Procedure, 1973 (hereafter CrPC) for instance, women of all communities, except divorced Muslim women, can claim maintenance from the Magistrates' courts throughout the country for themselves and their children. Divorced Muslim women can claim maintenance for themselves and children living with them under the Muslim Women (Protection of Rights on Divorce) Act, 1986. Under the fairly recently enacted Protection of Women from Domestic Violence Act, 2005 (hereafter PWDVA), women from all communities/religions can

---

[4] Section 3(b) of the Hindu Adoption and Maintenance Act, 1956, defines maintenance as:

3. Definitions-

   (a) …
   (b) 'maintenance' includes-

      (i) in all cases, provision for food, clothing, residence, education and medical attendance and treatment;
      (ii) in the case of an unmarried daughter also the reasonable expenses of and incident to her marriage;

The definition of maintenance in Sub-section (b)(i) has been widely referred to by the courts while dealing with cases under different personal laws.

[5] Under Section 125(d) of the CrPC, a mother also has a right to be maintained by her adult children if she is 'unable to maintain herself'.

[6] Sections 24 and 25, The Hindu Marriage Act 1955; Sections 36 and 37, The Divorce Act 1869; Sections 39 and 40, The Parsi Marriage and Divorce Act 1936; and Sections 36 and 37, The Special Marriage Act 1954.

[7] A Muslim wife can file a civil suit for maintenance under the *Sharia* law which is uncodified. A Hindu wife can file a petition for maintenance and separate residence under the Hindu Adoption and Maintenance Act 1956 for herself and any children living with her if she does not want to file a petition for divorce.

claim monetary relief in situations of violence.[8] They also have an explicit right to residence in their marital home under this Act and can further ask for injunctions stopping their spouses from evicting them from the marital home or ask for residence outside.[9]

Despite the many enactments governing the laws related to maintenance, it would not be incorrect to say that, in actuality, this right/remedy does not provide women, from any community, adequate financial support to be able to live in a manner similar to the manner in which they had lived during the subsistence of marriage. This is primarily because of the manner in which the courts have generally enforced this right and because of the procedural obstacles that women face in the courts and in accessing this right. Thus, women have complained that some of the major obstacles that they face are the length of time that the courts take to make awards of maintenance and the costs involved in fighting the litigation. Finally, the small and dismal amounts of maintenance that are routinely doled out by the courts almost make this effort worthless. One of the main reasons for this is that courts have a wide discretion in awarding maintenance amounts and are manned to a large extent by judges who themselves suffer from various degrees of gender bias and are not sensitised to the plight of women and children on separation/divorce. Another major hurdle that women face is a lack of access to courts. Even in cities, a sufficient number of courts do not exist to deal with family law cases. Women have to travel long distances to go to court. During our survey, working-class women also complained of losing their daily wages to attend court proceedings. The lack of financial resources does not allow a large number of women to file and pursue a case properly as they cannot afford legal fees. In a large number of cases, even when maintenance is awarded by the court, the women do not receive it and after pursuing the matter for a while, some women just abandon the case while others undertake another round of litigation in execution proceedings to recover the maintenance amounts. Some women also have to face appeals against the order of maintenance in High Courts and the Supreme Court which last almost as long as or longer than the original case. They, thus, have to go through tiers of litigation which may last anywhere between 3 and 20 years. It is not surprising, therefore, that many cases for divorce and maintenance get settled by the parties through official or unofficial mediation. Most family lawyers report that a majority of their cases get settled through negotiations

[8] Section 20, Protection of Women from Domestic Violence Act, 2005.

[9] Under the Hindu Adoption and Maintenance Act, 1956, the definition of maintenance in Sections 3(b) includes residence.

between the parties/their representatives or via the court mediation process or through the intervention of women's groups/other institutions like the State Commission for Women, or even in the Crime against Women Cell now set up in various cities to deal with dowry-related criminal cases and cases of cruelty and violence under Section 498A Indian Penal Code.[10]

The law relating to dowry, apart from specifying that the giving and taking of dowry is illegal, also states that all dowry given by the bride's family or anyone else on her behalf, at the time of marriage or at anytime thereafter, will be returned to her. Further, even under classic Hindu Law, gifts of jewellery or other movable or immovable items including land, etc., to a bride at the time of marriage or after this are her *stridhan*[11] and her sole and absolute property.[12] Not returning the *stridhan* of a woman by a person with whom she had left it has also been pronounced as a criminal act by the Supreme Court of India.[13] However, dowry often consists of consumable items which are of little value if and when they are retrieved. Money spent on weddings, gifts of cash and clothing and jewellery, and other items given to the in-laws are not retrievable and are often difficult to prove as the woman's *stridhan*. Even if this were not so, the retrieval of dowry is hardly sufficient for a woman and any children with her to survive. Thus, while the criminal law punishes the non-return of dowry and *stridhan* and stipulates that dowry and *stridhan* should be returned to the woman, this rarely happens.[14] Further, though Section 498A punishes harassment for dowry and

---

[10] Section 498A Indian Penal Code, 1860, defines cruelty as:

(a) any wilful conduct which is of such a nature as is likely to drive the woman to commit suicide or to cause grave injury or danger to life, limb or health (whether mental or physical) of the woman; or
(b) harassment of the woman where such harassment is with a view to coercing her or any person related to her to meet any unlawful demand for any property or valuable security or is on account of failure by her or any person related to her to meet such demand; and punishes it with upto three years imprisonment.

[11] 'Property given or bequeathed to a Hindu Female, whether during maidenhood, coverture, or widowhood, by her parents and their relations or by her husband and his relations is Stridhan.' See Mulla, *Principles of Hindu Law*, Vol. II (Nagpur: Butterworths India, 18th edition), 240.

[12] Ibid., Vol. I, 229.

Section 14 of the HSA confers full and heritable capacity on a female heir in respect of all property acquired by her, with the result that she now holds the property in her possession as full owner and not as a limited owner. The restraints and limitations on the powers of a female heir have ceased to exist even in respect of existing property.

[13] *Pratibha Rani v Suraj Kumar* AIR 1986 SC 628.

[14] Our surveyees overwhelmingly reported this.

severe cases of domestic violence, unless the wife dies or is killed due to the violence, this Section hardly ever leads to conviction.[15]

It is widely acknowledged that in general the financial position of women in the marital home leaves much to be desired. Neither Indian law nor government policy views their work within the home as productive work or work of any economic value. This is in spite of the fact that it is typically the wife who spends long hours in building up and maintaining the house and in supervising household work; she often has to cook food and do various household chores; she has to bear the double burden of household work and outside work if she has a job, etc.; and she solely or primarily looks after the children and elderly in the house. Meanwhile, by spending most of her time at home, a woman losses her capacity to earn and compete in the job market. Even working women tend to spend far less time than their male colleagues in advancing their careers and so miss out on promotions and other career opportunities. In carrying out her household tasks, women, in many instances, have to give up their career. Thus, non-recognition of household work and 'care' work results in reinforcement of gender discrimination and inequality.[16] The woman is not seen as an equal partner in the house. Her contributory efforts become 'transformed by the law into self-sacrifice'.[17]

Studies such as the *Time Use* studies carried out by the Central Statistical Organisation in 1998–1999[18] provide evidence of the enormous time spent by women in carrying out household activities. They reiterate the common experience that it is generally women who do the cooking and cleaning and taking care of children. Even women working outside the home bear the primary responsibility of looking after the house and caring for the children. Child care often requires a huge input of time, energy and supervision.[19] 'Working' women, thus, shoulder the double burden of both types of work.

---

[15] A survey undertaken by me of last five years of the divorce and matrimonial cases, a well-recognised and standard reference for family law and related criminal cases, shows that it is largely in dowry death, abetment to suicide or in dowry murder cases that conviction also takes place under Section 498A of the Indian Penal Code (IPC). Sometimes, when murder, etc., cannot be proved, conviction takes place under this Section.

[16] Neetha N. and Rajni Palriwala, 'Unpaid Care Work: Analysis of the Indian Time Use Data', in Debbie Budlender (ed.), *Time Use Studies and Unpaid Care Work* (London: Taylor and Francis, 2010), 92.

[17] Carolyn J. Frantz and Hanoch Dagan, 'Properties of Marriage', *Columbia Law Review* 104, no. 75 (2004), 99.

[18] Central Statistical Organisation, *Report of the Time Use Survey* (New Delhi: Ministry of Statistics and Programme Implementation, 2000).

[19] Neetha and Palriwala, *supra* note 16. Neetha and Palriwala argue that the Time Use Studies in fact undercount the time spent in child care.

It has been pointed out that though the nature of the contribution differs between classes, with poor and working-class women putting in more direct physical labour, women of the middle and upper classes, who may have recourse to domestic help, nevertheless perform a range of activities to maintain the family or household in terms of supervision and responsibility.[20]

In India, we are governed by the 'Separation of Property' Regime. A husband is the owner of his property and the wife is the owner of her property as they were even prior to the marriage.[21] The problem is that though a property may have been bought during the subsistence of marriage, the party in whose name an asset has been bought becomes the owner of the asset. This is typically the husband. Thus, though women through their efforts contribute to the building up of the household and thus to the buying of the assets, none of the movable and immovable assets like land, house, etc., that are acquired during the marriage belong to her equally with her husband unless it is acquired in her name also. As mentioned above, many of the assets, particularly houses and lands are bought in the husbands' names. Even working women, because of their vulnerable and subordinate position in the house, often let their husbands and in-laws dictate how their salary should be spent—typically, they spend their salaries on day-to-day household expenses while the husbands acquire assets in their own name. All the different personal/family laws that govern us uniformly deny women any rights to property/assets that are not acquired in their name. Indian family laws, thus, follow what is known as the 'Separation of Property' Regime, barring the State of Goa, which is still governed by the old Portuguese family laws enshrined in the Civil Code of 1867.

Thus, if an Indian woman is separated or deserted even years after marriage, she is left almost asset-less while her husband walks away with all the property. It is not surprising, therefore, that most separated or deserted women, usually along with their children, are forced to live with members of their natal family, such as parents and brothers, and are financially dependent on them. Often, they are not welcome even there and live as outcasts in the family. In Goa, where the 'Community of Property' Regime is in place, both spouses are equally entitled to marital assets. However, the problem in Goa is that in law and in fact it is the husband who controls and deals with the assets, though he can be stopped from alienating the marital home. The

---

[20] Economic Research Foundation, *Economic Rights and Entitlements of Separated and Divorced Women,* Report of Regional Seminar Proceedings (2008–2009) (New Delhi: ERF, 2010), 127–132.

[21] B. Sivaramaya, *Matrimonial Property Law in India* (New Delhi: Oxford University Press, 1999), 1.

couple can also opt not to be governed by the 'Community of Property' Regime through a contract. An additional problem is that the wife does not get her moiety[22] share of the property unless a divorce goes through, and this sometimes takes years. As a result, most women settle for less than their share.

Several countries have given legal recognition to the unpaid work done by women in the household and practise a 'Community of Property'[23] Regime when a marriage breaks down. This ensures that women at least have somewhat equal rights in the property acquired by the couple if the marriage breaks down, whether or not the asset or property has been bought in the woman's name. The law governing division of marital property in Ontario, Canada, for instance, explicitly states its legislative purpose in Section 4(7) of the Family Law Act. It states:

> The purpose of this section is to recognize that child care, household management and financial provision are the joint responsibilities of the spouses and that inherent in the marital relationship there is equal contribution, whether financial or otherwise, by the spouses to the assumption of these responsibilities, entitling each spouse to the equalization of the net family properties...[24]

In India, when a woman is separated from her husband, often with her children, she has to go to court for a long drawn-out battle to even get a small pittance as maintenance. While the courts have held that a woman or children with her have a right to the same standard of living as they were used to in the marital home,[25] the reality is that there is a sharp plunge in her status and standard of living. She is then forced to live with or depend on her relatives/natal family. Even there she is not welcome as her family thinks she has received her share of the family resources through dowry and the amount of money spent on her marriage and given as gifts to the groom and his family. No one seems to care how these women and often children are living and surviving. A lot of women, therefore, do not leave even violent marriages. They know it will be impossible to survive outside. When women approach the police to complain about domestic violence or for return of dowry, they often face hostility. The aim of the survey is to lay bare the lives

---

[22] Half of something.

[23] 'In the community of property, the wife and husband are regarded as partners with respect to the matrimonial assets; this however, is subject to a contract entered into between the spouses before the marriage.' Sivaramaya, *supra* note 21.

[24] 'Family Law Act', available at http://www.e-laws.gov.on.ca/html/statutes/english/elaws_statutes_90f03_e.htm (last accessed on 26 September 2012).

[25] *Mangat Mal (Dead) and Anr. v Smt. Punni Devi (Dead) and Ors.* AIR 1996 SC 172.

of these women and suggest reforms in law and policy to address these critical issues facing separated/deserted and divorced women in India.

The Indian state has reformed the laws relating to divorce in 1955, 1976 and even currently, the central government is trying to introduce further reforms. However, all these reforms have been focused on broadening the grounds for divorce and except in 1955 when the provision for maintenance was introduced in the Hindu Marriage Act (hereafter HMA) and the SMA, no reform regarding the marital property rights of women or reform to strengthen the maintenance laws were introduced. Recently, the central government has introduced an amendment to the HMA and the SMA to once again enlarge the grounds for divorce by introducing the irretrievable breakdown of marriage as a further ground for divorce.[26] They have also introduced an amendment which states that a woman can oppose this plea on the ground that it would result in 'grave financial hardship to her'.[27] A further amendment also states, 'the court may on a petition made by the wife, order that the husband shall pay to her as financial support such gross sum or share in the moveable or immoveable property towards settlement of property rights in respect of the property acquired during the subsistence of the marriage ...'[28] Just giving the woman a right to oppose divorce on the ground of financial hardship is not enough. The further introduction of a clause that the court may grant money or distribute marital property leaves the issue of distribution of property entirely to the discretion of the judge. As stated earlier, the Indian judiciary is manned, to a considerable extent, by judges with a largely patriarchal mindset. Petitioning women will be put through great hardship while trying to establish that they are entitled to a share in marital property. While very few will disagree with the concept of irretrievable breakdown of marriage per se; women's organisations and groups have pointed out that it is a wife's right to receive at least an equal share in the property acquired by the parties after marriage as she has to be considered an equal partner in the marital relationship. Women's groups and lawyers working in the area of family law have often found women opposing divorce petitions filed by their husbands because they have no viable economic alternative outside the marriage and because of the social stigma that is attached to a divorcee. It is well known that most divorce petitions are filed and initiated by men. Women, if they can afford to file a case, mostly file for maintenance and residence and return of *stridhan* and dowry.

---

[26] The Marriage Laws (Amendment) Bill, 2010, Bill No. XLI of 2010.
[27] Ibid.
[28] Amendment Introduced to the Bill No. XLI of 2010 on 24 April 2012.

During the period that this Bill on irretrievable breakdown of marriage as a ground for divorce had been referred to a standing committee,[29] women's organisations and groups had put forth a demand to this committee that a comprehensive legislation on a woman's right to marital property be enacted simultaneously or else the introduction of the new ground would result in greater financial hardship for women. They had suggested that this legislation should apply to women of all communities/religions, as an equal share in marital property is a recognition of the economic content of household work and of the wife's contribution to the family and no personal law can deny this. The legislation should also unequivocally provide that women should receive at least a half share of the marital property. It has also been suggested that this division should be allowed whenever a wife petitions for it after separation. Other clauses about what should constitute marital property would also form part of the standalone law. For instance, inheritance of the husband and wife and gifts to them could be left out of marital property. Other issues like whether the law should apply to persons living together also needs to be thought about. However, instead of having a proper discussion or debate on the issue, the government has hastily tried to push through the present amendments with some concessions.

Though this study does not focus on what a daughter/wife inherits from her natal home, it is pertinent to mention that women's property rights in inherited property are also unequal. Women's organisations and groups have been demanding equal rights in inheritance as the enforcement of this would, they felt, also have a negative impact on dowry. However, most personal laws relating to inheritance continue to have provisions which discriminate against women. The 2005 amendment to the Hindu Succession Act 1956 (hereafter HSA) sought to give equal rights in ancestral property to daughters by making them coparceners in the Mitakshara coparcenary.[30] It also gave the daughter a right to seek partition of a house she inherited. The earlier law had given daughters only an equal right of inheritance in self-acquired property of her father, a partial right in ancestral property and had restricted her rights in a dwelling house in which the joint family was living. However, even after the passing of this Act, it has been widely reported that sisters are

---

[29] The department related Parliamentary Standing Committee on Personnel, Public Grievances, Law and Justice, Rajya Sabha Secretariat.

[30] Originally, 'the conception of a joint Hindu family constituting a coparcenary is that of a common male ancestor with his lineal descendants in the male line within *four* degrees *counting from and inclusive* of such ancestor (or *three* degrees *exclusive* of ancestor).' The coparceners inherited the property of the coparcenary by birth and it remained joint property till a partition took place. See Satyajeet Desai, *Mulla's Hindu Law* (Nagpur: LexisNexis Butterworths Wadhwa, 2010, 21st Edition), 113.

routinely pressurised to give up their share of inheritance by their brothers and other members of their paternal family. Women also relinquish their shares in their ancestral property for keeping their relationships intact and maintaining peace and harmony.

Another obstacle in the way of women inheriting property is the right to will which was introduced in the HSA. This was earlier not available in Mitakshara law. The right to will was introduced by the British as a part of the Indian Succession Act, 1925, and has been a part of common law. The right to will has been used to disinherit daughters and their descendants and sometimes even wives. The right to will should accordingly be restricted.

Another important amendment in 2005 was the deletion of Section 4(2) of the Act which exempted land reform and ceiling Acts and the laws relating to devolution of tenancies in agricultural land from the purview of the HSA. These state Acts were highly discriminatory and privileged male lineal descendants over wives and daughters. However, even after the amendment, state governments have not amended the land laws and these laws continue to remain on paper in Delhi, Himachal Pradesh, Punjab and Haryana, Jammu and Kashmir and Uttar Pradesh. Other state laws on the subject allow devolution according to personal laws and discriminate against women. A recent positive judgment[31] by the High Court of Delhi held that the provisions of the HSA had an overriding effect over the Delhi Land Reforms Act and that the rule of succession in HSA would apply. However, state land laws continue to apply to women of other religious communities and should in any case be amended to ensure gender justice.

Another problem with the HSA is the discriminatory manner in which a woman's property devolves upon her heirs in comparison to the devolution of a male's property. Unlike the male, whose Class-I heirs are his wife, mother and children or their representatives in their absence, the woman's property devolves in the absence of her children and husband in a highly discriminatory manner. Her self-acquired property devolves upon the heirs of her husband and only in the absence of these heirs devolves upon her mother and father. A recent Supreme Court judgment[32] upheld this method of devolution while acknowledging the unfairness and injustice which this provision led to. In a case before the Supreme Court, a widow who had been ill-treated and deserted by her in-laws and thereafter lived with her parents and had worked and built up a career, died. The court held that her property would devolve upon her in-laws and not her parents. Thus, most women in India do not have or get equal rights in inherited property either.

---

[31] Nirmala and Ors v Government of NCT of Delhi and Ors. MANU/DE/2717/2010.

[32] *Omprakash v Radhacharan* (2009) 15 SCC 66.

Existing Studies

Though there is a dearth of primary and secondary data on the condition of separated and deserted women and their interaction with the law, some localised studies highlight the nature and extent of desertion of women and the dismal economic and social condition of these and other separated women. Some of these reiterate the findings of this survey.

A study[33] done by SOPPECOM, Pune, in the Daund Taluka of Pune District and Ghole Ward of Pune city in December 2008, to assess the extent and nature of desertion of women, is noteworthy. The percentage of deserted women in the Daund Taluka region was about 5.92 per cent. The highest incidents of desertion were reported amongst the Scheduled Castes (SCs), Denotified Tribes (DTs) and Muslims. All these women had come back to their natal homes. To begin with 50 per cent of the deserted women were non-literate, the remaining being within the category of secondary schooling. More than 70 per cent women were engaged in wage labour of some kind. The highest number of women; about 40 per cent were involved in agricultural labour and 33 per cent were involved in other labour activities, that includes working as unorganised workers in new small-scale industries, as construction labourers, etc. In Ghole Road area, 4,402 household across 16 *bastis* were covered. The percentage of deserted, divorced and widowed women to the total number of ever married women came to 26 per cent. The extent of desertion was 5.45 per cent and a large percentage of desertion was among SCs, that is, 7.20 per cent, and among the DTs. Most of the deserted women were engaged in domestic work in the neighbouring areas. Both in the rural and the city area, the general castes reported much lesser desertion. However, according to the report, this can be attributed to underreporting of the actual number of cases and the fact that women from the upper castes tried their best not to leave the marital home. After separation, life changed drastically for the woman as she belonged neither to the marital home nor to the natal one and she became more vulnerable than widows. It was found that most of these women had to work hard at home and give their entire income to their brothers if they lived with them. Very few women filed cases in court. Most of the cases that were filed were for maintenance followed by a share in the property. Even in Pune city, only 1.08 per cent of women received any monthly maintenance and the situation was even worse in Daund Taluka where only 0.08 per cent received

[33] SOPPECOM, *supra* note 2.

any monthly compensation. A minuscule number of women owned houses or benefited from any government schemes.

A legal study[34] of 1,129 cases decided under the HMA, 1955 during 1986 and 1987 was also carried out in the district of Pune. After excluding cases which had been filed under the provision of mutual consent or cases which had been dismissed or cases in which there were appeals pending, it was reported that the majority of these cases (570 out of 849)[35] had been initiated by the husband. The study also reported that maintenance had been asked by only women except in one case in which both the husband and wife had asked for it. During the course of the proceedings in the solitary case of maintenance asked by the husband, both parties gave up their claim of maintenance. Thus, we find that though the provision for maintenance had been deliberately made gender-neutral under the HMA for more than 30 years, the provision was used almost exclusively by women, showing that it was women who had an overwhelming need for maintenance. By and large, this clause is used to harass women during litigation. In the study, 400 cases of maintenance were analysed. Interim maintenance was asked for only in 297 cases and granted in 133 (44.78 per cent) cases. Thus, in almost half the cases interim maintenance was refused. Similarly though permanent alimony was claimed in 207 cases, it was only granted in 63 cases. In 28 of these cases, it was granted on monthly basis and in 35 cases on lump sum basis. The study noted that though interim maintenance had been asked for in 74.25 per cent cases, permanent alimony/maintenance had only been asked for in 207 (51.75 per cent) cases. Though interim maintenance should ordinarily be granted from the date of filing of the petition or the date of application for maintenance, it had also been granted from the date of the order for interim maintenance. Similarly for permanent alimony, the alimony was given from the date of order deciding the main petition in most of the cases without considering whether the woman had received interim maintenance earlier or not. This clearly showed how the court was biased in favour of the husband.

The study showed the inadequate maintenance that the courts had ordered. The amount of interim maintenance sanctioned by the court ranged between ₹75 and ₹300 when the wife was without children. The range of interim maintenance was between ₹100 and ₹500 when the claimants were a wife and children. This clearly showed that maintenance had been granted without any consideration of the number of children that the woman was

[34] Jaya Sagade, *Law of Maintenance: An Empirical Study* (Mumbai: N.M. Tripathi Pvt. Ltd., 1996).

[35] These cases pertain to nullity, restitution, judicial separation and divorce.

bringing up. This survey also highlights that the amount of maintenance had no connection with the income of the husband. A lack of application of the judicial mind was apparent in cases of permanent alimony also. The amount of permanent alimony per month ranged between ₹100 and ₹500 when the wife alone claimed it. Along with one child, it ranged between ₹200 and ₹750 and along with two children it was between ₹200 and ₹500.[36] One of the main reasons given for the dismal quantum of maintenance awarded under Section 125 CrPC was that the wife had no proof of the husband's income.[37] The study noted that the amount of maintenance granted to the wife should at least have supported her bare survival which it did not. In cases dealing with permanent alimony, the study noted that the sums that were awarded were negligible in terms of the income of the husband.[38] Even in cases of mutual consent where the wife was supposed to have agreed to the amount of permanent alimony, the amounts agreed upon had no relation to the income of the husband and were shockingly low. This showed the vulnerability and inability of the wife to negotiate a favourable settlement for herself and her children in a large number of cases.

The majority of divorce cases under the HMA, according to the study, were decided within three years from the date of the filing of the marriage petition. In fact out of the total of 400 cases under the HMA, 89 per cent cases were decided within three years.[39] Sagade's study also pointed out that in 24 per cent of the 258 cases filed under Section 125 of the CrPC, the wife remained absent/could not pursue her case after filing it and the case thus got dismissed[40]. The study, therefore, seems to support the argument that women lack access to the courts due to various reasons.

---

[36] Sagade, *supra* note 34, pp. 157 and 163.

[37] Ibid., 177. The suggested reasons were:

1. Income of the husband as claimed by the wife was always denied by the husband.
2. Many a times, there was no proof or record about the income.
3. Sometimes income was expressed vaguely or in abstract terms viz. good income.

[38] Ibid., 163, see Table 69.

[39] Ibid., 165–166. Most of the marriage petitions, that is, 231 out of 237 were decided within three years from the date of the filing of the petition. This means that 68 petitions were decided within one year, 83 in two years and 80 in three years. Further, if one looks at the disposal rate of the maintenance cases filed in different marriage petitions, out of 400 cases 352 (88.9 per cent) cases were decided within three years from their filing dates.

[40] Ibid., 181. The reasons attributed by her for such default were:

> She might have been unaware of the dates, lack of communication between the lawyer and the party, ill health, over technicality of the procedure, paucity of money, non-availability of time, and total frustration about whole judicial process.

A shorter study of 362 cases under Section 125 of the CrPC for maintenance had been done in Delhi in the Tis Hazari Courts in 1996. The study showed that even cases under this Section, which is supposed to provide a summary procedure for grant of maintenance, take a long time.[41] If the maintenance is not given, the wife has to file an execution proceeding, which the study showed, often takes as long as the main case 'because of the various manipulative malpractices'.[42] The study notes that a litigant has to spend an enormous amount of money, time and energy[43] for getting a paltry maintenance amount. In spite of the long execution proceedings, there were still substantial arrears of maintenance.[44]

Raheja also pointed out that though the 132nd Report of the Law Commission of India had suggested that no ceiling should be placed on the amount of maintenance that can be awarded by the court, the ceiling amount of ₹500 which could be paid as maintenance under this Section, had remained unchanged since 1898, with no reference to the inflation and cost of living in the meanwhile. This ceiling, it is pertinent to mention, was only removed over a century later in 2001. According to the report, the maintenance awards were therefore shockingly low, insignificant and unjust.[45]

The study takes account of the average amount spent on the proceedings under Section 125 of the CrPC and the average amount allowed under this provision for maintenance of the claimant wife and children and concludes that for getting an allowance of ₹1,563, a claimant needs to spend about ₹2,260 on various particulars, like lawyer's fee, conveyance to the court on each hearing, etc.

Another small study of 30 cases done between the years 1991 and 1992 in Calcutta[46] deals with 16 cases of maintenance—five cases of return of dowry/*stridhan* filed by 5 out of these 16 women and eight women struggling to get their inheritance right to their paternal property and six widows litigating to get a share of the property of their deceased husbands. The study seeks to

---

[41] 17.4 months. If the cases withdrawn or dismissed for default had not been taken into account, the average time of each case would have been even longer than 17 months. See, Devinder Raheja, *Who Is Maintaining Whom: An Analysis of the Working of Maintenance Provisions under Section 125 of the Criminal Procedure Code, 1973*, 2–3 Occasional Papers on Perspectives in Indian Development, No. XLIV (September) (for private circulation only, New Delhi: Centre for Contemporary Studies, Nehru Memorial Museum and Library, 1994).

[42] Ibid.

[43] Ibid., 3.

[44] Ibid., 8.

[45] Ibid., 5.

[46] Maitrayee Mukhopadhyay, *Legally Dispossessed, Gender Identity and the Process of Law* (Kolkata: Stree, 1998).

outline the struggle for family property that Hindu and Muslim wives, sisters/daughters and widows wage in the courts, the outcome of these contests and the basis on which entitlements are fixed. Under Section 125 of the CrPC, maintenance was awarded in 12 cases, ranging between ₹150 and ₹500 per month, as the ceiling of ₹500 was there at the time of this study, but only two out of these women were receiving these payments at the time of this study.[47] Almost all these women were rendered homeless and had to return to and depend upon their natal family for their shelter and support. All the women who had children, barring one, were left with their children but did not receive any financial support for the children. Though five women had asked for the return of their *stridhan*/dowry, only two were able to recover some property and only one of these two recovered her jewellery. Only 3 out of these 16 women could remarry and because of this they had to give up their right to maintenance from their ex-husbands.[48]

Although 4 of the 5 women who asked for their *stridhan* got the decree, only two were able to recover some property and only one of them recovered her jewellery (often constituting the most valuable part of her property).[49]

Patricia Jeffery, in her study[50] in rural Bijnor district of western Uttar Pradesh (UP) also makes the point that women, whether as daughters or as wives, scarcely ever own land, irrespective of the community or social class they belong to. She also highlights the extensive spread of the dowry system and the manner in which this is connected to notions of honour and propriety. She states:

> At all levels of the class hierarchy the most honourable marriage requires the bride's parents and their wider kin network to provide a dowry. This can entail major outlays for clothing and jewellery for the bride and members of her husband's family, household goods—bed, bedding, cooking utensils, etc.,—and amongst Hindus, cash.

She further makes the point that while a young married woman's work may be trivialised by her in-laws and even herself, the woman performs an 'important economic role' by 'cooking, rearing children, caring for livestock or working in the family fields'. Jeffery notes that most Hindu and Muslim

[47] Mukhopadhyay, *supra* note 46, p. 30 and pp. 40–41.

[48] Ibid., 41.

[49] Ibid.

[50] Patricia Jeffery, 'A "Uniform Customary Code"? Marital Breakdown and Women's Economic Entitlements in Rural Bijnor' in Imtiaz Ahmed (Ed.), *Divorce and Remarriage among Muslims in India* (New Delhi: Manohar, 2003), 101.

women from wealthy households work in the house while poorer women perform the double task of working in the house and also earning some money by stitching, spinning cotton, etc. She also observes that women from the poorest households seek employment as domestic servants or field labourers.

The study reiterates a significant finding of our study that women's options, whether they are Hindu or Muslims, are extremely limited on separation or divorce. Many of the informants of both communities in the Bijnor study did not seem to think that they had any option but to live in their marital homes even when they had problems. It relates how considerable time and energy is spent on avoiding separation. On the breakdown of marriage, the woman has to leave her husband's house and go to her natal family.[51] Jeffery states that the woman's dowry and other items presented to her may not be returned to her and the woman and her family generally have very little hope of retrieving even a small portion of the items. She makes a critical point, 'basically a separated woman, whether Muslim or Hindu faces almost certain penury unless she can persuade her natal kin to support her'.

She observes that in practice *mehr* is deferred and if a woman initiates separation she cannot get *mehr*. Many informants did not know what their *mehr* was; in many cases it was less than ₹500 and in one case it was ₹25.

> One-third of the key informants had forgiven or renounced the *mehr* mostly under pressure from their husbands. Even after divorce, women claimed, the *mehr* is not given. Thus in rural Bijnor, Muslim women are not protected from marital breakdown or from financial insecurity after it by the *mehr*.[52]

Jeffery says that the daughter is not welcome in her parents' home since after having been provided a dowry she is not expected to make further claims on her parents' property and land, and her parents and brothers do not expect to meet her expenses of daily living. 'Her natal kin, then, may provide shelter and support only grudgingly and temporarily.'

Sylvia Vatuk's study was carried out in the Chennai family courts on cases filed in 1993 and 1996 and randomly sampled cases of other years as well.[53] Vatuk too makes the point that almost all separated women live, usually with their child/children, in the household of their parents or an adult sibling. Her study shows that a small number of adult women live independently, but usually with their own teenage or young adult children.

---

[51] Jeffery, *supra* note 50, p. 113.

[52] Ibid., 115.

[53] Sylvia Vatuk, 'Muslim Women in the Indian Family Courts: A Report from Chennai', in Imtiaz Ahmed (Ed.), *Divorce and Remarriage among Muslims in India* (New Delhi: Manohar, 2003), 137.

She notes that the cases filed by Muslims and Hindus were similar and the patterns in their outcome were not very different either.[54] She also notes that marriages entailed a significant amount of expenditure on gold, silver, cash, clothing and other goods by way of dowry and liberal spending at wedding and associated feasts.

Methodology

The survey has been carried out on 405 women across the country in four different regions. All these women are separated/deserted or divorced. The survey primarily looks at the economic and financial status of these women. It interrogates where and with whom and how these women live and seeks to capture the stark reality of their lives. It seeks to record how these women have dealt with the police and the courts and what they feel about their experience. The survey was carried out between October 2008 and September 2009 in different metropolitan cities and some surrounding areas across the northern, southern, eastern and western regions of the country. It is, therefore, a survey of women living largely in urban areas.

The survey was conducted by researchers who were mostly lawyers and activists working with women's organisations. One of the limitations of the survey was that it has obviously relied on the version of the women surveyees, though the researchers tried to get to the truth by extensively questioning the surveyees and cross-checking their answers. Women who were approached for the survey were women who had sought help from the legal cells of women's groups and organisations, who had filed cases in the Crimes Against Women Cell, who had filed for maintenance in the family or other courts and in some cases women who had approached the State Women's Commissions. The surveyees were chosen at random and came from all income groups, as the responses show. However, they were women who were prepared, at least for some time, to fight for their legal right rather than give it up immediately. The vast majority of women who were surveyed came from low income groups. Table 1.1 shows the places in which the survey was carried out and the number of women who were surveyed.

Table 1.1 shows the four regions of India in which the survey has been conducted. In the north, the survey was conducted in Delhi and UP (Lucknow and Kanpur). In the south, it was conducted in Andhra Pradesh

[54] Vatuk, *supra* note 53, pp. 143–144.

Table 1.1 The States/Territories Covered by the Survey

Region	**States**				
North (44)	**Uttar Pradesh (19)** Kanpur Lucknow	**Delhi (25)**			
East (80)	**West Bengal** Kolkata (23) Darjeeling (24)	**Assam (9)** Guwahati	**Orissa (24)** Bhubaneswar Cuttack Jajpur		
South (134)	**Andhra Pradesh (24)** Hyderabad	**Karnataka (29)** Bangalore	**Tamil Nadu (59)** Chennai	**Kerala (22)** Thiruvanantha-puram	
West (147)	**Maharashtra (23)** Bhandup Pune Raigad	**Gujarat** Ahmedabad (30) Bhavnagar (17)	**Madhya Pradesh (30)** Bhopal	**Rajasthan (35)** Jaipur	**Goa (12)**

(Hyderabad), Karnataka (Bangalore), Tamil Nadu (Chennai) and Kerala (Thiruvananthapuram). In the east, it was conducted in West Bengal (Darjeeling and Kolkata), Assam (Guwahati) and Orissa (Bhubaneswar, Cuttack, Jajpur and other places). And, lastly in the western region the survey was conducted in states like Goa, Gujarat (Ahmedabad and Bhavnagar), Rajasthan (Jaipur), Maharashtra (Bhandup, Pune and Raigad) and Madhya Pradesh (MP) (Bhopal). The research for this book was originally conducted for a project on the *Rights and Entitlements of Indian Women on Separation and Divorce Including the Right to Spousal and Child Support and Right to Marital Property* for the Economic Research Foundation and supported by International Development Research Centre (IDRC).

The survey records information about the status and style of living of the spouses and children during the subsistence of marriage and after separation/divorce. It seeks to find out the amount of time spent by both the spouses doing domestic work and other employment, the income and assets of the marital home, and of the spouses post separation. It interrogates the manner in which the assets of the marital home get divided post separation and the amounts of spousal and child support received by the woman/child through the court or otherwise. It aims to record the change in the financial status of the separated wife/husband through household expenditure and assets post separation. It asks questions regarding the impact of being married on the careers of the spouses and the perceived loss of earning capacity of the female spouse. It attempts to record the experience of women with the law and the obstacles faced by them while interacting with the criminal justice system and the civil courts and other institutions.

At first a pilot survey was carried out on 15 separated/divorced women in Delhi. After this, with slight changes and some additions to the questionnaire, the survey was conducted throughout the country. The findings of the survey were also presented in four workshops at Kolkata, Delhi, Mumbai and Chennai.

Chapter 2 discusses the main findings of the survey.

Chapter 3 contains general information regarding the surveyees, including their occupation and income and their spouse's occupation and income, the age at which they got married and the date of their marriages. The law under which the marriage took place and whether it was an arranged marriage or a marriage by choice has also been documented. The chapter details where and with whom the surveyees are living after their separation/divorce, what their religion or caste is and their educational qualifications. The number of children and with whom these children are staying is also recorded. The date of separation of the surveyees and whether they have been divorced or not have also been recorded. The chapter also specifies the kind of cases that have been filed by the surveyees and their spouses and the laws under which they have been filed. Finally, details of the reasons for separation have also been included.

Chapter 4 is a report of Section II of the survey, which deals with the work status and earning capacity of both the spouses. It records the type of work both the spouses were engaged in prior to the marriage, during the marriage and the type of work they are currently pursuing. The number of hours spent in domestic work by both the spouses and the nature of domestic work that they were/are engaged in on a daily basis during the marriage and after the separation has also been recorded. The responses of the surveyees as to whether the burden of their work has increased after the separation and whether they have feelings of anxiety or stress or additional responsibility after the separation/divorce have also been included in this chapter. The details of the monthly income from employment and other sources of both the spouses have also been noted. In order to assess the 'loss of earning capacity', which the surveyees may have suffered due to the time spent in household work, the surveyees were asked a number of questions. These included the surveyees' opinion of whether their marriage had affected their work; whether they had to give up work during the marriage and how their work-status and income stood as compared with other colleagues. Finally, the surveyees were also asked if their separation had affected their careers and the benefits they thought their husbands had reaped because of their household work and their other talents in terms of his income, career, savings and assets.

Chapter 5 records the 'family status and lifestyle'[55] of the surveyees, both in the marital home and after separation. It records whether the family is nuclear or extended and the household expenditure during marriage and the expenses incurred in/by the husband and the wife after separation individually so as to record the extent to which the availability of resources for the surveyees has fallen. Specific questions to record the nature of assets that the surveyees and their spouses owned/enjoyed during the marriage and the nature of assets that the surveyees are left with were also asked from the surveyees. This chapter also details whether the surveyees currently own any immovable asset like the home they live in or a piece of land or movable assets like savings and investments or vehicles or jewellery or televisions/fridge. The chapter also details in whose possession these assets currently are.

Chapter 6 details the experience of women with the courts and other authorities that they approached to get financial support from their spouses. It pinpoints the amount of financial support that the women have been able to get for themselves or their children and the inadequacy of this sum. The process and length of time that the women have had to spend is also recorded. It has also been recorded whether the amount of maintenance granted by the court has been received by these women and the length of time that this recovery has taken and whether they have had to file further proceedings in order to be able to receive these amounts. Women have also described the difficulties and obstacles faced by them in the courts in trying to prove the income of their spouses and the various stratagems adopted by their spouse to conceal their income/transfer their assets, etc. Finally, the chapter records the opinion of the women about whether they think that they are entitled to an equal share of the household assets and whether the onus of proof should be on them to prove the income and assets of their spouses.

Women have also detailed the list of dowry and *stridhan* given to them by their various relatives and friends prior to the marriage, at the time of marriage, and after the marriage and the total value of these items. The value of dowry from the parents and siblings and other close relatives has also been sought to be recorded and this has been compared with the income of the parents. Specific tables regarding whether the surveyees' parents had to borrow money to acquire the dowry and *stridhan* gifts and whether this was

[55] This term is used in many court judgments in India to denote the standard of living and financial status of the family in the marital home.

a burden on their family are also a part of this chapter. The persons with whom the dowry and *stridhan* items are at present have also been recorded. Finally, the surveyees' experiences with the police and the length of time spent in pursuing the complaint to the police have been outlined.

Chapter 7 deals with the social status, mobility, skills and decision-making ability that the surveyees had during the marriage and after separation. It further records whether the surveyees faced any hostility or prejudice/ discrimination in their interaction with society and specifically in their interaction with other relatives, landlords, school authorities, employers or other authorities and persons. The surveyees have also described the nature of discrimination faced by them. They have further recorded whether they have a ration card or a voter ID or a driving license or a passport.

Chapter 8 is a recording of some of the main trends which we identified from different cities.

The survey comprehensively outlines the economic position of separated and divorced women and the lack of their rights and entitlements although since it is based only on answers by the women a certain margin of inaccurate reporting regarding certain questions may be presumed to exist.

2

Main Findings

Desertions and separations/divorces are increasing in India today. Yet, not much attention has been paid to the manner in which deserted and separated women live, often with their children, and what their rights and entitlements are in/from the marital home. Very few legal or sociological studies exist on the economic status of divorced and separated women in India. However, some studies describe the condition of separated/deserted women as even worse than that of a widow. This survey was necessitated by the absence of any reliable data on the economic status of these women.

To lay bare the lives of these women and suggest reforms in law and policy, the survey was carried out on 405 separated/deserted or divorced women across the country, in the four regions of north, south, east and west India. It included women in select cities and towns/villages of UP, Andhra Pradesh, Karnataka, Tamil Nadu, Kerala, West Bengal, Assam, Orissa, Goa, Gujarat, Rajasthan, Maharashtra and MP as well as Delhi. The survey was carried out by a team of researchers, women activists and committed lawyers from different parts of the country on behalf of the Economic Research Foundation, Delhi.

Under all Indian laws, a wife's entitlements on separation/divorce are extremely limited. Basically, the only legal right that an Indian woman has is a right to maintenance from her spouse, irrespective of the personal law that governs her religion, etc. Under the recent PWDVA, women can claim monetary relief in situations of violence and they also have a right to residence. However, in reality, the right to maintenance does not provide women, from any community, adequate financial support to be able to live in a manner similar to the manner in which they lived during the subsistence of marriage. Courts take years to award maintenance and routinely dole out dismal amounts. Actually obtaining maintenance usually requires further rounds of litigation that women generally cannot afford. The woman has a right to her *stridhan* and return of dowry but this right again is difficult to enforce and is hardly sufficient for a woman and any children with her to survive.

Women's economic position is adverse as neither Indian law nor government policy views their work within the home as productive work with economic value. Time Use studies by the Central Statistical Organisation provide evidence of the enormous time spent by women in carrying out household activities. Yet, the non-recognition of household work and 'care' work reinforces gender discrimination and inequality.

In India we are governed by the Separation of Property Regime. A husband is the owner of his property and the wife is the owner of her property. Typically, assets acquired during marriage, such as a house or other property, are bought in the husband's name. Thus, if an Indian woman is separated or deserted even years after marriage, she is left asset-less. Most separated or deserted women and their children are forced to live with their natal family, such as parents and brothers, and are financially dependent on them. Often, they are not welcome even there. Several countries have given legal recognition to the work done by women in building up, maintaining and managing the household and practise a 'Community of Property' Regime. This ensures that women have equal rights in the property acquired by the couple if the marriage breaks down.

The survey looks at the economic and financial status of these women and seeks to capture the stark reality of their lives. It seeks to record their experiences with the police and the courts. The survey was conducted between October 2008 and September 2009 by researchers who were mostly lawyers and women activists. The women interviewed were those who had sought help from women's organisations and State Women's Commissions and/or those who had approached the police and/or the courts. The surveyees were chosen at random and came from all income groups but the vast majority was from low income groups.

The survey records information about the status and style of living of the spouses and children during the subsistence of marriage and after separation/divorce. It seeks to find out the amount of time spent by both the spouses in doing domestic work and other employment, the income and assets of the marital home, and of the spouses post-separation. It interrogates the manner in which the assets of the marital home get divided post-separation and the amounts of spousal and child support awarded/received. It records the change in the financial status of the separated wife/husband through household expenditure and assets post-separation. It asks questions regarding the impact of being married on the careers of the spouses and the perceived loss of earning capacity of the female spouse. It attempts to record the experience of women with the law and the obstacles faced by them while interacting with the criminal justice system and the civil courts and other institutions.

Main Findings

In most parts of the country except the southern region, the majority of separated/divorced women (more than 60 per cent) were aged between 23 and 32 years, that is, they were separated/divorced in their twenties or early thirties. Whereas in the southern region, most women (64 per cent) surveyed were 28–42 years of age. When the same data has been looked at from the point of view of caste categories, more than 60 per cent of the Scheduled Caste (SC)/Scheduled Tribe (ST) and Other Backward Class (OBC) surveyees were divorced/ separated when they were younger than 32 years of age. The data showed a comparatively better picture among the surveyees from general category; about 50 per cent of these surveyees were separated/divorced at or below the age of 32 years.

The findings reveal that the majority live at the mercy of their husbands during the subsistence of marriage and post-marriage depend perforce on their parents, brothers, etc. Despite maintenance provisions, most women are financially dependent on their natal families and 63 per cent live with natal families, usually parents. Among general and OBCs, this data is similar except that in the SC/ST category where 71.4 per cent of the surveyees from this category live with their natal family post separation. Remarriage is extremely rare. The fact that 85.6 per cent of the surveyees had children living with them compounded their troubles. The miserable financial status of separated and divorced women is evident from the fact that even after separation 41.5 per cent had no income and 27.4 per cent earned less than ₹2,000 per month.

Work and Incomes

Although 58.5 per cent of the women surveyed were able to work outside their homes and earn something, their earnings were often too low for them to survive independently. Only 14 per cent of the surveyees were able to earn more than ₹6,000 per month. In the southern region, more separated/

divorced women were working and earning (66 per cent), whereas, in the northern region this percentage was the lowest at about 39 per cent. Not earning aggravates the distressed financial situation of these women, tending to make them more vulnerable. They are burdened with household tasks on returning to the maternal home and lack financial security for themselves and their children. In contrast, 93.5 per cent husbands were working and were financially independent.

Only 2.7 per cent of the women were in a better occupation like being a manager, engineer, professional and consultant, etc, and 4.9 per cent of the surveyees were advocates, teachers or doctors. About 15.6 per cent of our surveyees were working either as domestic workers or were labourers, 23 per cent of the women were in service or employed. In contrast, just 1 per cent of the husbands were labourers, 11 per cent were professionals like managers and 5 per cent were advocates, teachers or doctors. About 8 per cent of surveyees did not know the current occupation of their spouses.

More than 52 per cent of the 72 surveyees who were employed in various offices/enterprises earned less than ₹1,000 per month. Domestic workers generally earned less than ₹2,000 per month. Only 1.7 per cent of the surveyees were earning a 'handsome' salary of more than ₹35,000 per month. The majorities of our surveyees, approximately 80 per cent, had incomes of less than ₹4,000 per month. They and the children dependent upon them live in extreme deprivation, perpetuating a generational cycle of poverty.

Most of the spouses of the surveyees were in the higher income group with over 55 per cent of them earning ₹10,000 and above. In 32 per cent of the cases where the surveyees' incomes were less than ₹1,000 per month, the income of the male spouses was more than ₹10,000 per month. The contrast is stark. Separation/divorce clearly spells financial disaster for women and children but leaves the separated/divorced male with more income to spend on himself alone. About 87.9 per cent of the surveyees who knew about their male spouses' lifestyles said that they lived better than they had earlier or maintained the same lifestyle.

However, for around a quarter of the surveyees, division of assets and higher maintenance may not be an adequate solution. One percent of the men earned less than ₹1,000 per month and 23 per cent earned less than ₹6,000 per month, that is, about 24 per cent of the men earned incomes which can be considered to be below poverty line. A division of incomes between such spouses may not enable either of them to survive above the poverty line. These families will be in dire economic straits unless the state provides adequate social security to everyone living below the poverty line in general and to separated and divorced women and children in particular.

Surveyees' Background

Most of the surveyees were Hindus (75 per cent) followed by Muslims (19 per cent) and the rest belonged to other religious communities. A sizeable 42 per cent belonged to the SC/ST and OBC sections of society. Education levels varied from 17.1 per cent who had no formal education to 51.85 per cent with different levels of schooling, ranging from primary to higher secondary. Surprisingly, 29.7 per cent were graduates (10+2+3 years of education) and post-graduates. Thus, though 29.7 per cent of the surveyees were educated up to the graduate level or above, only 14.1 per cent of the SC/ST surveyees had studied beyond school.

Most (60.7 per cent) of the surveyees had 1–2 children, while 10.4 per cent of them had 3–4 children and a minuscule number (1.2 per cent) had more than four children. About 27.7 per cent of the women had no children. In comparison to OBCs and general category surveyees, more SC/ST surveyees, that is, 17.1 per cent of the SC/ST surveyees had more than two children.

A finding of great significance was that most separated women have to bear the burden of looking after their children single handed. Thus, most separations result in both women and children being abandoned and deserted. Any policy therefore regarding separated and divorced women must take into account this fact. As many as 429 (85.6 per cent) out of 501 children were living with their mothers while the rest were with their fathers (7 per cent) and others.

The majority of our surveyees (53.1 per cent) had got married between the ages of 23 and 32 years. However, in the north, 50 per cent of the surveyees got married fairly early, between the ages of 18 and 22. In 10 per cent of cases, at the time of marriage the surveyees were less than 18 years old, while 19.4 per cent of the SC/ST surveyees were younger than the legal age of marriage.

Most of the marriages (85.7 per cent) were arranged and 75.5 per cent were within the same caste and religion. Most of the surveyees married under Hindu Law (72.3 per cent) followed by Muslim Law (18.8 per cent). Only 4.2 per cent of the surveyees were married under the SMA which is the only civil law in the country. However, the fact that even from the couples who got married to a person of their choice, 61.1 per cent were married under Hindu Law followed by 13 per cent under Muslim Law and 11.1 per cent under other forms of marriage including customary forms shows that the civil law of marriage needs to be strengthened.

Separations and Extended Families

After marriage, the majority of surveyees or 87.92 per cent lived in marital homes with someone from the in-laws' side, like husband's mother, or brother or sister or brother's family, etc., that is, in extended families. While one could surmise from this data that the typical Indian family is extended, the survey seems to suggest that it is in these extended families that the most number of separations currently take place. This could lead to the startling revelation that the majority of the separated and deserted women were living in extended families and faced the maximum harassment there.

Most women in India do not want a divorce even if they have faced violence in their marital homes as they feel both financially and socially insecure outside the marriage. This is why most women's groups are strongly opposed to the introduction of any law which permits irretrievable breakdown of marriage as a ground for divorce. Contesting a divorce petition and not giving a divorce is also the only tool that separated women have to negotiate terms of settlement with their spouses as their legal rights are insignificant. Not surprisingly, therefore, only 73 out of 405 (18 per cent) surveyees were divorced while 81.7 per cent were separated. When we tried to have a look on these figures from the point of view of caste categories, we found that among OBCs 90.4 per cent of the women were separated whereas among the general category 80 per cent of the surveyees were separated. Even amongst the SC/ST surveyees, 73.4 per cent of them were living separately without a divorce though the highest percentages (26.6 per cent) of the divorced were also amongst this social caste group.

However, more than half the women surveyed had gone to the courts mostly asking for maintenance and a few for custody. This shows that, in spite of the inefficiency of the legal system, women are still dependant on it for accessing their rights to maintenance and underscores the need to improve the justice delivery system for women.

A total of 516 cases were filed by 326 surveyees. Multiple cases were filed by some women, mostly (213) asking for maintenance. Thus, the overwhelming need of our surveyees was for financial support. The second largest number of cases (94) was for harassment for dowry and for recovery of dowry. Although the PWDVA, was only brought into force on 26 October 2006, quite a few (46) cases had been filed under the Act.

The finding that only 18.5 per cent of the surveyees asked for divorce reiterates the assertion by many women's groups that very few women ask for divorce because of social and financial insecurity. In sharp contrast,

77.03 per cent of the total 135 cases filed by male spouses were for divorce. The male spouse asked for maintenance/compensation in only two cases. This shows the lack of relevance this remedy has for men.

Causes for Separation/Divorce

The survey highlights the startling reality that 83 per cent of the surveyees were separated due to cruelty or domestic violence in their marital homes. The violence took place even though 87.92 per cent of our surveyees were living in extended families. About 13.5 per cent of the surveyees reported that they had been deserted by their husbands. Some women from the north-eastern states reported that their husbands deserted them and fled to the neighbouring country of Bangladesh; consequently they cannot even go to court to seek maintenance. They do not know the whereabouts of their spouses.

Cruelty was the main reason for separation in 85.3 per cent of the cases in the SC/ST category of the surveyees whereas other kinds of reasons were the cause of separation in about 15 per cent of these cases. Amongst OBCs, in 81.8 per cent of the cases, cruelty was the main reason for separation, whereas in 13.2 per cent of the cases desertion was also an additional reason for the separation.

Domestic violence/cruelty cut across all communities and religions as a reason for separation. Physical violence was present in 64.5 per cent of marriages and approximately two-thirds of the surveyees had suffered physical violence while mental violence was present in almost all the cases. The highest incidence of cruelty was reported from Hindu families; 84.5 per cent of the Hindu surveyees and 79.2 per cent of the Muslim surveyees reported that they had been subjected to cruelty/domestic violence of various kinds. Also, SC/ST surveyees reported that they had to face mental violence in almost all of the cases, whereas in about 90 per cent of the OBC cases the surveyees had faced mental violence. The situation was just a bit different in general category where the surveyees had faced mental violence in about 95 per cent of the cases. In all, we can say that mental violence was present in almost all of the cases. In comparison to the general and OBC categories, more SC/ST surveyees reported that they had to face physical violence, that is, in 73.1 per cent of the cases. Also, 65.8 per cent surveyees in the general category faced physical violence. A total of 56.1 per cent of the surveyees belonging to the OBC category faced physical violence resulting in forced separation.

The main reasons for cruelty/domestic violence were dowry/extra-marital affairs/second marriage of their spouse and the suspicious nature of the spouse. Other reasons for separation were drug addiction, alcoholism of the male spouse, etc. Amongst the various reasons for domestic violence and cruelty, the surveyees in all the caste categories reported that dowry-related harassment remained a major cause of cruelty. Closely following this reason for cruelty was the reason that the male spouses of the surveyees had an extra-marital relationship or had a second wife and hence subjected the surveyees to various forms of cruelty. Extra-marital affair was a reason for cruelty in about 35 per cent of the cases among SC/ST category, whereas other reasons (30.8 per cent) as well as dowry-related issues (28.8 per cent) were also significant causes for cruelty. Our surveyees from the OBC category said that dowry-related issues were the main cause for the cruelty in 42.2 per cent of the cases. The husband perpetrating cruelty because he had a suspicious nature and constantly doubted his wife was a cause for cruelty amongst the OBC surveyees in 14.5 per cent of the cases. In the general category, while dowry accounted for cruelty in about a quarter of the cases, an extra-marital affair or second marriage of the husband was a cause in 36 per cent of these cases. A total of 12.7 per cent of the cases in this category reported that they were subjected to cruelty by their husband because of his unduly suspicious nature.

A majority of our surveyees were engaged in housework and did not work for gain. A total of 69.3 per cent did not work even before their marriage. During the subsistence of marriage, a larger number of them (74.3 per cent) reported that they were not working outside their marital homes and were involved in household chores, in maintaining the house and in looking after the children/elderly. After separation, however, many more surveyees (58.5 per cent) had to again start working or working afresh even though they never worked before. This indicates the lack of financial support post separation.

Value of Housework

The truism that almost all women do the housework and care for the children and elderly is borne out by the fact that 98.2 per cent of our surveyees reported that they did housework during the weekdays and 95 per cent also did housework on holidays. In contrast, only 10.4 per cent of their male spouses helped with occasional household chores like buying vegetables or cooking non-vegetarian food on Sundays. A total of 35.5 per cent of surveyees reported that during their marriage they had to work for 8–12 hours in a day doing housework like cooking, cleaning and washing clothes, besides constantly supervising the children. Quite a few also had to get up in the night to look after the child. Only 25.3 per cent worked between 4 and 8 hours a day in the house.

Our surveyees reported that a considerable amount of time was spent on cooking (4 hours 6 minutes on an average) and household chores (4 hours 45 minutes on average) during the subsistence of their marriage. On an average, another 4 hours approximately were spent on elderly care and approximately 3 hours on child care. Cleaning, reportedly, took about 3 hours on an average. Some women also had to fetch water and/fuel for their household and they spent on an average 1 hour and 27 minutes for these activities.

Our surveyees reported that on an average they spent comparatively less time on these activities after their separation. This showed that the burden of household work had actually decreased. However, more surveyees had to take employment outside the house. On an average, they spent 2 hours and 40 minutes on cooking and 3 hours 19 minutes on household chores. Another 3 hours approximately on an average was spent on elderly care and some minutes more than 3 hours on child care, whereas cleaning reportedly took approximately 2 hours on an average.

The burden of housework was reduced post separation in 39.7 per cent cases. However, an almost equal number (41.2 per cent) said that their burden had increased as they had to do both household and outside work and take care of the children and elderly parents, etc.

Stress and Anxiety Levels

Separation often results in acute feelings of anxiety and stress in women. They are generally insecure about the future. Many are traumatised by what they have undergone. They feel guilty about the break-up and their dependence on their natal families. They worry about the children's emotional and physical upbringing. An average 60.5 per cent of the surveyees reported feelings of stress and anxiety. A heavy burden of responsibility was also felt by 53.4 per cent of women. A total of 34.3 per cent of the surveyees reported feeling emotionally burdened with responsibility for their children. A minority of the surveyees (9.4 per cent), however, felt that getting out of their marital home was a positive experience for them. They felt free after the separation.

Loss of Career Opportunities

A contentious issue that arises on the breakdown of a marriage is the manner in which a wife should be compensated for the loss of earning capacity that she has suffered during the subsistence of marriage by not being able to earn, or spend enough time on her career. The surveyees gave examples to show how marriage had affected their career opportunities as they could not work after marriage or could work only in a very limited way. Over half, that is, 62.7 per cent in all of the cases, and in 75.6 per cent from the north, 67.5 per cent from the south, 59.3 per cent from the east and 54.9 per cent from the west said that they had suffered a loss of earning capacity. Some of the surveyees reported that their in-laws and spouses did not keep their promise to let them study. During marriage, the women's housework and care work had left the men free to pursue their careers. A total of 80 per cent of the women felt that their male spouses had benefited because of their contribution to the household. Their spouses' lifestyle also did not change for worse in 203 out of 231 cases in which the surveyees had knowledge about the lifestyle.

One positive thing about career-oriented women can be inferred from the data: women who were employed at the time of their marriage did not have to leave the job. A total of 47.3 per cent of these 182 surveyees said that they did not have to resign from their job after their marriage. Other surveyees responded that they left their jobs on their own, not due to the marriage. They gave the explanations like parents asking them to resign before the marriage, or quitting after marriage to care for a sick child, or because they did not wish to pursue a career, or because the job was not transferable while her male spouse was working in another city, etc.

When we analysed the data according to the caste category of the surveyees, we found that 60 per cent of the OBC category surveyees and around 54 per cent of the SC/ST category surveyees had to give up their job during their marriage. A smaller number of surveyees (39.4 per cent) from the general category of surveyees reported that they had to leave their job after their marriage.

Ownership of Property

In India in the absence of any laws for division of marital property, when a separation or divorce takes place, the male spouse/husband usually walks away with all the movable and immovable assets of the household.

Most of the surveyees lived in marital homes acquired and owned either by themselves or the parents of their spouses or their own parents. However, 59.8 per cent of marital homes had been acquired by the in-laws. Surprisingly, only 15.3 per cent of the surveyees reported that their marital homes had been acquired by their spouses or themselves. A total of 13.8 per cent of the marital homes had been rented either by the surveyees or by their male spouses or by both of them.

The fact that such a vast majority of surveyees from the lower and lower-middle income groups in urban areas live in houses which belong to the male spouse's parents will have an impact on any law for division of marital property and also on the implementation of the right to residence under the PWDVA. The PWDVA has in explicit terms given a right of residence in the shared household, that is, the household in which the parties were living during their marriage whether it belonged to either or both of the parties or not. The Supreme Court has, however, in a judgment[1] not allowed this right of residence to a wife even though the residence was a shared household. Even though the effect of this judgment has been subsequently whittled down by another Supreme Court judgment,[2] such judgments will keep on reappearing given the patriarchal nature of sections of our judiciary. Only a few surveyees reported that they lived in their parents' homes.

Ownership of Other Assets

A total of 23 per cent of the surveyees owned land during the subsistence of their marriage but only 20.5 per cent of them had current possession of the land at the time of this survey. The land had been acquired by either the surveyees' parents or herself or her spouse or in-laws. While the male spouses and the surveyees' in-laws had bought land in only 25.8 per cent of the cases, they managed to grab much more land in another 14.8 per cent of the cases.

Of the 161 surveyees who said that they had owned vehicles (cars, scooters/motor-cycles, bi-cycles), in a surprising 42.8 per cent of the cases either the surveyees or their parents had bought the vehicles. The buying of immoveable and moveable properties in 24.8 per cent of the cases by the parents of the surveyees for them and their male-spouses, shows the extent

[1] S.R. Batra v. Taruna Batra MANU/SC/0007/2007: (2007) 3 SCC 169.

[2] V.D. Bhanot v Savita Bhanot (2007) 3 SCC 169.

to which dowry is flourishing. Most of the vehicles (65.3 per cent) remain with the in-laws and male spouses.

Jewellery was owned by most of the surveyees and had been acquired by her or her parents in 59 per cent cases while the male spouses/in-laws had given her jewellery only in 10 per cent of the cases. However, after separation the wife and her parents retained the possession only in 27 per cent of the cases.

When we look at the data regarding financial assets, in 19 per cent of the cases the surveyees had cash in the bank but the source was they themselves (or their parents in 57.2 per cent of the cases). Probably, that is the reason why they retained the possession of the cash in an almost similar percentage of cases, that is, 58.4 per cent.

Maintenance

Only 213 surveyees had asked for maintenance in which 150 had also asked for maintenance for their children. A total of 47.4 per cent of the surveyees, that is, almost half had not even asked for maintenance. The reasons ranged from not knowing that they were entitled to ask for maintenance, to not having the money to approach the courts or wishing not to be dependent on the spouse.

As many as 48.8 per cent of these maintenance cases were pending; in 41.8 per cent of the cases maintenance had been allowed and in 9.4 per cent of the cases their applications had been dismissed. In the 89 cases where maintenance was allowed, only 12 women reported receiving a satisfactory amount.

Of the 60 surveyees who answered the question on the quantum of maintenance awarded to them, those with no income at all received merely 13 per cent of the salary on an average, for their financial support. Women who earned less than ₹1,000 but whose spouses earned between ₹5,000 and ₹56,000 were awarded an average of 11 per cent of their male spouse's salary.

Surveyees who earned more than ₹10,000 per month but whose spouses earned between ₹100,000 and ₹250,000 per month, received an average maintenance of 4.5 per cent of the man's income! In one case from Kerala, the surveyee fought for 17 years to be awarded maintenance of ₹900 per month even though her male spouse was earning ₹56,000 per month.

In 35.6 per cent of the 87 cases which were filed in court, maintenance was granted within a year. The rest took anywhere from 1 to 5 years. Through the conciliation process, however, many more (55.6 per cent) of the 18 cases got solved within a year.

Only 25 surveyees appealed for increase of maintenance although 72 out of those who were granted maintenance were dissatisfied with the quantum of maintenance. Three appeals took as long as 5–10 years for a decision.

Out of 101 decided cases, in 14 cases lump sum amounts were granted and in 87 cases monthly maintenance was allowed. In 9 out of these 14, the court ordered the lump sum amount whereas in 4 cases the surveyee got it through settlement. In one case, the surveyee got a lump sum order but it was not implemented as she went back to her husband. While 55.4 per cent of these 101 surveyees said that they had received the payment, 43.6 per cent said that they had not. Out of a total of 56 surveyees, 26 (60.5 per cent) claimed that though their spouses pay monthly maintenance, usually they do not receive the payment regularly.

In 59.1 per cent of the 186 cases, in which the surveyees replied to the given question, the wife could not prove the income of the husband for a variety of reasons including not knowing the income and not having access to his income documents. In more than half (57.8 per cent) of the 187 cases, the spouses tried to conceal their income. A large number of them, approximately 18 per cent, had also transferred assets to other people during the court proceedings.

A total of 90 per cent of the 276 women felt the burden of proving spousal income should not fall on them. When we asked the surveyees whether they should share the household assets equally with their spouses, an overwhelming percentage (79.3 per cent of 372 surveyees) answered in the affirmative.

Stridhan and Dowry

The value of *stridhan* was reported to be between ₹100,000 and ₹500,000 in 23.5 per cent of the 264 cases, less than ₹100,000 but over ₹50,000 in 15 per cent of these cases and more than ₹500,000 in 9.8 per cent of these cases. One-fourth of the surveyees did not know the value of their *stridhan*.

Cash dowries ranged from ₹50,000 to over ₹500,000, with regional variations. The highest cash dowries were given in south India, followed by northern India.

Parental incomes on the other hand were low. In 42.7 per cent of the 222 cases, the parents' earning was between ₹1,000 and ₹5,000 per month and in another 19.6 per cent it was between ₹500 and ₹10,000 per month.

In 53.8 per cent of the 338 reported cases, the parents had to borrow money to acquire dowry or *stridhan* for their daughter's marriage.

In over 69 per cent of the 309 reported cases, the dowry and *stridhan* was in the possession of the male spouse and in-laws and in 30 per cent cases it was with the surveyees. In quite a few cases, it had been sold off by the in-laws/spouse.

Only 40.1 per cent of the 367 surveyees went to the police for recovery of dowry, *stridhan* or gift items but their experience was not positive. The initial hitch was to get the case registered and the women had to take the help of women's groups/organisations or State Commissions for Women. One woman said that it took one year to get the case registered due to non-cooperation of the police and no recovery had been made by them. The court had not passed any order despite several requests for recovery of at least her clothes!

In 54.4 per cent of the 370 reported cases, women had to face hostility or prejudice from various people on account of their separation. This was most prevalent in northern India and least in eastern India. During marriage the women had limited decision-making powers. Decisions regarding expenditure inside the house and outside the house were made by the surveyees in 20.5 per cent and 18.2 per cent of the cases respectively. Matters regarding their children's education were decided by the surveyees in about 40 per cent cases. After separation, however, the picture changed and in the majority of cases the surveyees were taking decisions on expenditure (in about 60 per cent cases), children's education (in about 75 per cent cases), etc. Their mobility also increased sharply. The women were changing their lives and learning new skills, independently going to work, going out to pay bills and making new friends and new social connections beyond their marital and natal families.

The survey also brings out various regional similarities and differences which are discussed in the following chapters.

3

General Information about the Surveyees

This chapter provides a broad overview of the status of the women surveyed in the four regions of the country. The surveyees were mostly young separated women who had approached various women's groups and organisations, State Women's Commissions and lawyers for help or who had gone to the family courts to file their claims. Thus, the survey was conducted only amongst those women who had approached either a group or other authorities and therefore lacks data about those women who may not have approached these groups. Although the surveyees cut across all class and caste groups and communities, the majority belonged to the lower income groups. The survey is based on the information that was given by the surveyees to the researchers which was duly filled into a detailed questionnaire.

The survey highlights the lack of control that most women have over their lives prior to, during and post marriage. A majority of the surveyees reported that they lived with and were dependent on their natal families after separation. A reporting of great significance was that the overwhelming majority of surveyees had been separated, deserted and abandoned along with their children and thus the children had also become homeless along with their mothers. As many as 85.6 per cent of the children were living with their mother while only 7.9 per cent were living with their father at the time of the survey. A large number of these surveyees, around 40 per cent, were not working. The miserable financial status of the surveyees became evident from the fact that 41.7 per cent of the surveyees did not have any income at all while 27.4 per cent of the surveyees were earning less than ₹2,000 per month. Again, although the vast majority of surveyees were not responsible for whom they were married to, since their marriages were arranged marriages, they had to suffer the social and economic consequences of the breakdown of the marriage and lived with the natal family on sufferance. Another finding of importance is that a significant number of our surveyees were not divorced but had been living apart from their husbands, sometimes for several years. Only 188 of the 405 surveyees said that they had filed cases and most of these were cases claiming maintenance or spousal and child support from their husbands. This finding again highlighted their dismal economic status. Finally, domestic violence was found to be the primary reason for separation, regardless of whether the surveyee had been forced to leave the house or had left on her own.

Current Age Group of the Surveyees

Graph 3.1(a) gives a region-based distribution of the surveyees by their current age. In most parts of the country, except in the southern region, the separated/divorced women were aged between 23 and 32 years. In the southern region, in most of the cases the surveyees were between 28 and 42 years of age. In the north, 59.6 per cent of the women were less than 32 years of age. In the east and west, 61.4 per cent and 62.4 per cent of the women, respectively, were less than 32 years of age. In the southern region, however, the picture was different. Here, in most cases (64.2 per cent), the surveyees were between 28 and 42 years of age. It is pertinent to mention that while there were only a few surveyees in the east and west and none in the north above 42 years of age, 7.5 per cent of the surveyees were between 48 and 52 years of age in the south. Graph 3.1(a) further shows that the current ages of the surveyees were less than 32 years in 54.6 per cent cases, and in 31.1 per cent cases they were between 32 and 42 years of age. Thus, most of the women who approached us were divorced or separated fairly early in their lives, in their twenties or thirties. In 14.5 per cent cases, the surveyees were more than 42 years of age. In three cases, the women did not know their age so they did not respond to the question. It appears that women across ages approach the courts and women's groups/organisations and other institutions. However, the largest numbers of women who seek help are relatively young. Only in 14.5 per cent cases, the surveyees were older than 42 years.

Graph 3.1(b) shows that the majority (61.9 per cent) of the SC/ST surveyees were in the age group of 18–32 years at the time of their interview. Another 27 per cent of them belonged to the age group of 33-42 years and only 11 per cent were 43 years of age or even older.

Among OBCs also, more than 60 per cent of the surveyees were in the age group of 18–32 years at the time of interview, 28.3 per cent of them were in the age group of 33–42 years and only 11.3 per cent were of 43 years of age or older.

Graph 3.1 (a) Percentage Distribution of the Surveyees by Their Age Groups in Different Regions

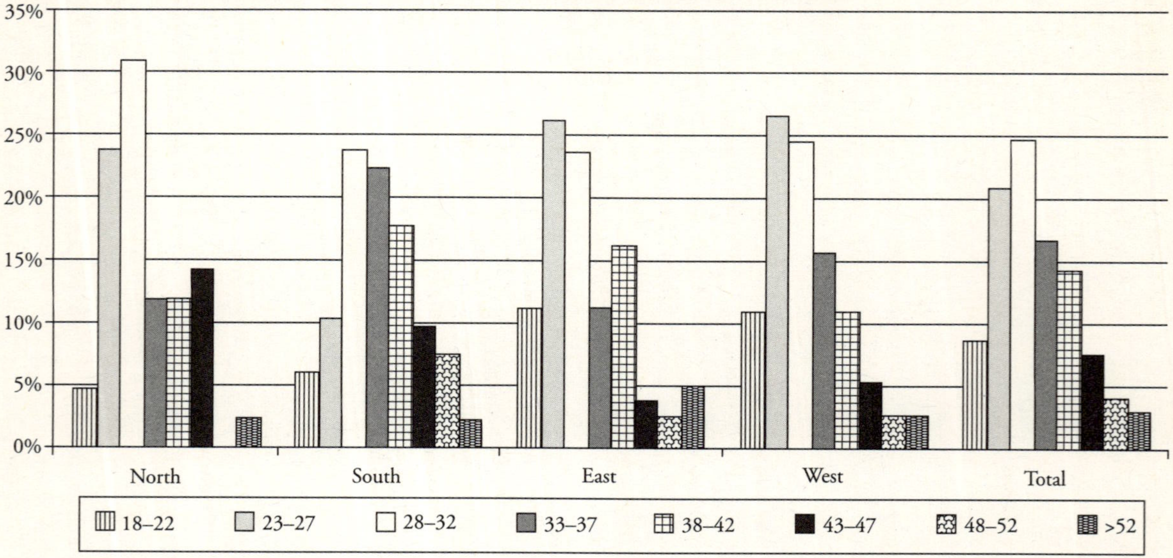

Note: The age of the surveyees in three cases has not been reported and these have been excluded from the age distribution in this graph.

Graph 3.1(b) Age-wise Percentage Distribution of the Surveyees by Their Social Caste Groups

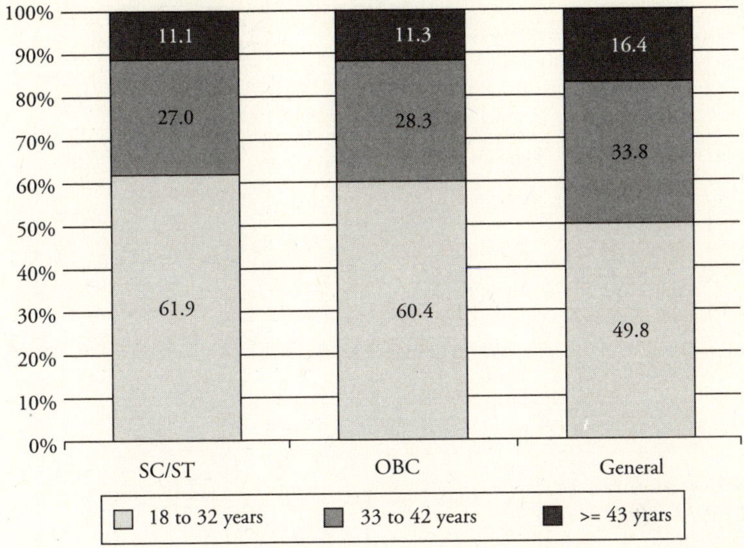

Among the surveyees belonging to the general category, this distribution was only slightly different and about 50 per cent of the surveyees were in the age group of 18–32 years and another 34 per cent surveyees were in the age group of 33–42 years. Only 16 per cent of these women were 43 years of age or even older.

Current Residential Status of the Surveyees

One of the main findings of the survey confirmed what had often been reported by women's organisations, groups and lawyers working in the area of family law. Graph 3.2(a) shows that most of the separated and divorced women in India are economically dependent and have no place to live. They live at the mercy of their husbands during the subsistence of marriage and thereafter with their parents, brothers, etc., after being forced to leave their marital home.

This stark reality became evident in our survey as in 63.1 per cent of the cases we found that the surveyees were living with their natal families (parents in 239 cases and siblings in 16 cases) and in 11.9 per cent (48) cases with

Graph 3.2(a) The Current Residential Status of the Divorced and Separated Women (Surveyees) in Different Regions

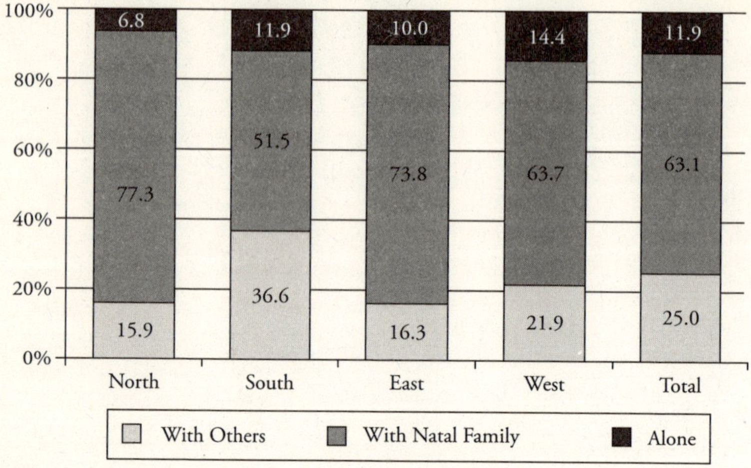

Note: There was only one case of non-reporting in the graph.

others. When we further clarified these others we found that in 6 out of these 48 cases, the surveyees were living with their second husbands, 26 with minor children (which means they were living on their own) and 13 were living with their major children (usually these were children in their twenties and thirties), and 3 with other relatives. Thus, we can say that 31.4 per cent of the surveyees were living alone whereas 3.96 per cent were living with others including major children. A study done in Pune, in the district courts showed that a majority of women took refuge in their natal homes, often along with their children.[1] This was also found in another study[2] from certain parts of Pune. This was also found in the SOPPECOM study done in certain parts of Pune. The SOPPECOM study reported that in the Daund taluka and Ghole Road ward of Pune city 50 percent and 65 percent deserted women respectively were living with their natal families.

Graph 3.2(a), therefore, corroborates both anecdotal evidence and findings of previous micro-studies that most Indian women are forced to take refuge in their parental home as they have no other place to go to. The lack of resources that women suffer from has also been shown by certain government

---

[1] Jaya Sagade, *Law of Maintenance: An Empirical Study* (Mumbai: N.M. Tripathi Pvt. Ltd., 1996).

[2] SOPPECOM, Hindola, 'Assessing the Extent and Nature of Desertion in Daund Taluka and Ghole Road Ward of Pune City' (Pune: SOPPECOM, December 2008), 89.

studies.[3] The fact that in only six cases the surveyees had remarried and were living with their second husband reflects the social discrimination faced by these women.

Graph 3.2(b) shows the residential status of the surveyees according to the caste categories they belong to. Though the majority of women in each caste live with their natal family, more OBC women (30.2 per cent) lived alone, followed by women in the general category (24.7 per cent).

Most (71.4 per cent) of the SC/ST surveyees were living with their parents and/or siblings after their separation/divorce. The difference between them and the other caste categories was about 10 per cent. The trend of living with the natal family, therefore, cut across caste lines and seems to be reflective of the dependent status of separated women.

Graph 3.2(b) Distribution of the Surveyees Belonging to Different Social Caste Groups by Their Residential Status after Separation

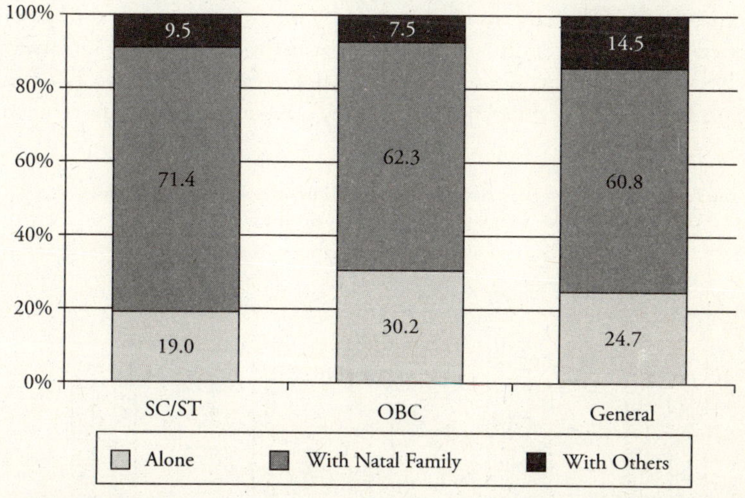

[3] Government of India, Report: *Gendering Human Development Indices: Recasting the Gender Development Index and Gender Empowerment Measure for India*, Part III (New Delhi: Ministry of Women and Child Development, 2009), 47. Available at www.wcd.nic.in (last accessed on 13 July 2010). The Gender Empowerment Measures (GEM) scores for India estimated by UNDP are a very low at 0.228 (UNDP *Human Development Report*, 1998). It uses the indicators:

i. Percentage of Female/Male with Operational Land Holdings;
ii. Percentage of Females/Males with Bank Accounts in Scheduled Commercial Banks (with credit limit above ₹2 lakh); and
iii. Share of Female/Male Estimated Earned Income Share per capita per annum.

Current Activity Status and Income of the Surveyees and Their Spouses

Graph 3.3(a) shows that in total 58.5 per cent of the women surveyed were working outside their homes and thus earning something. The rest presumably continued to perform household chores, etc., at home. In the southern region, we found that more separated/divorced women were working outside their home and in approximately 66 per cent cases they were earning whereas in the northern region this percentage was the lowest, that is, about 39 per cent. Not earning obviously aggravates the already distressed financial situation of these women, tending to make them more vulnerable. It was reported by several women that their dependant status forced them to continue to perform household tasks, though now in their maternal homes, and yet they had to continuously worry about their and their children's security and future. The amounts earned by the surveyees were also rather limited and were certainly not sufficient for them to live in the same way as they were earlier living in their marital home except in a few cases (see Graph 3.6). The stark difference between the percentages of men and women

Graph 3.3(a) The Current Activity Status of the Surveyees and Their Spouses after Divorce or Separation in Different Regions

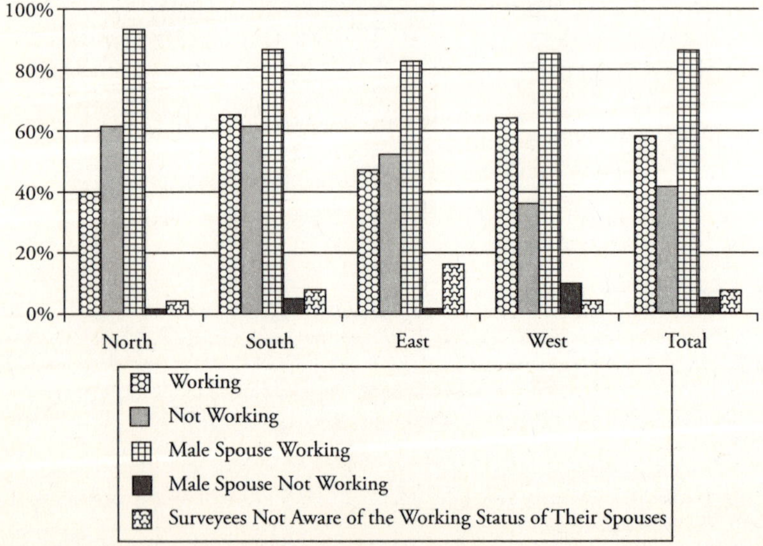

who work outside the home became evident when we conducted the survey. Even though many more women are forced to work after their separation/divorce (see Graph 4.1 in Chapter 4), their numbers were still rather limited. However, a total of 85.9 per cent of the male spouses worked outside the house. In the eastern region, only 1.3 per cent of the husbands were not working and in the western region 10.2 per cent husbands were not working. However, in the east, almost 16 per cent of the surveyees were either not aware of the working status of their spouses or did not respond to the question on the working status of their spouses. In the northern region, the largest proportions of the husbands (93.2 per cent) were working. However, 4.5 per cent of the surveyees in this region also could not respond or were not aware of the activity status of their spouses.

Graph 3.3(b) shows that there was no major difference with respect to the working status of the surveyees when we compare them according to their caste groups/categories. Among the SC/ST category, 40.6 per cent of the surveyees were currently not-working and similar percentages in the other two caste categories were also not working. A total number of 397 surveyees answered this question.

Graph 3.3(b) Percentage Distribution of the Surveyees Belonging to Different Caste Groups by Their Current Work Status

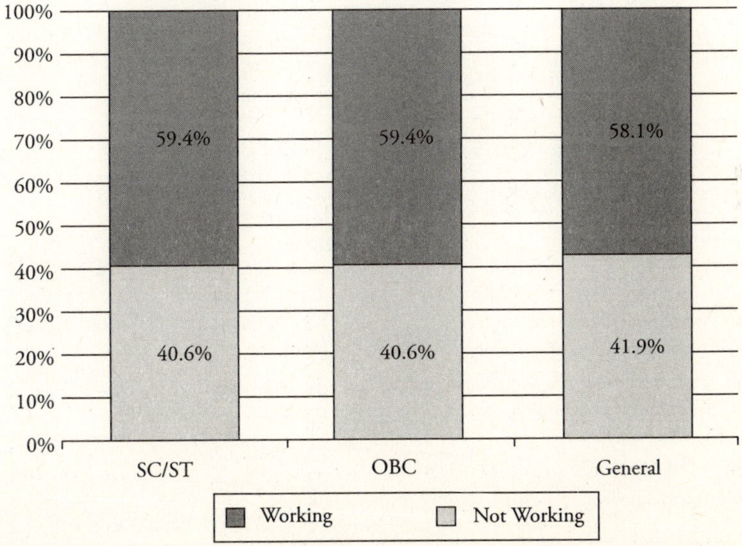

The data in Graph 3.4 shows that most of the surveyees either did not earn or were employed in low paying jobs such as domestic work or were self-employed workers. Not many of the surveyees were engaged in large public and private enterprises. A total of 8.70 per cent of the surveyees worked as either labourers or as self-employed workers. This graph also reiterates that 40 per cent of the surveyees remained housewives, while 14.1 per cent were working as domestic workers outside their homes. In 16 per cent of the cases, the surveyees were involved in an occupation which paid them a moderate to high income. Of these, 2.7 per cent of the women were in a more lucrative occupation like being a manager, engineer, professional and consultant, etc., and another 4.9 per cent of the surveyees were professionals like advocates, teachers or doctors. A total of 3.20 per cent women had small/petty businesses, or were doing the job of an accountant, clerk, goldsmith, or providing tiffin service, etc. In 2 per cent of the cases, she was a seller. Also, 2 per cent of the surveyees were studying at the time of the survey. A total of 21.23 per cent of our surveyees were working either as domestic workers or were labourers while 17.5 per cent of the women were in service or employed.

Table 3.1 shows the distribution of the surveyees in different regions by their current activity status/occupation. In both the northern and eastern

Graph 3.4 Percentage Distribution of the Surveyees by Their Current Activity Status/ Occupation

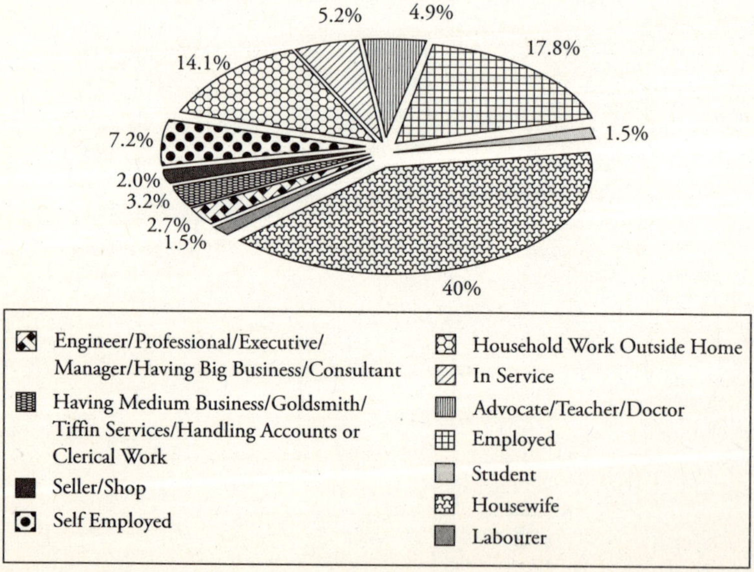

Table 3.1 Distribution of Surveyees by Their Current Occupation in Different Regions

	Number of the Surveyees					*Distribution Within the Region*				
	North	*South*	*East*	*West*	*Total*	*North*	*South*	*East*	*West*	*Total*
Engineer/Professional/Executive/ Manager/Having big business/ Consultant	1	9	0	1	11	2.3	6.7	0.0	0.7	2.7
Having medium business/Goldsmith/ Tiffin services/Handling accounts or clerical work	0	6	1	6	13	0.0	4.5	1.3	4.1	3.2
Seller/Shop	0	3	2	3	8	0.0	2.2	2.5	2.0	2.0
Self-employed	3	13	2	11	29	6.8	9.7	2.5	7.5	7.2
Household work outside home	3	12	14	28	57	6.8	9.0	17.5	19.0	14.1
In service	1	10	0	10	21	2.3	7.5	0.0	6.8	5.2
Advocate/Teacher/Doctor	3	5	8	4	20	6.8	3.7	10.0	2.7	4.9
Employed	6	25	11	30	72	13.6	18.7	13.8	20.4	17.8
Student	1	1	2	2	6	2.3	0.7	2.5	1.4	1.5
Housewife	26	45	40	51	162	59.1	33.6	50.0	34.7	40.0
Labourer	0	5	0	1	6	0.0	3.7	0.0	0.7	1.5
Total	44	134	80	147	405	100.0	100.0	100.0	100.0	100.0

regions, approximately 50 per cent and 59 per cent of the surveyees, respectively, were housewives. However, in the south and west, only 33.6 per cent and 34.7 per cent of the surveyees were housewives and in these regions more than 60 per cent of the surveyees were working.

Graph 3.5 shows that in sharp contrast to the high percentage of the women who had remained housewives and were working in lowly paid jobs, their spouses were not only working in an overwhelming majority of cases but were also in far better jobs. A total of 15 per cent of the male spouses were employed with companies whereas 21 per cent were employed in some other kind of work. Another 15 per cent of the spouses were self-employed. In 11 per cent of the cases, the spouses either had a medium business or ran tiffin services, etc. They were also goldsmiths, accountants or clerks. Another 11 per cent were engineers, professionals, managers, consultants or running a big business. A total of 4 per cent of the male spouses were traders or had shops or were engaged in selling one thing or the other. About 4.7 per cent of the male spouses were advocates or doctors or teachers. Only 3 per cent of the spouses were engaged in agriculture and a minuscule 1 per cent were

Graph 3.5 Percentage Distribution of Surveyees by the Current Activity Status of Their Husbands

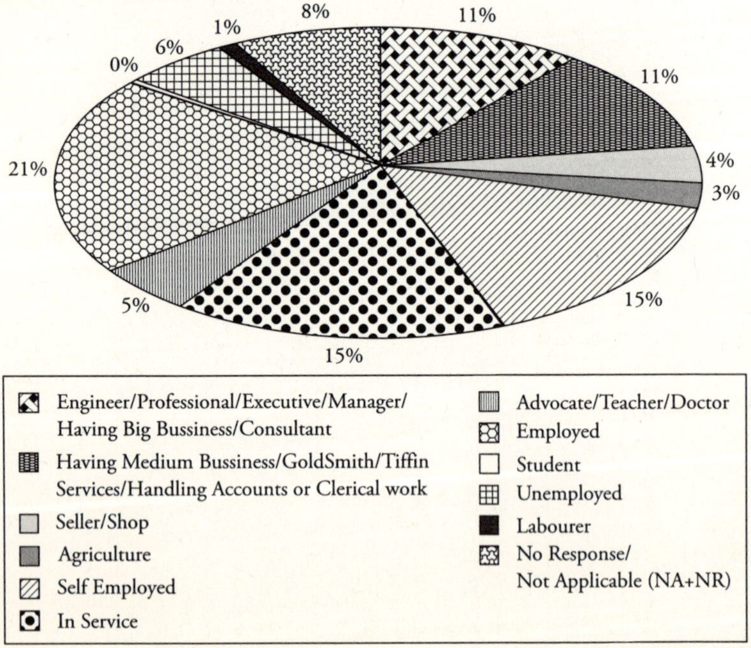

labourers. Merely 6 per cent of the men were unemployed. The women did not know about the occupation of their husbands in 8 per cent of the total of 405 cases.

Graph 3.6 and Table 3.2 highlight the miserable financial status of separated and divorced women in India today. In 41.7 per cent of the cases, the surveyees did not have any income and in 27.4 per cent of the cases the surveyees were earning less than ₹2,000 per month. Region-wise comparison again highlights the fact that in the south the surveyees were better off, as a lesser percentage (34.3 per cent women) did not earn in contrast to the north where a majority of 61.4 per cent of those surveyed had no income. In 20.5 per cent of the cases, the women were earning a moderate salary of ₹2,000 to ₹10,000 per month (see Box 3.1). In 10.1 per cent cases, they were earning a better salary of more than ₹10,000 per month. The majority of our surveyees, therefore, belonged to the lowest income group/poorest sections of our society. Only two of the surveyees did not respond to this question.

To put it in another way, 29.6 per cent of the surveyees had an income between ₹1,000 and ₹4,000 per month, 9.9 per cent of them had an income between ₹4,000 and ₹10,000. Only 5.2 per cent of the surveyees had an income between ₹10,000 and ₹20,000, while 4.4 per cent got between ₹20,000 and ₹35,000. Only 1.7 per cent of the surveyees were earning a 'handsome' salary of more than ₹35,000 per month. The majority of our surveyees, approximately 80 per cent, earned less than ₹4,000 per month and were living in poverty.[4]

Graph 3.7 contains the responses of the surveyees regarding the income level of their male spouses after the divorce or separation. Table 3.3 shows that as many as 111 surveyees (27.4 per cent) could not answer the question or stated that they were not aware of their spouses' income.

In Table 3.3, the income of the female spouse has been kept static and the income of the male spouse is the variable showing that when the separated/divorced wife's income falls in one category how the income of the husband varies. We found that in cases in which the surveyees had no income, their spouses earned varying amounts. In 4.5 per cent of these cases, even the male spouses did not earn, in about 2.2 per cent of these cases they earned less

---

[4] Rukmini Shrinivasan, '55% of India's Population Poor: Report', *TNN*, 15 July 2010. Available at http://timesofindia.indiatimes.com/articleshow/6169549.cms (last accessed on 21 July 2010). Also see, Human Development Report 2009, *Overcoming Barriers: Human Mobility and Development*, Table I, p. 177. Available at http://hdr.undp.org/en/ (last accessed on 23 July 2010).

See also, Utsa Patnaik, 'Poverty and Neo-Liberalism in India'. Available at http://www.ideaswebsite.org/pdfs/neoliberalism(2).pdf.

Graph 3.6 Percentage Distribution of the Surveyees by Their Current Monthly Income (in Rupees) Categories in Different Regions

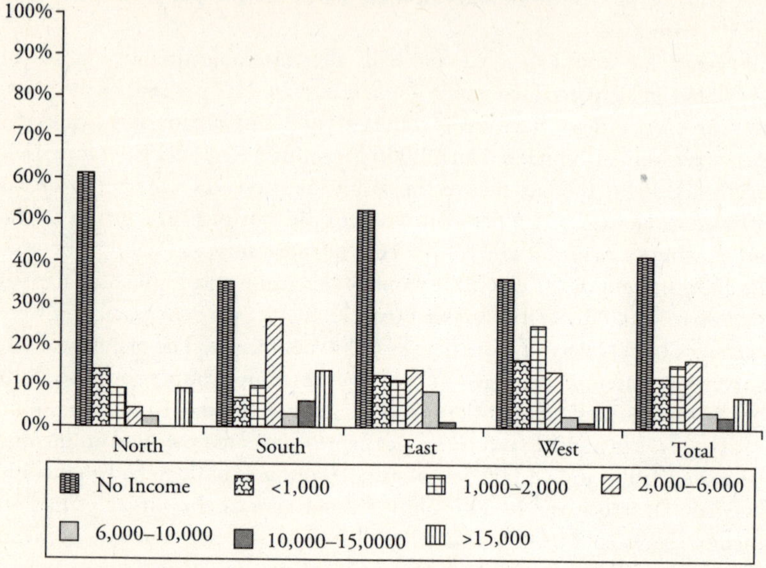

Table 3.2 Percentage Distribution of the Surveyees by Their Current Monthly Income (in Rupees) Categories in Different Regions

	No Income	*< 1,000*	*1,000–2,000*	*2,000–6,000*	*6,000–10,000*	*10,000–15,000*	*> 15,000*	*Non-Response*	*Total*
North	61.4	13.6	9.1	4.5	2.3	0.0	9.1	0.0	100.0
South	34.3	6.7	9.7	25.4	3.0	6.0	13.4	1.5	100.0
East	52.5	12.5	11.3	13.8	8.8	1.3	0.0	0.0	100.0
West	36.1	16.3	24.5	13.6	2.7	1.4	5.4	0.0	100.0
Total	41.5	12.1	15.3	16.5	4.0	2.7	7.4	0.5	100.0

than ₹2,000 per month, in another 29.1 per cent of these cases they earned between ₹2,000 and ₹10,000 per month, whereas in 23.1 per cent cases they earned between ₹10,000 and ₹15,000 per month and in an astounding 41 per cent of these cases the spouses earned more than ₹15,000 per month whereas the surveyees had no income at all.

In 25.8 per cent of the cases where the surveyees' incomes are less than ₹1,000 per month the incomes of the male spouses are more than ₹10,000 per month. In approximately 48.4 per cent of the cases the incomes of the male spouses are between ₹2,000 and ₹10,000 per month. Thus, their spouses are far better placed than the separated/divorced wife after the separation.

Graph 3.7 The Current Monthly Income (in Rupees) of Spouses of the Surveyees after Divorce or Separation in Different Regions

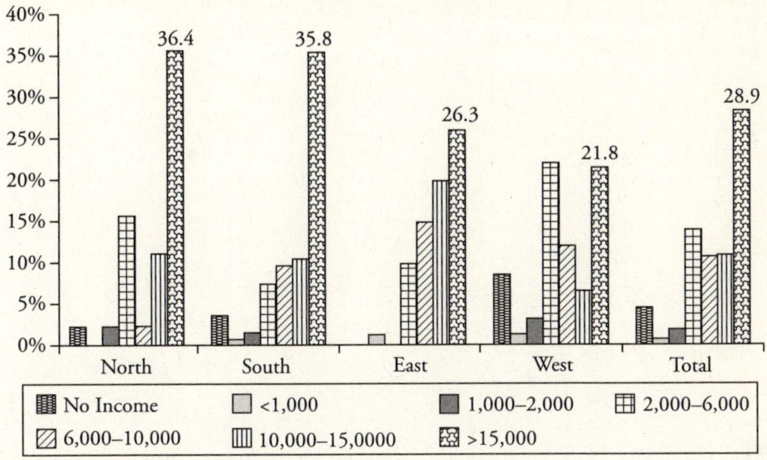

Similar is the case when the incomes of the separated/divorced wives are between ₹1,000 and ₹2,000 per month. The spouses are earning more than ₹10,000 per month in 29.3 per cent of the cases. In more than 51.2 per cent cases, the male spouses are earning between ₹2,000 and ₹10,000 per month. Thus, their earnings are much more than the surveyees' incomes.

The situation is similar for women in the income group of ₹1,000 to ₹6,000 per month.

When the incomes of the surveyees are between ₹6,000 and ₹10,000 per month, the spouses are currently earning more than ₹15,000 per month in 50 per cent of the cases, ₹6,000 to ₹10,000 per month in 25 per cent cases and ₹10,000 to ₹15,000 per month in the other 25 per cent cases.

When the incomes of the surveyees are between ₹10,000 and ₹15,000 per month, the male spouses fall in the highest income category in approximately 66.7 per cent of the cases. Only 11 per cent of the male spouses were earning less than then the surveyees, whereas the rest, that is, 22.2 per cent of them were earning the same as the surveyees.

In the highest category of income, that is, more than ₹15,000 per month the husbands are in the same band in 81 per cent cases and in other cases they are earning less than the women. A total of 9.5 per cent of the male spouses are earning between ₹6,000 and ₹15,000 per month whereas 4.8 per cent of them are earning as little as ₹1,000 or ₹2,000 per month and a similar percentage have no incomes.

Table 3.3 Percentage Distribution of Male Spouses in Different Income Levels by the Current Income of the Surveyees

Income of the Surveyees	*Income of the Spouse*							
	No income	*< 1,000*	*1,000–2,000*	*2,000–6,000*	*6,000–10,000*	*10,000–15,000*	*> 15,000*	*Total*
No Income	4.5	0.7	1.5	19.4	9.7	23.1	41.0	100.0
< 1,000	19.4	3.2	3.2	29.0	19.4	3.2	22.6	100.0
1,000–2,000	12.2	0.0	7.3	31.7	19.5	12.2	17.1	100.0
2,000–6,000	2.0	2.0	2.0	18.4	26.5	6.1	42.9	100.0
6,000–10,000	0.0	0.0	0.0	0.0	25.0	25.0	50.0	100.0
10,000–15,000	0.0	0.0	0.0	0.0	11.1	22.2	66.7	100.0
>15,000	4.8	0.0	4.8	0.0	4.8	4.8	81.0	100.0
Total	6.5	1.0	2.7	19.5	15.0	15.4	39.9	100.0

Note: The table includes only those cases where the surveyees have reported their incomes and the income of their spouses. There were only 293 such cases (72 per cent of the total sample of 405).

Table 3.4 Current Monthly Income of the Surveyees in Rupees

Present Occupation of Self	*No Income*	*<1,000*	*1,000–2,000*	*2,000–6,000*	*6,000–10,000*	*10,000–15,000*	*> 15,000*	*Total*
Engineer/Professional/Executive/Manager/Having big business/Consultant	0.0	0.0	0.0	18.2	0.0	0.0	81.8	100.0
Having medium business/Goldsmith/Tiffin services/Handling accounts or Clerical work	0.0	15.4	30.8	15.4	7.7	7.7	23.1	100.0
Seller/Shop	0.0	25.0	25.0	50.0	0.0	0.0	0.0	100.0
Self-employed	0.0	17.2	31.0	27.6	6.9	10.3	6.9	100.0
Household work outside home	0.0	35.1	38.6	24.6	1.8	0.0	0.0	100.0
In service	0.0	0.0	14.3	28.6	9.5	19.0	28.6	100.0
Advocate/Teacher/Doctor	0.0	5.0	5.0	35.0	25.0	5.0	25.0	100.0
Employed	0.0	23.9	28.2	32.4	5.6	2.8	7.0	100.0
Student	100.0	0.0	0.0	0.0	0.0	0.0	0.0	100.0
Housewife	100.0	0.0	0.0	0.0	0.0	0.0	0.0	100.0
Labourer	0.0	40.0	20.0	20.0	20.0	0.0	0.0	100.0
Total	41.7	12.2	15.4	16.6	4.0	2.7	7.4	100.0

Note: The table has excluded the two cases where the surveyees have not reported their incomes.

Table 3.4 shows that a sizable number of the surveyees (49) earned less than ₹1,000 per month in spite of the fact that they were employees in various offices/enterprises. Most (76.3 per cent) of the domestic workers earned less than ₹2,000 per month. However, the majority (67, i.e. 16.6 per cent) of those surveyed earned between ₹2,000 and ₹6,000 regardless of the profession they were in.

Religion of the Surveyees

Most of the 405 surveyees were Hindus (75 per cent) followed by Muslims (19 per cent), Christians (4.4 per cent), Buddhists (0.2 per cent) and others (1 per cent). The highest numbers of Hindus were in east (92.5 per cent) and highest numbers of Muslims were in the western region (35 per cent). The highest numbers of Christians were surveyed in the southern region (see Graph 3.8).

Graph 3.8 Distribution of the Surveyees by Their Religion in Different Regions

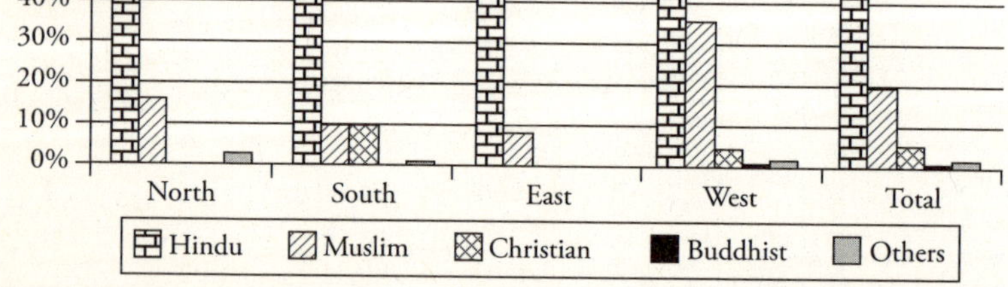

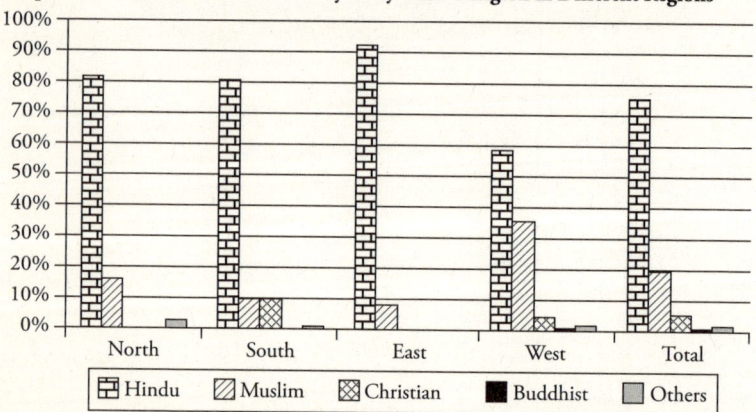

As per the data in the Provisional Census 2011 of India, Hindus constitute 80.5 per cent of the population whereas Muslims constitute 13.4 per cent, Christians 2.3 per cent, Sikhs 1.9 per cent and Buddhist 0.8 per cent, Jains 0.4 per cent and others 0.6 per cent[5] of the population. The religious

[5] Census Data 2001, India. Available at http://censusindia.gov.in/Ad-Campaign/drop_in_articles/04-Distribution_by_Religion.pdf.

Box 3.1: No Maintenance for a 'Working' Woman!

Amita Basu's (name changed) case illustrates the sharp fall in living standards because of separation. The wife of a business tycoon, at her mid-forties, she works in a hospital as a receptionist earning ₹8,000 per month. She got married in 1986 when she was 22 years old. It was an inter-caste marriage of her choice. The marriage was performed under the Hindu law and was registered. Since she had eloped, no dowry was given to her by her parents. She has two daughters aged 19 and 16 years and a son aged 11 years. She separated from her husband in 2005. He filed for divorce and she filed for maintenance under Section 125 CrPC. She has also filed for residence and a criminal complaint for domestic violence under the PWDVA. Amita's husband was involved in an extra-marital affair. He used to beat her and the children and always used to come home drunk.

Amita was a post-graduate and worked in an office before marriage, earning about ₹6,000 and making an additional ₹2,000 by giving tuitions. After marriage she stopped working and became dependent on her husband for money. She states that she became 'an unpaid housekeeper, a nanny for the children, and a hostess at parties'. She said she worked for 14 hours a day doing household chores, looking after children and elders. Her husband did not do any domestic work. She did not know how much he spent on the household. Post separation she spends ₹12,000–13,000 per month and works for ten hours a day, earning, doing household chores and caring for the children. During marriage, she had a house, vehicle, jewellery, TV, fridge, etc., earned by her husband. Later, he gave her a house to live in and the use of these assets. However, he withdrew all the fixed deposits in their joint names. Her husband owns a tea estate, has other houses, land, vehicles, jewellery, electronic goods and money that he has earned or got from his father.

During her married years she says, 'I had lost the habit of working. I lost the confidence to work but had to start working again after separation.' She did not get any maintenance from her husband as she is working. She got ₹15,000 per month for her three children and actual expenditure for their education, career and marriage. The interim maintenance case took two years. The main reason for delay was that dates after dates were given. The maintenance is supposed to be paid monthly but it is irregular. She feels that she is entitled to share the household assets equally with her husband. She neither had knowledge, nor proofs of her husband's income. She feels that her husband should be asked to disclose his income instead of her proving it.

It is ironic that Amita should be denied maintenance for herself as she is now 'working'. She earns a very small salary while her husband is rich. She is currently earning as much as she did 20 years ago when she was unmarried (i.e., her real income has fallen, given inflation). Maintenance must be given to working women keeping in mind the woman's lesser earning capacity—which is often a consequence of marriage, childbearing, domestic duties, etc.,—so that she maintains the same standard of life as before. To deny maintenance on the grounds that a woman is earning—when in fact she is struggling to re-establish herself in the world of work—is often a gross injustice.

distribution of our surveyees was, therefore, similar to the religious distribution of India's population as reflected by the recent Provisional Census 2011 figures.

Caste Distribution of the Surveyees

A total of 16 per cent of our surveyees stated that they belonged to the SCs and STs while 26 per cent reported that they belonged to the OBCs. Thus, a sizable 42 per cent of the surveyees belonged to the SC/ST and OBC sections of our society. Graph 3.9 highlights the representative character of the survey.

As per NFHS III, 19 per cent of heads of households belonged to the SCs, 8 per cent to the STs and 40 per cent to the OBCs. About one-third did not belong to any of these three groups.[6]

Graph 3.9 Distribution of the Surveyees by Their Caste in Different Regions

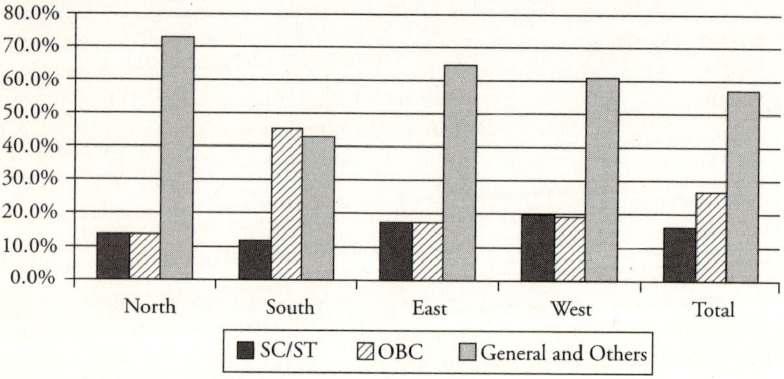

Education Levels of Our Surveyees

Among the surveyees, 17.1 per cent did not have any formal education. About 17.15 per cent of the surveyees were educated up to the primary level, 22.8 per cent of them were educated up to the secondary level and

[6] International Institute for Population Sciences (IIPS) and Macro International, *Summary of Findings*, National Family Health Survey (NFHS-3), India, 2005–2006 (Mumbai: IIPS, 2007), xxix–xxx. Available at www.measuredhs.com/pubs/pdf/FRIND3/00FrontMatter00.pdf (last accessed on 16 November 2012).

11.9 per cent were educated up to the higher secondary level. About 31 per cent of the surveyees had education of more than 12 years. A total of 13.4 per cent and 16.3 per cent of the women surveyed were graduates and post graduates respectively (see Graph 3.10).

Graph 3.10 Distribution of the Surveyees by Their Educational Level in Different Regions

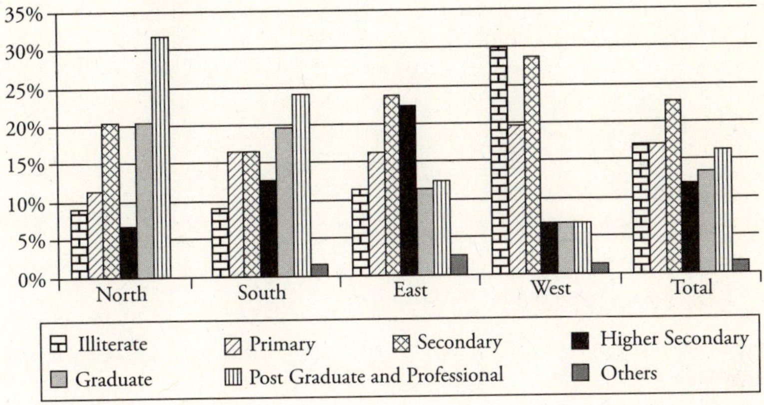

As per the NFHS III, 40.6 per cent women did not have any education, 23 per cent had primary education, 14 per cent had secondary education, 10.4 per cent had higher secondary and 12 per cent had education for more than 12 years.[7]

According to the 532nd Report of the National Sample Survey Organisation (NSSO) of India, 0.9 per cent of women were without formal education, 7.3 per cent were educated but not up to the primary level of education, 14 per cent were educated up to the primary level, 13.3 per cent were educated up to the middle level. A total of 9.5 per cent were educated up to the secondary and 5 per cent up to the higher secondary level, 3.5 per cent of the surveyees were graduates and 1.1 per cent of them post graduates or had more education.

Graph 3.11 shows that 18.8 per cent of our SC/ST surveyees were illiterate. Slightly lesser percentages of surveyees in the other categories were also illiterate. A total of 26.6 per cent of our surveyees had only had primary school education in contrast to 16 per cent of our OBC surveyees and

[7] Table 3.2.1: Respondent's Le vel of Education: Women, *National Family Health Survey (NFHS-III), 2005–06, India*, Vol. I. Available at http://www.rchiips.org/NFHS/NFHS-3%20 Data/VOL-1/India_volume_I_corrected_17oct08.pdf (last accessed on 16 November 2012).

Graph 3.11 Distribution of the Surveyees Belonging to Different Caste Groups by Their Educational Status

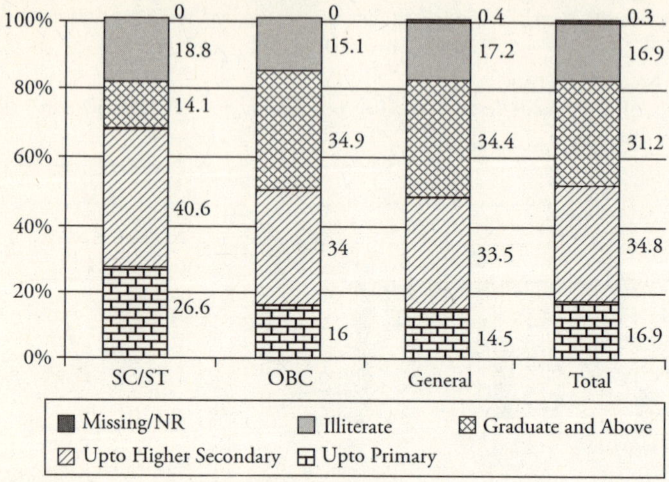

Note: Graph 3.11 represents the 396 cases which have reported their social caste as well as their educational levels.

14.5 per cent of the surveyees who belonged to the general caste category. Only 40.6 per cent of our surveyees who belonged to the SC/ST category had studied up to the higher secondary level. Thus, the overwhelming majority (85.9 per cent) of our SC/ST surveyees were either illiterate or had studied up to the primary and/or secondary level of education. Though 31.2 per cent of the surveyees were educated up to the graduate level (10+2+3 years of education) or above (see Graph 3.10), only 14.1 per cent of the SC/ST surveyees had studied beyond school.

Children of the Surveyees

Graph 3.12(a) portrays the number of children all the 405 surveyees had. Most (60.7 per cent) of the surveyees had 1–2 children while 27.7 per cent of them did not have a single child. We found that only 10.4 per cent of them had 3–4 children; a minuscule number of them (1.2 per cent) had more than four children. The age of surveyees and the fact that most of those who contacted us were young perhaps had a direct relation to the number

Graph 3.12(a) Percentage Distribution of the Surveyees by the Number of Children They Have in Different Regions

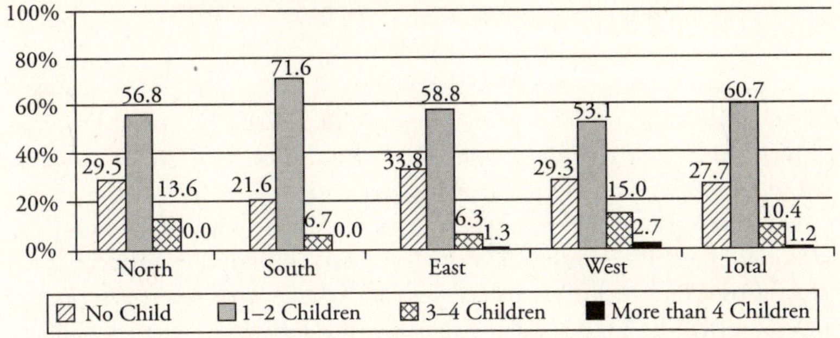

of children that the surveyees had. However, the majority of the surveyees surprisingly did not have more than two children.

As per Graph 3.12(b), 25 per cent of our SC/ST surveyees had no children as compared with 29.2 per cent of the OBC surveyees and 27.8 per cent of the general category surveyees. The majority of our surveyees belonging to all caste categories had only one or two children. The survey surprisingly showed that only 7.5 per cent of surveyees who belonged to the OBC social caste category had more than two children whereas 11.9 per cent of the surveyees who belonged to the general category had more than two children. However, 17.2 per cent of the surveyees belonging to the SC/ST social caste category had more than two children.

Graph 3.12(b) Distribution of the Surveyees Belonging to Different Caste Groups by the Number of Children They Have

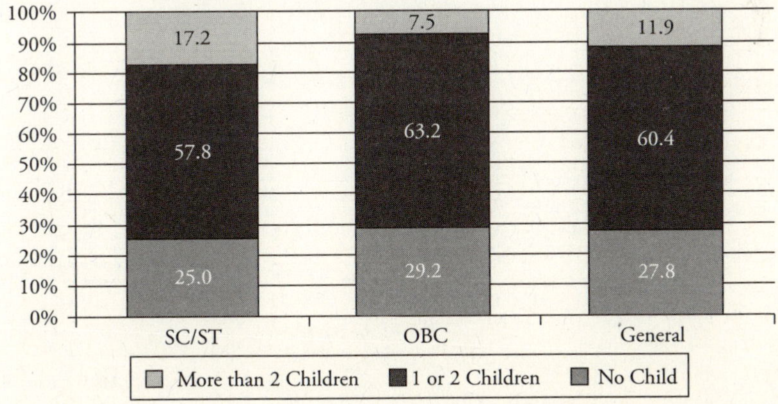

Graph 3.12(c) shows the number of children that the 405 surveyees in particular age groups had. In the age group of 18–22 years, 51.4 per cent of the women did not have any children, 37.1 per cent of them had one child and the rest (11.4 per cent) had 2 children each.

In the age group of 23–32 years, an almost equal number of surveyees either had no children (35.9 per cent) or had one child (37.5 per cent) while 19 per cent had two children, 4.9 per cent had three children, 2.2 per cent had four children and 0.5 per cent had five children.

In the age group of 33–42 years, most (39.2 per cent) of the surveyees had only one child, another 33.6 per cent had two children, and 13.6 per cent did not have children. In 6.4 per cent of the cases, the surveyees had three children, in 5.6 per cent of the cases the surveyees had four children and 0.8 per cent of surveyees had five children.

In the age group of 43–52 years, 15.2 per cent surveyees had no children, 26.1 per cent surveyees had one child and 30.4 per cent surveyees had two children, while 15.2 per cent surveyees had three children. In another 8.7 per cent and 4.3 per cent of the cases, the surveyees had four children and five children, respectively.

In the age group of 52 years and above, 41.7 per cent surveyees had 2 children, while 16.7 per cent surveyees had no children; the same percentage had only one child while another 16.7 per cent surveyees had three children. Only 8.3 per cent of those surveyed in this age group had four children.

Graph 3.12(c) Percentage Distribution of the Surveyees by Their Age and the Number of Children They Had

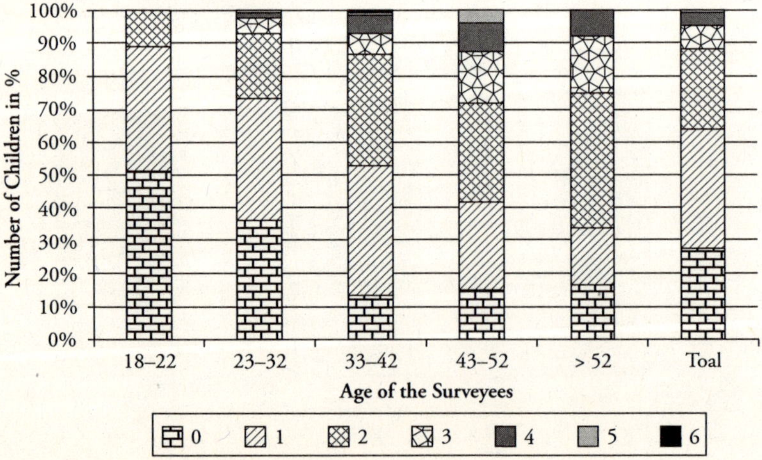

Residential Status of the Children of the Surveyees

A finding of great significance, which reiterates what women's groups and those working with separated women have, time and again, been saying is that most separated women have to bear the burden of looking after their children single handed. Thus, most separations result not only in the women getting abandoned and deserted but also children being deserted along with them. Any policy regarding separated and divorced women must take into account this fact. Graph 3.12(d) highlights this stark reality. A total of 429 (85.6 per cent) out of 501 children were living with their mother while only 40 (7.9 per cent) were living with their father. Twenty (3.9 per cent) children had to find refuge with others—in four cases the children were living with their grandmother or grandparents, the others were studying at a boarding school or were majors, or were married. Surprisingly in four cases, 12 (2.4 per cent) children were living with both parents. In one case, the surveyee had got married again and was staying with the second husband along with the children, in another case the surveyee had recently reconciled with the husband and in yet another she was separated but living in the same house.

Graph 3.12(d) Parent With Whom the Children of the Surveyees Are Staying

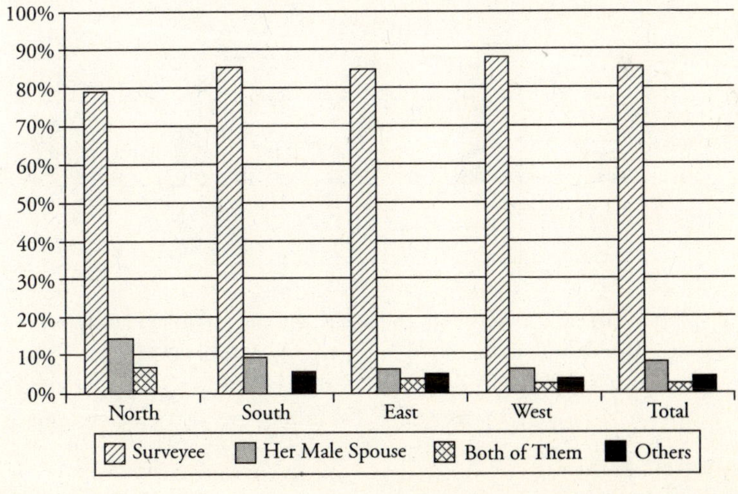

Age at the Time of Marriage

According to the NFHS-III figures, more than one-quarter (27 per cent) of Indian women between ages 20 and 49 got married before age 15, while over half (58 per cent) got married before the legal minimum marriage age of 18 and three-quarters (74 per cent) got married before reaching age 20. The median age of marriage ranges between 16.5 years to 18.3 years for the women aged between 20 and 49 years.[8]

Following a somewhat similar pattern, the majority (53.1 per cent) of our 399 surveyees had got married between the ages of 23 and 32 years. However, in the north, 50 per cent of the surveyees got married between the ages of 18 and 22. In another 32.5 per cent of the cases, the surveyees got married between 23 and 32 years of age. In 10 per cent of the cases, however, the ages of the surveyees at the time of marriage were less than 18 years and they were thus minors when the marriage took place. Only in 7.5 per cent of the cases, the surveyees were more than 33 years of age at the time of marriage (see Graph 3.13[a]).

Graph 3.13(a) Percentage Distribution of the Surveyees by the Age of Marriage in Different Regions

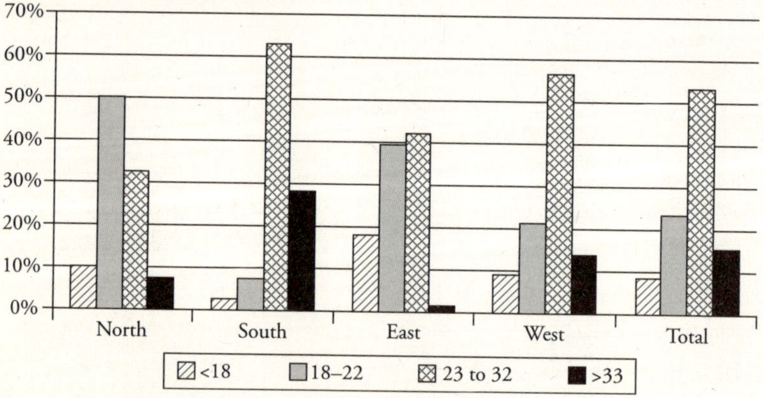

Graph 3.13(b) provides us with the age at the time of marriage as per the caste of the surveyees. Among SCs/STs the trend of child marriage was more than in other caste groups. A total of 19.4 per cent of the SC/ST surveyees got married at less than 18 years of age. But, there was also a large group of

[8] *Supra* note 7, p. 163.

Graph 3.13(b) Distribution of the Surveyees Belonging to Different Caste Groups by Their Age at the Time of Marriage

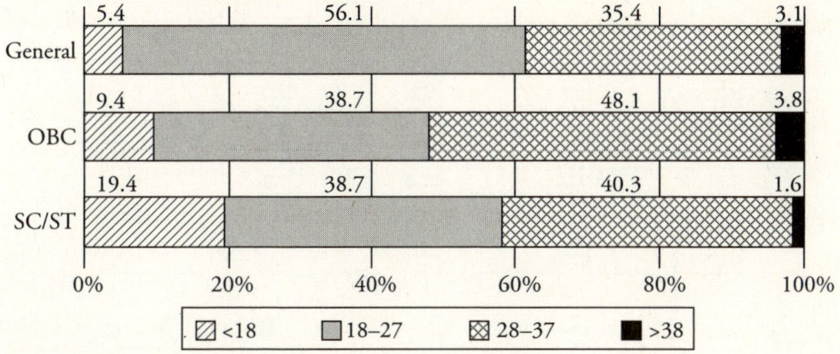

Note: Graph 3.13(b) represents 391 cases in which the surveyees reported their age at the time of marriage and their social caste group.

surveyees of these caste categories (40.3 per cent) who got married in their late twenties or thirties. A significant number of our OBC (48.1 per cent) surveyees reported that they had got married between the ages of 28 and 37 years. In the general category, a majority (56.1 per cent) of our surveyees got married when they were aged between 18 and 27 years.

Type of Marriage

In India, most marriages are arranged and over half (58 per cent) of the women get married before the legal age of marriage, that is, 18 years. The survey also reflected this reality. Most of the marriages (85.7 per cent or 347 out of 405) amongst the women surveyed were arranged and only 13.6 per cent (55 out of 405) of the surveyees had got married to men they had chosen. A total 0.7 per cent of the surveyees said that their marriage was neither arranged nor of their own choice. Graph 3.14(a) elucidates this.

Graph 3.14(a) shows that the highest percentage of arranged marriages (93.2 per cent) had taken place in northern India while a relatively less number of arranged marriages (78.8 per cent) had taken place in the eastern part of India. Arranged marriages obviously mean that the girl and boy do not get to choose each other. In India, these marriages take place within the same caste, same religion and community. Even within the same caste, certain restrictions are followed within certain groups. For instance, the Jat community in Haryana and many other communities across India do not

Graph 3.14(a) Percentage Distribution of 405 Surveyees by the Type of Marriage They Had in Different Regions

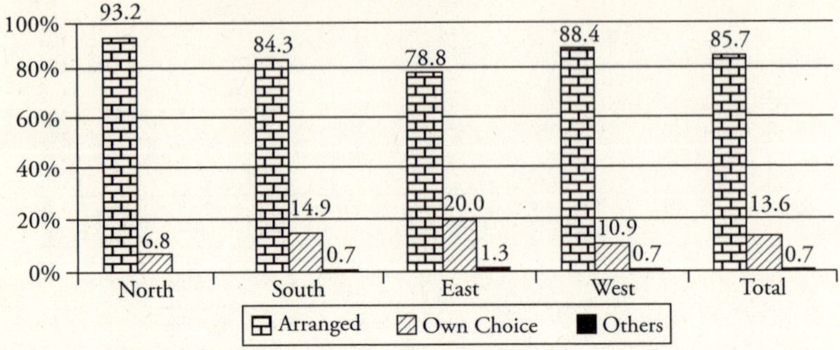

marry within the same *gotra*.[9] Even in the same caste and within the same village young boys and girls who do not follow the rules pertaining to marriages are dealt with harshly, and subjected to various forms of harassment including 'honour' killings. It is a well-known fact that in most arranged marriages traditional customs and practices are followed including the giving of an appropriate amount of dowry from the girl's side. Thus, often arranged marriages have a direct and adverse impact on the practice of dowry and both go hand in hand.

Marriages in which our surveyees had chosen their own partners were the highest in the east (20 per cent), followed by the south (14.9 per cent). The least number of marriages by choice came from the north (Delhi and UP). Some respondents (0.7 per cent) stated that their marriage was neither arranged nor by choice as their marriage contained elements of both arranged marriages and marriages by choice. Some of our surveyees had been asked/allowed by their parents to meet the proposed bridegroom. This phenomena of taking the consent of a girl, particularly in urban areas, to the boy chosen by the parents of the girl is a relatively new phenomena, as earlier only the girl was shown to the boy and his family for approval in several parts of the country.

As shown in Graph 3.14(b), arranged marriages are most often performed within the same caste and religion. This is also reflected in our survey as

[9] In Sanskrit, *gotram* means family, race, lineage, a mountain, a cow-pen and so on. According to Sherring, one legend has it that all the chief Brahmin *gotras* are descended from the *Saptarishis* (seven sages). A *gotra* could, therefore, be composed of several hundred thousand people. The Hindu Marriage (Removal of Disabilities) Act 1946 specifically stated that marriages within the same *gotra* were completely legal. This position was reiterated by the courts.

Graph 3.14(b) Distribution of Surveyees by the Type of Marriage (Inter-religion/ Inter-caste) They Had in Different Regions

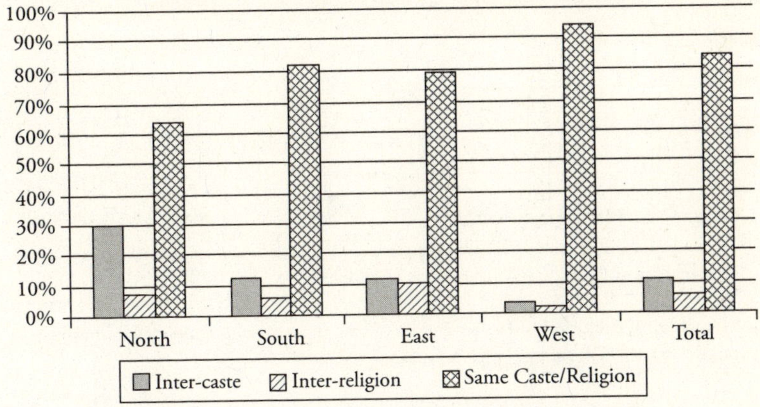

75.5 per cent of the marriages (340/405) were also marriages within the same caste and religion. Only 10.6 per cent of marriages were inter-caste and even smaller percentages (5.4 per cent) of the marriages were inter-faith. Most of the inter-caste marriages had taken place in the north (29.5 per cent) followed by the south (11.9 per cent). The least number of inter-caste marriages were reported from the west (3.4 per cent) in this survey.

Inter-faith marriages, on the other hand, were the highest in the east (10 per cent) followed by the north (6.8 per cent) and the south (6 per cent). Only 2 per cent of the surveyed cases were of inter-faith marriages from the west.

Most of the surveyees were, as expected, married under Hindu Law (72.3 per cent) followed by the Muslim Law (18.8 per cent) (see Graph 3.15[a]). Only 4.2 per cent of the surveyees were married under the SMA which is the only civil law in the country. This shows the stranglehold of custom and tradition in various parts of the country and the lack of use of the SMA despite it being passed as far back as 1954. Another factor which inhibits the use of this law is the cumbersome procedure which the Act stipulates. Many young couples who want to marry in a hurry, therefore, do so under the various religious personal laws. It is not surprising therefore that Graph 3.15(b) shows that even a number of marriages by choice were performed under Hindu and other personal laws.

The SMA was passed in 1954 to also specifically allow marriages between persons who belonged to different religions or different castes, by the civil law without either party having to give up their religious persuasion; prior to

Graph 3.15(a) Distribution of Surveyees by the Law under Which They Married in Different Regions

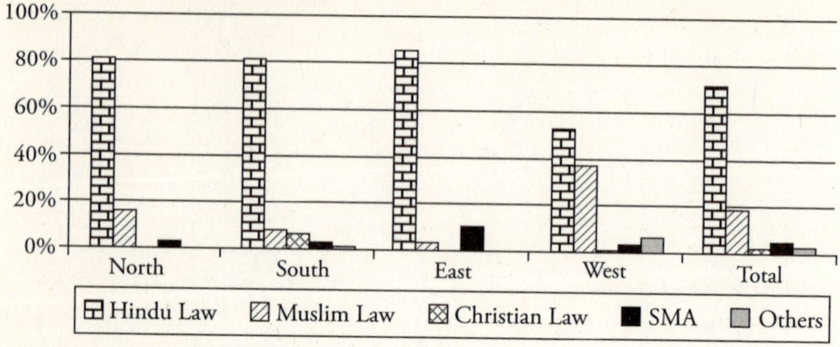

Note: Graph 3.15(a) accounts for a distribution of 404 surveyees who responded to the question on the law under which they got married.

Graph 3.15(b) Distribution of Surveyees by the Law under Which They Married by the Type of Marriage They Had

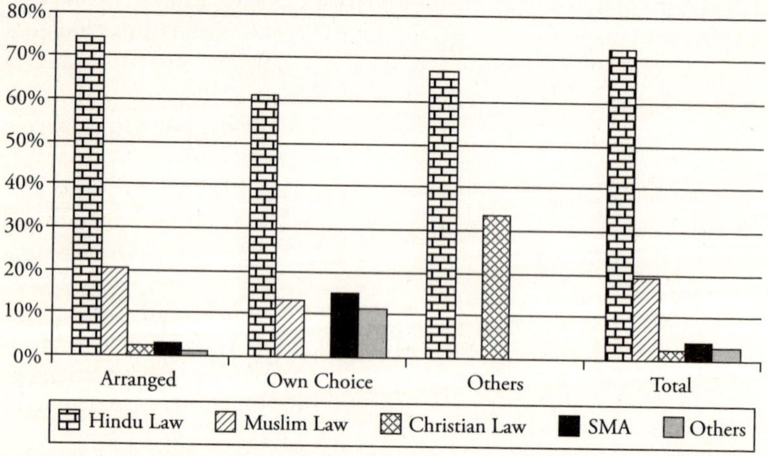

Note: Graph 3.15(b) accounts for 404 surveyees.

this a civil marriage could not be performed between two persons belonging to different religions.[10]

Despite the limitations in the SMA, it is not surprising that the highest percentages of civil marriages under SMA were performed in cases in which

[10] Tahir Mahmood, *Civil Marriage Law: Perspectives and Prospects* (Bombay: N.M. Tripathi Private Ltd., 1978).

couples exercised their choice in getting married to the person they wanted. However, the fact that even from the couples who got married to a person of their choice 61.1 per cent were married under the Hindu Law followed by 13 per cent under Muslim Law and 11.1 per cent under other forms of marriage including customary forms shows that the civil law of marriage needs to be strengthened. While some of the couples, particularly those involved in inter-caste marriage and those marrying within the same religion, may prefer a religious ceremony, others particularly those marrying across religion may prefer to marry under the civil law. The reasons for couples not marrying under SMA need to be analysed. It has been pointed out that as there is a requirement of a one-month notice under the SMA[11] and the marriage notice is pasted for a month in the marriage registry to invite objections, if any, many young couples do not get married under this Act. Even in inter-faith marriages one of the parties to the marriage often converts to the religion of the other party to get married quickly. In the recent past, women's groups have demanded that the requirement of one-month notice be done away with.[12]

---

[11] Sections 5 and 6 of the Special Marriage Act 1954 read as under:

5. Notices of intended marriage: When a marriage is intended to be solemnized under this Act, the parties of the marriage shall give notice thereof in writing in the Form specified in the Second Schedule to the Marriage Officer of the district in which at least one of the parties to the marriage has resided for a period of not less than thirty days immediately preceding the date on which such notice is given.
6. Marriage Notice Book and publication:

(1) The Marriage Officer shall keep all notices given under Sec. 5 with the records of his office and shall also forthwith enter a true copy of every such notice in a book prescribed for that purpose, to be called the Marriage Notice Book, and such book shall be open for inspection at all reasonable times, without fee, by any person desirous of inspecting the same.
(2) The Marriage Officer shall cause every such notice to be published by affixing a copy thereof to some conspicuous place in his office.
(3) Where either of the parties to an intended marriage is not permanently residing within the local limits of the district of the Marriage Officer to whom the notice has been given under Sec. 5, the Marriage Officer shall also cause a copy of such notice to be transmitted to the Marriage Officer of the district within whose limits such party is permanently residing, and that Marriage Officer shall thereupon cause a copy thereof to be affixed to some conspicuous place in his office.

[12] AIDWA, etc. This has also been incorporated in a recent Bill proposed by the government but not yet approved by the Union Cabinet/Government of India.

Size of the Marital Home

The NFHS-III India had put the number of non-nuclear families, that is, joint families in India at approximately 39.5 per cent.[13] Over 80 per cent of the surveyees reported that their marital homes were extended and comprised of members of three generations, or were families in which brothers and their families lived together.[14] Most of our surveyees lived in marital homes in which 3 to 8 members lived and the vast majority of our surveyees lived in joint or extended marital homes. While on the one hand one could surmise that the normal state of the Indian families is joint or extended, on the other hand perhaps what the survey shows is that it is in these extended families that the most number of separations currently take place. This could lead to the startling revelation that most of the separated and deserted women were living in extended families and faced the maximum harassment there.

Most of the surveyees as per Graph 3.16 lived in extended families. An analysis of the data showed that 43 out of 356 (excluding surveyees who did not answer), that is, only 12.08 per cent surveyees were living in a nuclear family. The nuclear family is defined for the purposes of the survey as families in which only husband–wife and their children lived. The majority or 87.9 per cent surveyees were living in extended families during the subsistence of their marriages. This trend was similar in almost all parts of the country. However, in the eastern region 54 out of 56, that is, 96.4 per cent of the surveyees lived in extended families while in the northern region 28 out of 32, that is, 87.5 per cent of the surveyees, in the West 127 out of 140, that is, 90.7 per cent of the surveyees and in the south 104 out of 128, that is, 81.25 per cent of the surveyees lived in extended families.

Graph 3.17 shows the number of years that the surveyees lived with their male spouses before getting separated or divorced. This has been compiled by taking into account the date of marriage and the date of separation/divorce.

In 28.7 per cent of the cases, the marriages lasted less than two years, whereas in the other 30 per cent of the cases the surveyees were married for 2–6 years, while some 26 per cent of the surveyees were married for more than 10 years.

---

[13] *Supra* note 7, p. 23. *NFHS-III), 2005–06, India* says:

'Nuclear households are households comprised of a married couple or a man or a woman living alone or with unmarried children (biological, adopted, or fostered) with or without unrelated individuals.'

[14] John Van Willigen, 'Social Ageing in India and America', *Seminar* No. 488, April 2000. Available at http://www.india-seminar.com/2000/488/488%20willigen.htm#top (last accessed on 12 December 2010).

Graph 3.16 Distribution of Surveyees by the Type of the Marital House in Different Regions

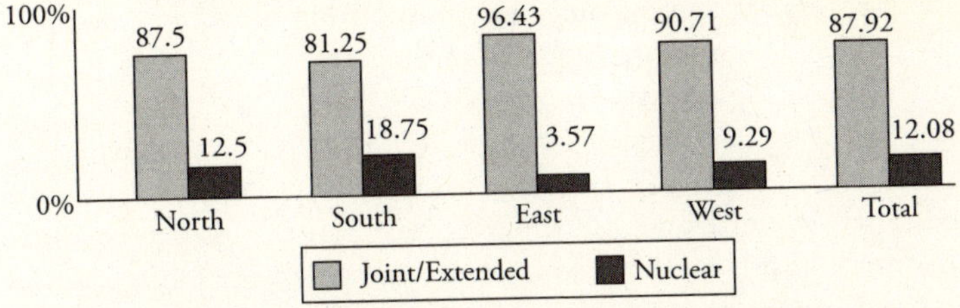

Note: Graph 3.16 represents the 356 surveyees who responded to this question.

Graph 3.17 Distribution of Surveyees by the Time Duration of Marriage in Different Regions (Years)

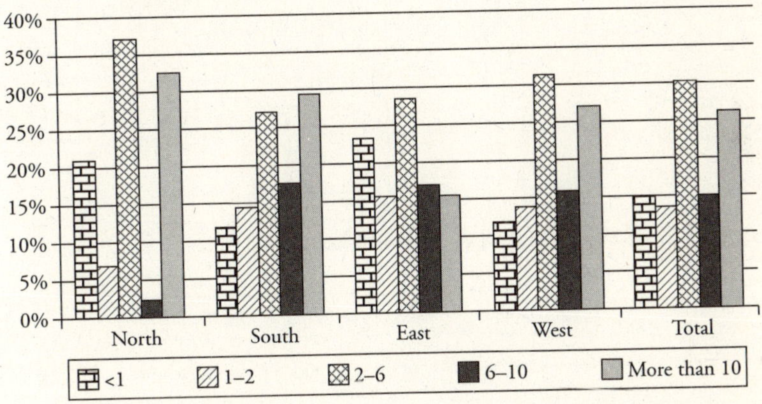

Note: Graph 3.18 represents 390 surveyees who responded to this question.

In northern and southern India, in more than 20 per cent of the cases the surveyees got separated within one year of their marriage. Also, most of the surveyees who separated after 10 years of their marriage were from these regions.

A large number of women that we interviewed were not divorced even though they had been separated. Most women in India do not want a divorce even if they have faced violence in their marital homes as they feel both financially and socially insecure outside the marriage. They are looked down upon in society and their standard of living plummets after separation/divorce. Separated women are also not willing to divorce their spouses as they feel that they will gain nothing from it whereas their husbands will have a standard of living which is as good as or better than it was while the parties were living together. Not giving a divorce is also the only tool that separated women have to negotiate terms of settlement with their spouses as their legal rights are insignificant and the procedures involved in accessing even those rights are long and complicated apart from the fact that they often have to face gender bias in the courts.

As per the survey, 18 per cent of the surveyees were divorced and 81.7 per cent were separated. The maximum divorces took place in western India followed closely by north and east, while the least were surprisingly reported from the south. However, the maximum percentages of cases of separation were reported from southern India (see Graph 3.18[a].

Graph 3.18(a) Percentage of Surveyees by the Status of Their Separation in Different Regions

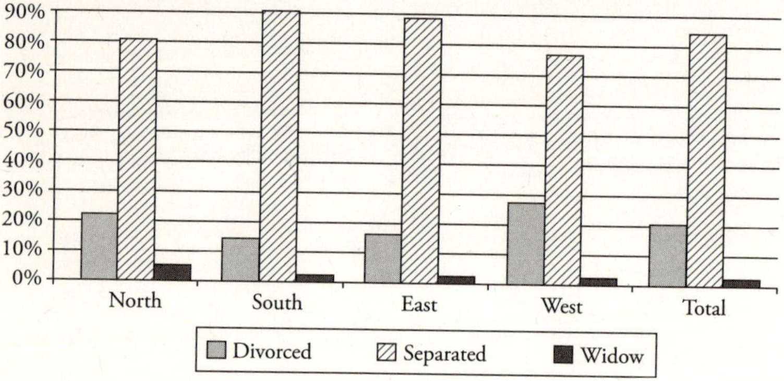

Note: Graph 3.18(a) represents 400 surveyees who responded to this question.

Several legal experts and women activists have pointed out that because of the stigma related to divorce, the accompanying fall in social status of the woman and her natal family and the lack of remarriage options, most women prefer a separation to a formal divorce.[15]

An interesting aspect of Graph 3.18(b) is that the percentage of SC/ST surveyees who reported that they were divorced was greater than the percentage of OBCs and general surveyees. However, it cannot be ruled out that these divorces may have been the outcome of traditional divorce practices and not through the legal procedures. Among OBCs, 90.4 per cent of the women were separated whereas only 9.6 per cent of them were divorced.

[15] Economic Research Foundation, *Economic Rights and Entitlements of Separated and Divorced Women,* Report of Regional Seminar Proceedings (2008–2009) (New Delhi: ERF, 2010), 127–132.

Graph 3.18(b) Distribution of the Surveyees Belonging to Different Caste Groups by the Status of Separation

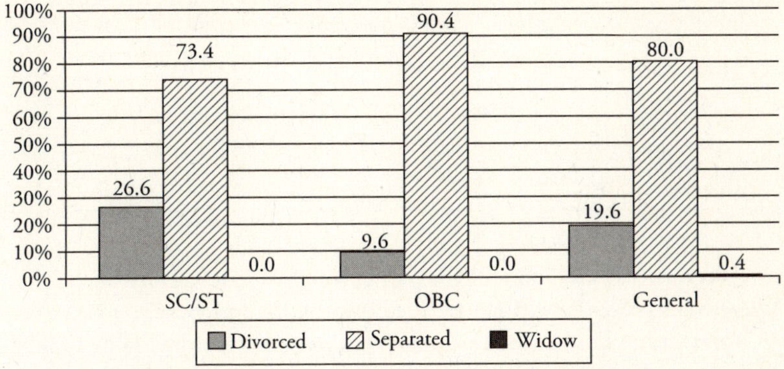

Note: Graph 3.18(b) represents 393 surveyees who responded to this question.

Among the general category, 80 per cent of the surveyees were separated and 19.4 per cent of the surveyees were divorced. Even amongst the SC/ST surveyees, 73.4 per cent of them were living separately without a divorce though the highest percentages (26.6 per cent) of the divorced were amongst this social caste group.

Cases Filed by the Surveyees and Their Male Spouses

In Table 3.5, we found that 283 of our surveyees had approached the courts, while 120 women had not gone to the court at all. Most of the surveyees who had approached the courts had filed cases for maintenance and custody. Since about 30 per cent of the women had not approached the court, we can presume that they lacked access to courts or some other reasons prevented them from approaching courts or other authorities, apart from women's groups. This shows that, in spite of the inefficiency of the legal system, women are still dependant on it for accessing their rights to maintenance/alimony. This finding also underscores the need to improve the justice delivery system for women.

In 79 cases, neither the surveyees nor their husbands took their dispute to the court of law. In 41 cases, only the husbands filed cases against the

Table 3.5 Number of Cases in Which Matrimonial Dispute Was Taken to the Court of Law

Regions	*Both had filed*	*Only husband filed*	*Only wife filed cases*	*No case filed*	*No response*	*Total*
North	18	0	22	4		44
South	25	19	64*	24	2	132
East	36	1	36	7		80
West	16	21	66*	44		147
Total	95	41	188	79	2	405

surveyees. In 95 cases, both of the parties sought a relief against each other. There were 188 cases which were filed only by the surveyees.

Apart from going to the court, a few of our surveyees had gone to institutions which try to help with counselling and settlement of cases. Quite a few of the women approach institutions like the Women's Commissions simultaneously with or before or after going to the court. Some women only go to these institutions; e.g., a woman in Hyderabad had filed in the State Women's Commission and another in Kerala had similarly filed with the State Women's Commission. In two cases in Jaipur the matter was pending with the Family Counselling Centre. In 16 cases in Ahmedabad, the husband had divorced his wife under the personal law or customary law and the matter is not pending in courts.

Only 13 surveyees reported to us that their cases had come to an end.

Table 3.6(a) shows that 516 cases were filed by the surveyees. This is because, often, more than one case is filed by a separated woman or her spouse.

Under each personal law a person can ask not only for a divorce or judicial separation or restitution of conjugal rights but also for certain ancillary reliefs like maintenance/alimony, custody, etc. Apart from this, a woman of any religion can ask for maintenance from her husband under Section 125 of the CrPC. Even after a divorce a woman, regardless of the religion she belongs to—apart from a Muslim woman—can file for maintenance under this Section of the CrPC. A divorced Muslim woman can file for maintenance, custody and return of *mehr* under the Muslim Women (Protection of Rights on Divorce) Act 1986. A woman can also file a case for maintenance, protection orders against violence, custody, damages, etc., under the Protection of Women from PWDVA. The criminal law also allows a wife to register a case against her husband for harassing her for dowry, and for physical and mental cruelty under Section 498A of the Indian Penal Code. A woman can also file for return of dowry and *stridhan* under the Dowry

Table 3.6(a) Types of Cases Filed by the Surveyees

Region	*Custody*	*Rest.*	*Div.*	*Sep.*	*Maint.*	*Resd.*	*Dowry Haras. 498A*	*Dom. Viol. Civil*	*Cruelty 498A*	*Dow. Reco.*	*Ors*	*Total*
North		3	9		28	4	12	8	5	12		81
South	5	7	28		56	10	14	14	6	16	7	163
East	1		17		61	4	14	11	9	15	2	134
West		3	21	6	60	5	3	13	10	8	9	138
Total	6	13	75	6	205	23	43	46	30	51	18	516

Note: Rest.: Restitution, Div.: Divorce, Sep.: Separation, Maint.: Maintenance, Resd.: Residence, Dowry Haras.: Dowry Harassment, Dom. Viol. Civil: Domestic Violence Civil, Dow. Reco.: Recovery of Dowry, Ors: Others.

Prohibition Act and certain provisions of the criminal law (Section 406[16] Indian Penal Code 1860).

Table 3.6(a), therefore, shows these various provisions under which a separated woman can ask for relief. It is, however, telling that a majority of the surveyees asked for the relief of maintenance. In many (205 of maintenance + 23 of residence) cases, the surveyees went to the court for financial support, and in 8 cases the surveyees appealed for maintenance through conciliation proceedings in Women's Commissions and other similar forums.[17] Thus, the overwhelming need of our surveyees was for financial support. The second-largest number of cases (94) was for harassment for dowry and for recovery of dowry. It is relevant to mention that, though the PWDVA is of recent origin, having been only brought into force on 26 October 2006, quite a few (46) cases had been filed under the Act.

Table 3.6(a) shows that in six further cases the woman had asked for the custody of children. In three cases, the child/children was/were with their mother and in the other three cases the child/children was/were living with their father. In Graph 3.12(d) earlier it was shown that 429 (85.63 per cent) children out of 501 children were living with their separated mothers, thus, indicating that the surveyees had been left/deserted along with their children.

The finding that only 18.5 per cent (75 out of 405) of the surveyees asked for divorce reiterates the assertion by many groups working with separated women that in India very few women ask for divorce because of social and financial insecurity.

The other types of cases that were filed by the 18 surveyees included cases for nullity of marriage, a criminal case for bigamy, adultery and reports with the police that their husbands had disappeared and were missing, etc. Some further cases were either police complaints, or were pending with the Mediation Centres or Women's Commission. As stated, 79 women had not approached the court for any relief. Altogether 516 cases had been filed by 326 surveyees.

In sharp contrast to the surveyees, out of a total of 135 cases filed by their male spouses, the majority were for divorce (See Table 3.6[b]). In Ahmedabad, we found that in five cases husbands had divorced the surveyees under customary law and in Jaipur in one case the husband had divorced

[16] Section 406—Punishment for criminal breach of trust: 'Whoever commits criminal breach of trust shall be punished with imprisonment of either description for a term which may extend to three years, or with fine, or with both.'

[17] Mediation Centre and NGOs like AIDWA, etc.

Table 3.6(b) Types of Cases Filed by Husbands of the Surveyees

Regions	*Custody*	*Divorce*	*Maintenance*	*Restitution*	*Separation*	*Other*	*Total*
North	3	10	1	6	1		21
South	3	29	1	4	1	2	40
East		28		8	1		37
West		37					37
Total	6	104	2	18	3	2	135

the surveyee under the tribal law—these husbands had not gone to court. Similarly 16[18] of the male spouses had obtained divorce under personal laws, without going to court. In five cases the male spouse asked for judicial separation and nullity of marriage.

Restitution of conjugal rights is an old outdated remedy which cannot be physically enforced under the law in India but if despite a decree of restitution of conjugal rights a male spouse and wife do not live together the court can grant a divorce after a year of the decree.[19] This 'remedy' is sometimes used under legal advice by male spouses as a step towards divorce. Sometimes the male spouses also ask for restitution of conjugal rights to pressurise their wives to return to the marital home. We found that in 18 cases the male spouse had asked for restitution of conjugal rights.

Only in two cases (one of Delhi and another of Chennai), the male spouse had asked for maintenance/compensation. This showed the lack of relevance this remedy has for the male spouse.

---

[18] Two from Jaipur, seven from Ahmedabad, five from Bhopal, one from Bhandup and one from Thiruvananthapuram.

[19] Section 13, HMA.

Section 13: Divorce,

> (1A) Either party to a marriage, whether solemnized before or after the commencement of this Act, may also present a petition for the dissolution of the marriage by a decree of divorce on the ground:
>
> (i) that there has been no resumption of cohabitation as between the parties to the marriage for a period of [one year] or upwards after the passing of a decree for judicial separation in a proceeding to which they were parties; or
>
> (ii) that there has been no restitution of conjugal rights as between the parties to the marriage for a period of [one year] or upwards after the passing of a decree for restitution of conjugal rights in a proceeding to which they were parties.

Reasons for Separation

As per the NFHS-III data, almost all ever-married women who had experienced violence reported a current or former husband as the person who inflicted violence. Eighty-five per cent of ever-married women who have experienced violence since the age of 15 have experienced it from their current husband. Only 2 per cent mentioned in this study that a mother-in-law was the perpetrator, though the father-in-law was violent in 0.6 per cent of the cases and other in-laws were violent in 1.5 per cent cases.[20]

The Pune study had identified the main reasons for desertion in the Daund Taluka as second marriage or extra-marital relationships of the husband, alcoholism and harassment, husband not willing to live with wife, mental and physical torture by the husband and his family, no male child or infertility and demands for dowry. In the rural area also, similar reasons existed and were labelled as manifestations of the patriarchal system. A lot of the women also said that they had been forced to leave their marital homes without any apparent reason by their husbands or in-laws.[21] The study done by Jaya Sagade more than two decades ago had found that the ground pleaded in almost all cases was cruelty. Along with cruelty, the other ground pleaded in maximum cases was desertion and adultery.[22]

One of the questions that we posed to the surveyees was asking them why they had separated. The overwhelming majority of the surveyees reported that they had been treated with violence and forced to leave the marital home (see Graph 3.19). This was in tandem with what many social activists and lawyers and others working with women have also been reporting. For instance Shipra Sharma, an activist from Gujarat, identified violence as the 'high-tide' reason for separation. Vimala K.S. of AIDWA, Karnataka, observed that while conducting the survey they had come across many shocking cases of torture by in-laws. Jayashree Bora of Assam, described cases where wives had been beaten and had their limbs broken by abusive husbands. Kiran Bhatty, economist, referred to cases of harassment, abuse and violence related to dowry demands post-marriage.[23]

Graph 3.19 and Table 3.7 reveal the startling reality that 83 per cent of the surveyees were separated due to cruelty or domestic violence in their marital homes (see Box 3.2). More than 90 per cent of these surveyees were living in

---

[20] *Supra* note 7, p. 500.
[21] SOPPECOM, *supra* note 2, p. 74.
[22] Sagade, *supra* note 1, p. 164.
[23] Economic Research Foundation, *supra* note 15, pp. 91–93.

Graph 3.19 Percentage Distribution of Surveyees by the Reasons for Separation

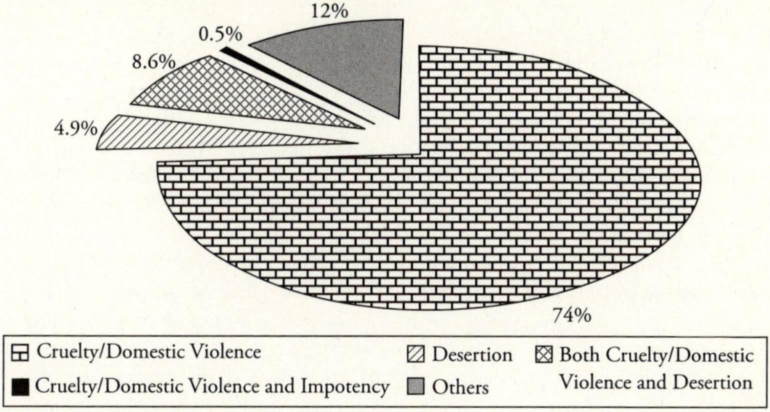

Note: Graph 3.19 represents 384 surveyees who answered the questions on the reasons for separation.

Table 3.7 Frequency Distribution of Surveyees by Reasons for Separation

Reasons of Separation	*Frequency*	*Percent*
Cruelty/Domestic Violence	284	74.0
Desertion	19	4.9
Both Cruelty/Domestic Violence and Desertion	33	8.6
Cruelty/Domestic Violence and Impotency	2	0.5
Others	46	12.0
No Response/Missing	20	
Not Applicable	1	
Total	405	
Total (Excluding NA, Missing, NR)	384	100.0

extended families. A total of 13.5 per cent of the surveyees reported that they had been deserted and 8.6 per cent out of these 13.5 per cent deserted women reported that they had also been subjected to physical and mental violence.

The frequency of various forms of cruelty, ranging from mental to physical abuse within marriages in India, has been documented by some researchers. A total of 9,938 married women with at least one child, from rural areas, urban slums and urban non-slums, were surveyed between 1997 and 1999 by research teams from medical colleges in seven major Indian cities and towns.[24]

[24] International Clinical Epidemiologists Network (INCLEN), *Domestic Violence in India 3: A Summary Report of a Multi-Site Household Survey* (Washington DC: International Center for Research on Women and the Centre for Development and Population Activities, 2000).

Box 3.2: Domestic Violence/Drug Addiction Destroys Marriage

Aarti Singh (name changed for privacy) from Bhopal, in her late twenties, is a divorced Hindu woman who has studied up to the 10th standard and lives with her parents. She could not complete her studies due to her early marriage. Post separation she has started studying for her high-school examination. She had done a short stint as a school teacher during the marriage and says that if she had continued she would have been earning ₹1,000 per month. As of now, she is unemployed. She says that everybody tells her that she saved her life by coming back to her parents' place.

She has one son. Aarti's husband was a drug addict and was unemployed most of the time. He used to beat her under the influence of drugs. It was her father-in-law who took care of their household expenses. Her husband used to ask her to get money for his drugs. He forcibly took her jewellery and sold it to buy drugs.

Aarti did not work before marriage. During marriage she worked for two months. Presently, she is not working. Before marriage, her husband was self-employed. Later, he began to work as a driver and earned ₹4,000–5,000 per month. His present monthly income is not known to her. Aarti says that there is no change in her husband's lifestyle now as he is still addicted to drugs.

During marriage she and her husband enjoyed the facilities of a house and car owned by her father in-law, jewellery (given by her parents and in-laws and presently in husband's possession), TV and other electronic goods (belonging to her father-in-law). In her parental home, there is a TV, fridge and other electronic goods.

Aarti was ordered maintenance of ₹1,400 for herself and the child. She is not satisfied with the quantum of maintenance awarded. She did not face any difficulty in proving her husband's income because her father-in-law himself told the court that his son earns ₹5,000 per month. The court took three years to award maintenance because her husband was not willing to pay. She had to file an execution application. The application took about a month's time. The judge issued an arrest warrant against her husband and thereafter he started paying the maintenance. However, he does not come regularly to the court to make the payment.

Aarti's parents and siblings had given a television, fridge, clothes and jewellery on her marriage. Her in-laws had given her jewellery. Her husband was given a gold ring, watch and suit and her in-laws were given clothes. The total value of *stridhan* from her parents was nearly ₹100,000 and from in-laws was over ₹25,000. The total value of her dowry was ₹100,000. She feels that her marriage was a great financial burden on her family. Her parents borrowed ₹30,000 for her marriage. Her father is retired and gets a pension of only ₹500 per month. *She has not recovered the dowry and* stridhan *items which are with her husband.*

She complained to the police once when her husband beat her very badly and asked her to hang herself. However, the police did not lodge the complaint. They told her that her husband had behaved like that because he was drunk and would be fine later. Aarti approached an AIDWA worker because of whose help the police official was finally compelled to lodge the complaint.

The study found that in many marriages there was either psychological —psychological violence was defined as insulting, demeaning, threatening, threatening someone else she cares about, making her feel afraid, abandoning her, and/or being unfaithful—or physical violence—physical violence was defined as slapping, hitting, kicking, beating, using or threatening to use a weapon and/or forced sex—or both. Overall, about 50 per cent of women reported experiencing some psychologically violent or physically violent behaviour at least once in their married life; 43.5 per cent reported psychologically abusive behaviour at least once and 40.3 per cent reported at least one form of violent physical behaviour.[25]

Of the 9,938 women in the survey, approximately one out of every four (2,596 women or 26 per cent) had experienced slapping, kicking, hitting, beating, threat or use of a weapon, or forced sex in the last 12 months. Women living in rural and urban slum areas reported similar rates that were higher than for women living in urban non-slum areas.

Nearly 15 per cent of the total sample of women reported one or more incidents of forced sex during the previous 12 months, and this rate was consistent across the three strata.[26]

It needs to be pointed out that the research was conducted among married women who continued to live with the violence, unlike our surveyees who had either left the marriage because of violence or had been violently thrown out. Our survey is almost unique in its focus on separated and divorced women.

Out of the cases from the eastern states, a few of the surveyees reported that their husbands deserted them and crossed over the border into Bangladesh, so going to court to seek maintenance would be fruitless. Their spouses are simply untraceable. In 12 per cent of the cases, the reasons for separation were drug addiction, alcoholism of the male spouse, incompatibility between the spouses, etc.

Other reasons for separation were desertion by the husband, husband's intolerance of non-stereotypical behaviour by the wife, impotence, his being of unsound mind, repeated demands of money from the wife and his wanting to get rid of the wife for a variety of reasons. Lack of privacy in the joint family was also listed as one of the reasons for separation.

As per this graph, cruelty was the main reason for separation in 85.3 per cent of the cases in the SC/ST category whereas other kind of reasons were the cause of separation in about 15 per cent of the cases. Amongst OBCs, in 81.8 per cent of the cases cruelty was the main reason for separation, whereas

---

[25] *Supra* note 24, p. 9.

[26] Ibid., 11.

in 13.2 per cent of the cases desertion was also an additional reason for the separation. Graph 3.20(a) shows that similar reasons for separation exist amongst women belonging to all the social caste categories.

A study carried out in the Pune district courts had found that in the majority of cases the wives had pleaded physical beating, ill treatment, providing no food, second marriage of the husband, his drinking habits, demand for dowry, no permission to visit parents, etc. In reply, the husband usually pleaded that the wife had insulted him and his relatives, was short tempered, refused to do household work or made demands for separate stay, etc.[27]

Graph 3.20(a) Distribution of 377 Surveyees by the Reasons of Separation in Different Social Caste Groups

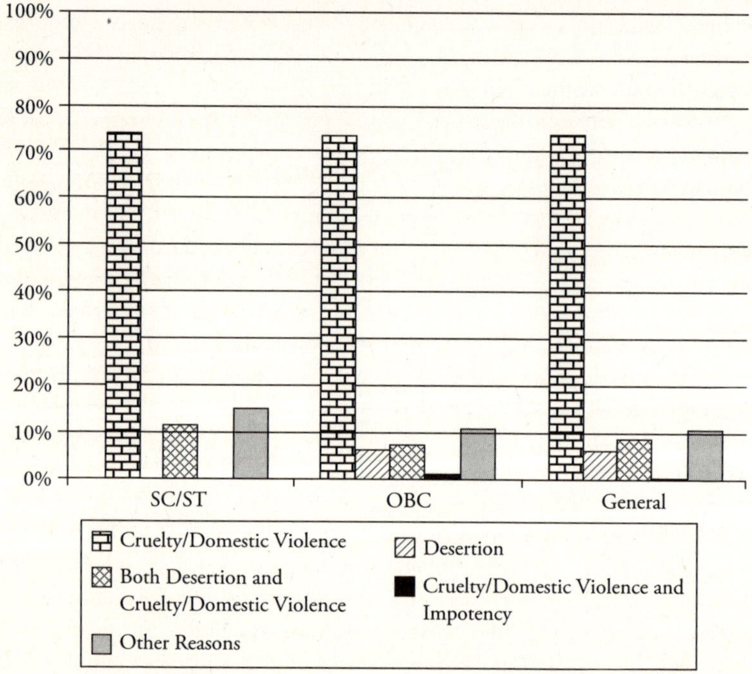

Graph 3.20(b) highlights the fact that domestic violence/cruelty cuts across all communities and religions as a reason for separation. However, the highest incidents of cruelty were reported from Hindu families. A total of 84.5 per cent of the Hindu surveyees and 79.2 per cent of the Muslim

[27] Sagade, *supra note* 1, p. 177.

Graph 3.20(b) Percentage Distribution of Surveyees by the Reasons for Separation in Different Religions

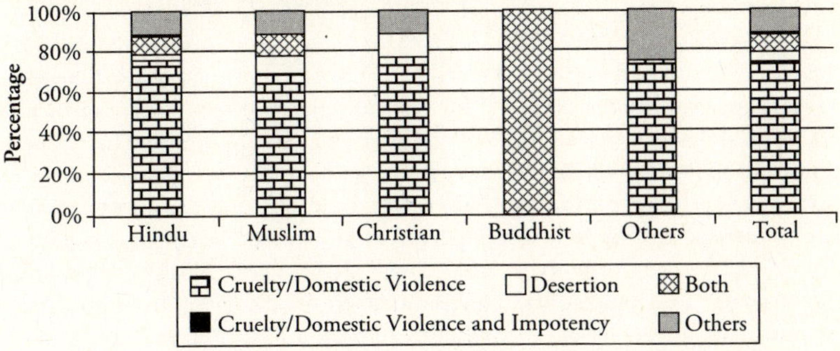

Note: Graph 3.20(b) is a representation of 384 cases, reporting the religion and the reasons for separation.

surveyees reported that they had been subjected to cruelty/domestic violence of various kinds. Though the sample for separated women who were Christians and others was fairly small, 75 per cent of those surveyees also reported cruelty/domestic violence as a major cause for separation. Desertion as a cause for separation was the highest amongst the Muslims surveyees (19.5 per cent) followed by Hindu surveyees (11.9 per cent) and the Christian surveyees (11.8 per cent) though the percentage differences were not much. Both the Buddhist surveyees reported that they had been deserted.

Other reasons for separation were also cited by approximately the same percentage of surveyees.

Graph 3.21 shows that 35.5 per cent of the 321 surveyees—who suffered cruelty/domestic violence and reported it as a reason for separation—reported that they had suffered mental cruelty while 57.9 per cent of the surveyees reported that they had suffered both mental and physical cruelty. Another 6.6 per cent reported that they had only suffered physical cruelty. The percentages of women suffering from both physical and mental cruelty were similar amongst both our Hindu and Muslim surveyees. However, 69 per cent of 13 Christian surveyees and 75 per cent of four of the surveyees who belonged to the category of other religions reported that they had suffered both types of cruelty. Thus, physical violence was present in 64.5 per cent of the surveyed cases and approximately two-thirds of the surveyees had suffered physical violence while mental violence was present in almost all the cases (see Box 3.3).

Graph 3.22 shows that both aspects of cruelty, that is, mental and physical were present in 71.2 per cent of the cases. The data here clearly shows that

Box 3.3: Fat Dowry Does Not Bring Wedded Bliss

Shabana Amin (name changed for privacy) aged about 35 years from Ahmedabad got married when she was just 14. Her parents forced her to marry a man who was 38 years old. After marriage there were all kinds of mental and physical cruelties. She had two miscarriages by the age of 19. Six years into the marriage the man divorced her without giving her anything. She later remarried and now lives with her second husband and two children. She runs a beauty parlour. She feels that because of a bad marriage her whole life was affected. She could not study and do things that she wanted to do. She feels that her divorce has spoilt her image for no fault of hers. She says that the girls who studied with her have done much better in life.

Shabana's first husband was a goldsmith and earned ₹30,000 to ₹50,000 per month. Her father was also a goldsmith and had a factory as well. He earned approximately ₹100,000 to ₹150,000 per month. Her parents gave her husband a flat, a vehicle and partnership in a shop. They also gave her jewellery, electronic goods, utensils and clothes. Her relatives gave her gold items. Her in-laws gave her 15 *tolas* of gold. The total value of dowry from her parents was between ₹800,000 and ₹1,000,000. The total value of *stridhan* including jewellery from her parents was ₹65,000, from her relatives was ₹25,000 and from her in-laws was ₹10,000. Her parents did not borrow any money for her wedding. Her marriage was not a great financial burden on them.

During her first marriage she worked all day in the house, from 7.30 am till 10 pm, while her husband only worked from 9.30 am till 12 noon and did no housework.

Shabana did not get anything from her husband. She feels that she should have been entitled to share the household assets equally with her husband. She feels that marriage means that whatever the couple possess, they possess equally. Instead of being given anything she has lost so much. Her in-laws have kept all her dowry/*stridhan* items. They have not returned the flat and vehicle given at the time of marriage either. She and her family have not made any legal attempt to recover all this property.

She faced some hostility and prejudice on account of her separation. It affected her interaction with her relatives, parents and sister as they blamed her for the divorce and consequent loss of face. Post separation she rebuilt her life, completed her education, did a beautician's course and remarried.

Now she is fairly independent despite being remarried. She drives a two-wheeler, runs her beauty parlour, shops for household goods, goes to the children's school and visits friends. She does the household accounts and even acquires assets in her own name.

almost all our surveyees from SC/ST category barring 1.9 per cent of them were subjected to mental violence. Among the surveyees who belonged to the OBC category, 46.3 per cent had to face both kinds of cruelty. However, in 10 per cent of the cases the surveyees reported that they faced only physical

Graph 3.21 Percentage Distribution of Surveyees by Type of Cruelty Faced by Them Forcing Them to Separate from Their Spouses

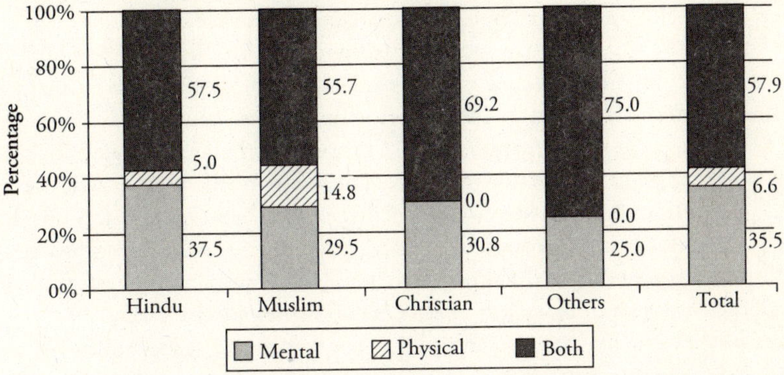

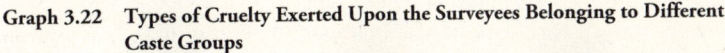

Note: The above is a graphical representation of the 321 cases reporting their religion and the type of cruelty faced by them.

Graph 3.22 Types of Cruelty Exerted Upon the Surveyees Belonging to Different Caste Groups

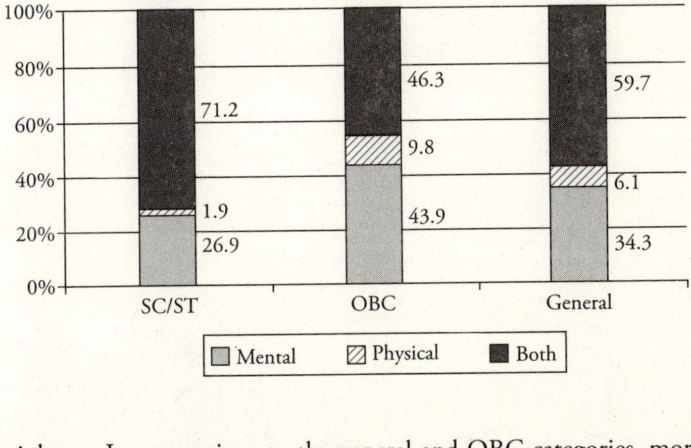

violence. In comparison to the general and OBC categories, more SC/ST surveyees reported that they had to face physical violence, that is, 73.1 per cent of surveyees. Among the general category, 65.8 per cent surveyees also faced physical violence. A total of 56.1 per cent of the surveyees belonging to the OBC category faced physical violence resulting in forced separation.

Various reasons due to which they suffered cruelty were described by the surveyees in the different regions. The reasons for cruelty included dowry-related issues, spouses' extra-marital affair or second marriage, the suspicious nature of the husbands, not having a male child, alcoholism, drug-addiction, etc.

Graph 3.23(a) is a general graph that shows the various reasons because of which the surveyees have been treated with cruelty. While dowry-related cruelty accounted for around 53.8 per cent cases in the north, an extra-marital affair/second marriage was the reason why 43.5 per cent of the surveyees in the east were treated with cruelty. Surprisingly, being ill-treated for not having a male child was not very prevalent in any of the regions, with only 2.5 per cent of the 322 surveyees reporting ill-treatment on this account. In the west, this reason accounted for ill-treatment in 3.4 per cent of the cases. Ill-treatment/cruelty of the surveyees because of the suspicious nature of their spouses was a reason given in 21.3 per cent of the cases in the south. Other reasons for cruelty were present in 27.7 per cent of the cases.

Amongst the various reasons for domestic violence and cruelty, the surveyees in all the categories reported dowry-related harassment as a major cause. Closely following this reason for cruelty was the reason that the male spouse had an extra-marital relationship or had a second wife. Extra-marital affair was a reason for cruelty in about 35 per cent of the cases in the

Graph 3.23(a) Reasons for Cruelty among Surveyees in Four Regions of India

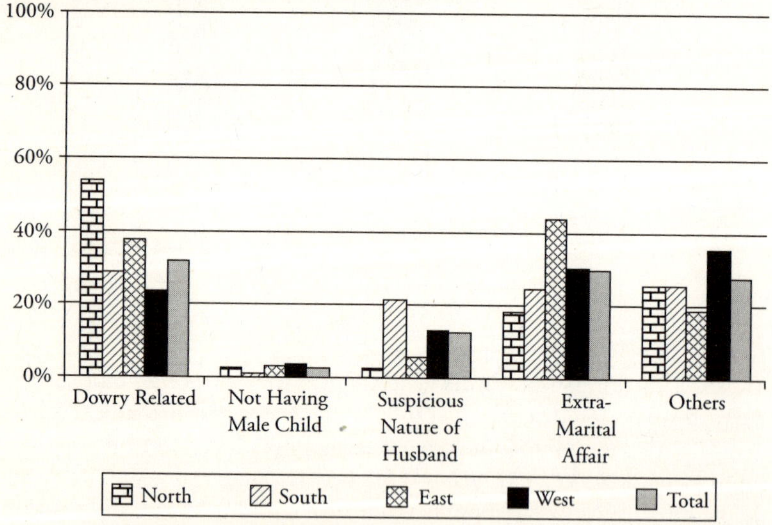

Note: Graph 3.23(a) is a graphical representation of the reasons for cruelty reported by 322 surveyees across different regions. The sum of the percentages across the regions will be more than 100 per cent as there are multiple answers to the question.

SC/ST category, whereas other reasons (30.8 per cent) as well as dowry-related issues (28.8 per cent) were also significant causes for cruelty.

Our surveyees from the OBC category said that dowry-related issues were the main cause for cruelty in 42.2 per cent of the cases. The husband perpetrating cruelty because he had a suspicious nature and constantly doubted his wife was a cause for cruelty amongst our OBC surveyees in 14.5 per cent of the cases.

In the general category while dowry accounted for cruelty in about a quarter of the cases, an extra-marital affair or second marriage of the husband was a cause in 36 per cent of these cases. In 12.7 per cent of the cases in this category, it was reported that they were subjected to cruelty by their husband because of his unduly suspicious nature. Some other reasons were given by another 27.1 per cent of our surveyees in the general category such as the husband's profligacy, pressure from the in-laws to file for divorce, husband being of unsound mind, no privacy in the joint family, etc (see Graph 3.23[b]).

Graph 3.23(b) Percentage Distribution of Reasons for Cruelty Resulting in Separation among Surveyees Belonging to Different Caste Groups

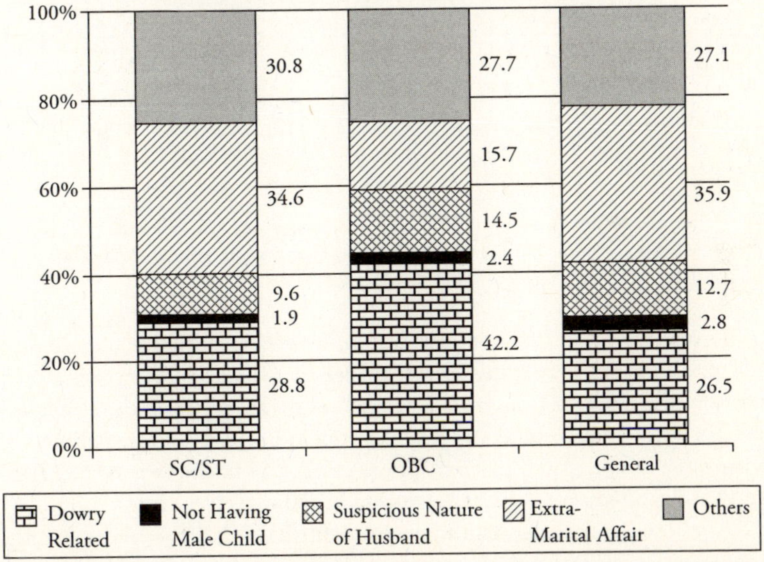

Note: Graph 3.23(b) is a representation of the 316 cases reporting the social caste group and the type of cruelty exerted upon the surveyees. As this was a multiple-response question the percentage will add up to more than 100 per cent.

Among Hindus, the main reason for cruelty/domestic violence in most cases was dowry (33.7 per cent). Women were also subjected to cruelty due to extra-marital affairs/second marriage of their spouse in 27.4 per cent of the cases. In 12.3 per cent of the cases, women reported that they were harassed as their spouse was constantly suspicious of them and imagined that they were being unfaithful. Not having a male child being a reason for cruelty was reported by 2.9 per cent of the surveyees. The other reasons for cruelty that the women reported were alcoholism of the husband, and in some cases the husband's frustration due to reasons such as unemployment. Women who did not behave as per conventional norms were also subjected to cruelty (see Graph 3.23[c]).

Graph 3.23(c) Reasons for Cruelty as One of the Reasons for Separation among Hindu Surveyees

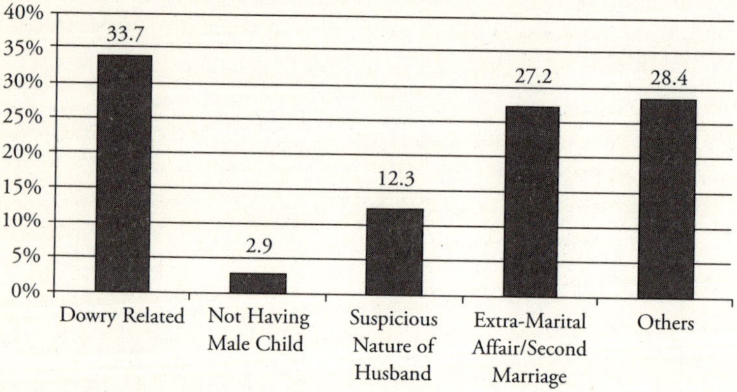

Note: As the question of the reason for separation was a multiple response question, the percentage distribution is more than 100. Two-hundred and forty-three Hindus out of the 304 Hindus in the sample responded to this question.

A total of 39.3 per cent of our Muslim surveyees reported that extra-marital affair/second marriage was the main reason for cruelty. However, dowry was another major reason in 26.2 per cent of the cases. Again the suspicious nature of the male spouse and the consequent ill-treatment perpetrated by him was a reason in 6.5 per cent of the cases. Not having a male child was reported as a reason in only 1.6 per cent of the cases (see Graph 3.23[d]).

Anecdotal experience reinforces some of these findings. Aarti Pandey, who works with the Muslim community in Bhopal, speaking at the Mumbai seminar, pointed out that since Muslim men are entitled to more than one

Graph 3.23(d) Reasons for Cruelty as One of the Reasons for Separation among Muslim Surveyees

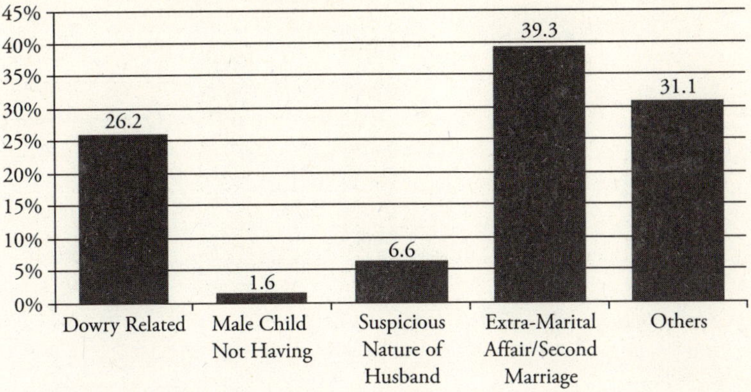

Note: As the question of the reason for separation was a multiple response question the percentage distribution is more than 100. Sixty-one Muslims out of the 78 Muslims in the sample responded to this question.

wife, they feel free to initiate extra-marital affairs. Advocate Badr Sayeed of Chennai made a strong case for an end to polygamy, describing it as the sword that hangs over every married woman's head.[28]

Our Christian surveyees reported that the suspicious nature of the male spouse was a major cause for perpetration of cruelty in 35.7 per cent of the cases. A similar percentage of surveyees reported that the reason they were subjected to cruelty was because their male spouse was involved in an extra-marital affair or because he had got married again. Twenty-one per cent of the surveyees reported that dowry was a main reason for cruelty and ultimately for separation. A total of 7.1 per cent of the surveyees, however, cited other reasons for cruelty (see Graph 3.23[e]).

Surveyees belonging to other communities described extra-marital affairs/second marriages as a main reason for cruelty and separation in 2 cases and in another case the suspicious nature of the male spouse was the main reason for cruelty whereas in the fourth case other reason was cited (see Graph 3.23[f]).

[28] Economic Research Foundation, *supra* note 15, pp. 155–156 and 207–211.

Graph 3.23(e) Reasons for Cruelty as One of the Reasons for Separation among Christian Surveyees

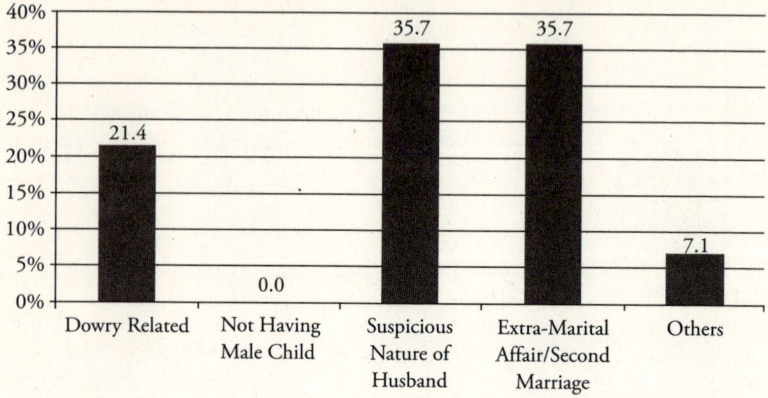

Note: As the question of the reason for separation was a multiple response question, the percentage distribution is more than 100. Fourteen Christians out of the 18 Christians in the sample responded to this question.

Graph 3.23(f) Reasons for Cruelty as One of the Reasons for Separation among Surveyees of Other Religious Groups

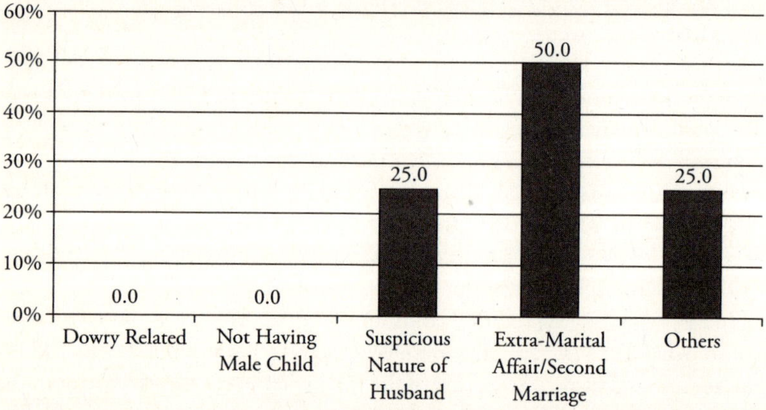

Note: As the question of the reason for separation was a multiple response question, the percentage distribution is more than 100. Four surveyees belonging to other religions out of the 5 cases in the sample responded to this question.

4

Work Status and Earning Capacity

In the majority of cases, women's time and energies in the post-marriage period become focused on the marital family and household because of social conditioning, family expectations, a narrow interpretation of gender roles and capabilities, as well as the imperatives of childbirth and nursing of the young. As a consequence, their role as workers and producers in the larger economy suffers. They become confined to domestic work, care work and the household economy.

The highly productive nature of housework and its contribution to the GDP of nations has been variously measured by feminist economists. *Time Use* studies have been devised to quantify the endless tasks of the householder including the 'own account production of domestic and personal services'. The female's tasks in the home enable the male worker to reproduce his labour in the non-domestic sphere but the woman's work is invisibilised and remains largely uncounted and unacknowledged. Little value is ascribed to it as it fetches no direct monetary returns. Economists such as Dr Jayati Ghosh of the Economic Research Foundation, New Delhi, and Prof. Maitreyi Krishnaraj, formerly of the SNDT University, Mumbai, have made substantial contributions to research on the productive nature of housework in India. This reinforces the argument for equal rights to property and adequate financial support to separated and divorced women.[1]

Employment and Work Status

A majority of our surveyees reported that they were mostly engaged in housework and did not work for gain (Graph 4.1). Thus, 69.3 per cent of

[1] Economic Research Foundation, *Economic Rights and Entitlements of Separated and Divorced Women*, Report of Regional Seminar Proceedings (2008–09) (New Delhi: ERF, 2010), 70–73 and 127–134.

Graph 4.1 Work Status of Surveyees at Various Stages of Their Marriage in General

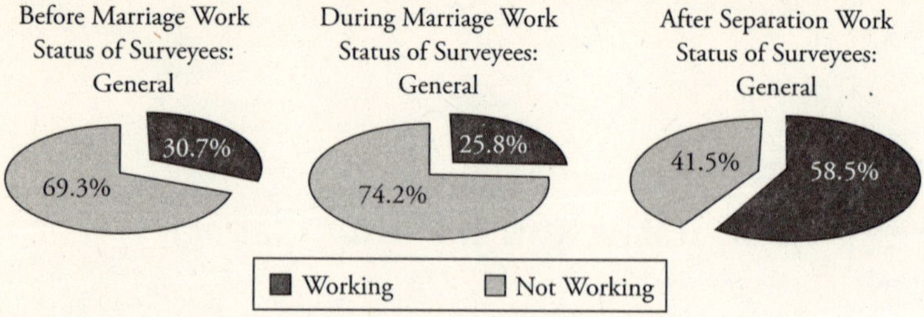

Note: The distributions across all categories in the entire chapter have been adjusted for the non-response cases. There were only an insignificant (0%–2%) number of surveyees who did not respond to this question.

our surveyees did not work even prior to their marriage. However, during the subsistence of marriage a larger number (74.3 per cent) reported that they had to stop outside work and were mostly involved in household chores and in looking after and maintaining the house and in looking after the children/elderly. After they separated from their spouses, however, many more women reported that they had to start working (58.5 per cent). This would indicate the lack of financial support that women receive after they separate from their spouses.

North

The surveyees from north India (44) reported that most of them, approximately 79.5 per cent, could not take employment/work outside their homes during their marriage (Graph 4.2). However, 65.9 per cent of the surveyees did not work for gain either before marriage or even after separation. Almost 61.4 per cent of the surveyees were not working even after separation. This would lead to the inference that during the subsistence of marriage most

Graph 4.2 Work Status of Surveyees at Various Stages of Their Marriage in Northern India

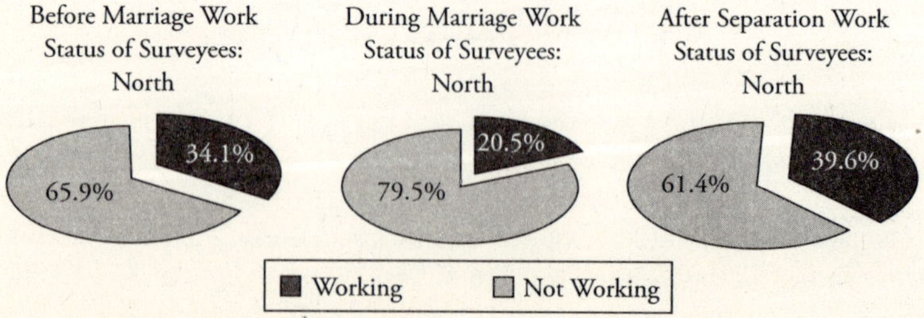

women, due to a variety of reasons, stop working and earning. Though they perform household work and look after the children and elderly during this period, this is not seen as productive work or work which is as important as the work done by their spouses. This increases their economic dependency on the male spouse and/or on the in-laws with whom they mostly reside. The percentage of our surveyees who were employed and working for gain were less in northern India than in some other parts.

South

In southern India, more women reported that they were working outside the home and for an income (Graph 4.3). Prior to the marriage, 44.8 per cent of the women reported that they were working. During marriage, however, this percentage was reduced to 34.6 per cent. Women from all regions have reported how they were either asked to stop working for monetary gain or were so burdened by household work that they could not work outside their homes. During the marriage, only one-third of the surveyees were working for financial gain. However, when they separated, the surveyees were suddenly bereft of any financial support from their spouses and many more women were forced to go back to work and earn their living. The majority of women in the south, that is, 55.2 per cent, reported that they were working after separation.

Graph 4.3 Work Status of Surveyees at Various Stages of Their Marriage in Southern India

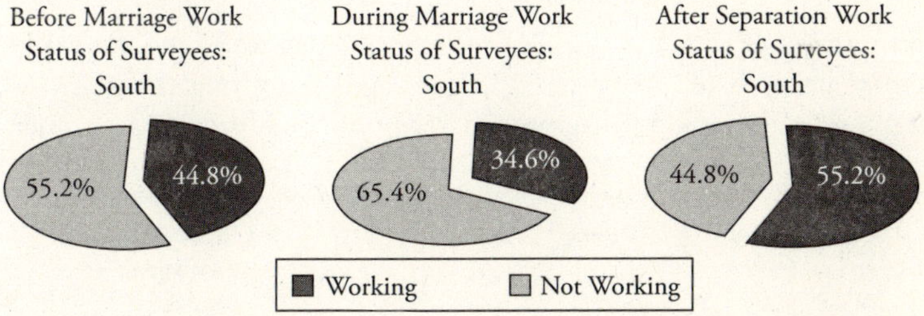

Note: There was an insignificant number of non-response cases (0%–1%) in this category.

East

The largest number of surveyees who were not working came from the east (Graph 4.4). A total of 78.2 per cent of the women reported that they were not working prior to the marriage, whereas 75.9 per cent reported that they were not working during the marriage. This number was, however, reduced after the separation when more women (47.5 per cent) had to work. In Darjeeling, 79.1 per cent of the surveyees were not working before the marriage while during marriage this percentage increased to 87.5 per cent. However, after separation 33.3 per cent of the surveyees were not earning. In Guwahati, 66.7 per cent of the surveyees were not working before the marriage, 44.4 per cent were not working during marriage and 66.7 per cent were not working after separation. In Kolkata, 65.2 per cent of the surveyees were not working before marriage, 56.5 per cent were not working during the marriage and 17.4 per cent of the surveyees were not earning after separation.

Graph 4.4 Work Status of Surveyees at Various Stages of Their Marriage in the East

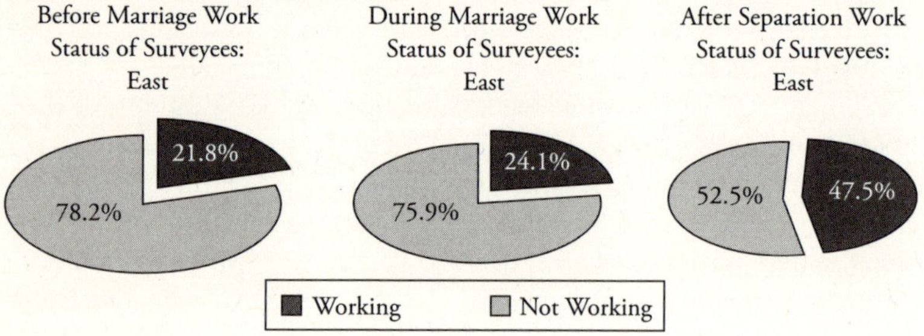

Note: There was an insignificant number of non-response cases (0%–1%) in this category.

West

A large number of women from the west reported that they were not working either prior to the marriage (78.6 per cent) or during the marriage (79.9 per cent) (Graph 4.5). Approximately, only one-fifth of the women

Graph 4.5 Work Status of Surveyees at Various Stages of Their Marriage in the West

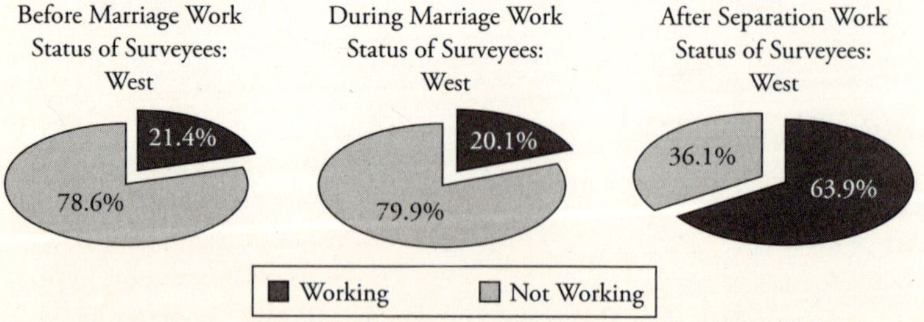

Note: This question was answered by all but 1%–2% of surveyees in this category.

worked for financial gain during these periods though there was a slight decrease of women working during the marriage. However, after the separation, the percentage of women working outside the home increased to 63.9 per cent, that is, an increase of 43.8 per cent if compared to the percentage of women working during marriage (see Box 4.1).

Box 4.1: From Housewife to Factory Worker

Shalini Sharma, 21, lives with her parents in Kanpur and works in a *pan masala* factory to support herself and her five-year-old son. She was married at 16 and separated three years later in December 2005.

Shalini alleges that her husband was a habitual drinker. He was unemployed and lived off his mother. He was involved in criminal activities. He would beat Shalini and force her to bring money from her parents. He threatened her with a knife on two occasions.

Shalini did not work outside the house during marriage but did the domestic work for the household which comprised her parents-in-law, brother-in-law and husband. She now works all day in the factory and earns ₹1,000 per month. The expenses on her and her child are ₹2,500 per month approximately and her parents pay for much of it.

Her parents had given dowry worth ₹50,000 in her marriage. They had borrowed ₹20,000 for the marriage. They gave her a TV, fan, utensils, clothes, music system and suitcase. Her husband sold the dowry and *stridhan* items.

She has not filed any case against her husband. She knows that he currently works in a cosmetic shop but has no idea what he earns. She feels entitled to share the household assets equally with her husband because most of the household goods were given by her parents.

She worries about her son's future as her parents earn little and her own income is meagre.

Domestic Work and Burden of Work

The truism that almost all women do the housework and care for the children and elderly is borne out by Graph 4.6. As many as 98.2 per cent of our surveyees reported that they were busy with housework during the weekdays and 95 per cent reported that they performed household chores even on holidays.

In sharp contrast, only 10.4 per cent of their male spouses helped with household chores. Our surveyees mostly reported that their men helped only once or a few times during the week, doing chores like buying vegetables or cooking non-vegetarian food on Sundays or occasionally helping at times of crises.

Graph 4.6 Contribution of the Surveyees and Their Spouses to Household Work

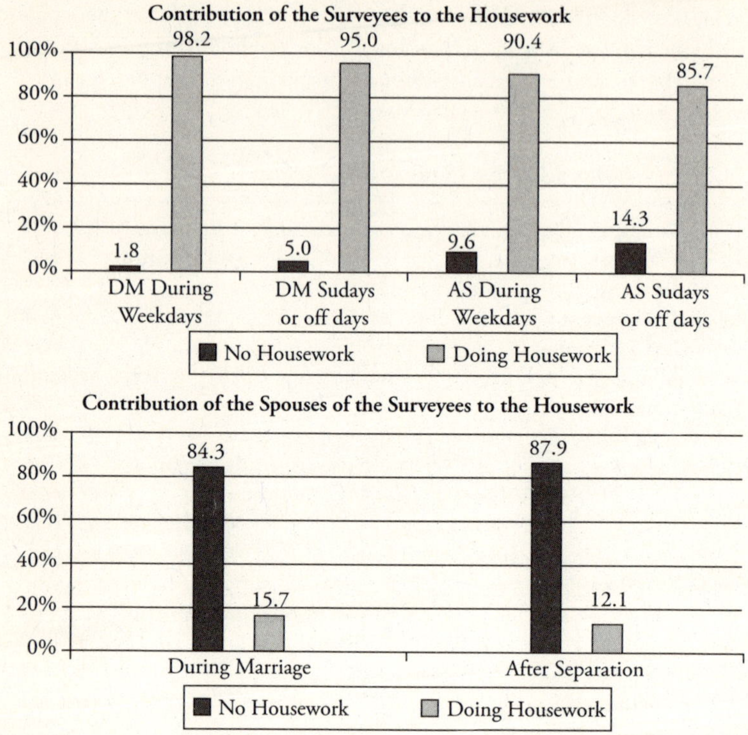

Even after separation, 90.4 per cent of the surveyees reported being engaged in housework. However, after separation, there was a slight decrease in housework on holidays, although 85.7 per cent of the women reported that they worked on those days too. The surveyees also informed us that after separation only 5.2 per cent of the male spouses had to do the domestic work. A lot of the women (232) said they did not know how their spouses spent the day, post-separation.

More than 90 per cent of surveyees reported their working status during marriage and after separation. More than 92 per cent of the surveyees reported the working status of their spouses during marriage but only 43 per cent of them knew the working status of their spouses after separation.

Table 4.1 shows the enormous number of hours spent by most of our surveyees doing housework during their marriage. However, 25 surveyees did not respond to this question. The time spent by our surveyees doing housework generally lessened after their separation, though 41 surveyees

Table 4.1 Number of Hours Spent on Housework by the Surveyees/Their Spouses during Marriage and after Separation

	Wife					
	During Marriage		*After Separation*		*Male Spouse*	
Hours of Work	*During Weekdays*	*Sundays or Off Days*	*During Weekdays*	*Sundays or Off Days*	*During Marriage*	*After Separation*
Not working at home	7 (1.8%)	19 (5.0%)	35 (9.6%)	52 (14.3%)	334 (88.8%)	152 (87.9%)
Working at home	373 (98.2%)	361 (95.0%)	329 (90.4%)	311 (85.7%)	42 (11.2%)	21 (12.1%)
Working hours						
<= 4 hrs	16 (4.2 %)	20 (5.3%)	73 (20.1%)	63 (17.4%)	33 (8.8 %)	14 (8.1 %)
4 to 8 hrs	96 (25.3 %)	82 (21.6%)	154 (42.3 %)	139 (38.3%)	6 (1.6 %)	4 (2.3 %)
8 to 12 hrs	135 (35.5 %)	132 (34.7 %)	67 (18.4%)	70 (19.3%)	1 (0.3 %)	1 (0.6 %)
12 to 16 hrs	94 (24.7 %)	95 (25.0 %)	27 (7.4 %)	31 (8.5%)	2 (0.5 %)	2 (1.2 %)
> 16 hrs	32 (8.4 %)	32 (8.4 %)	8 (2.2%)	8 (2.2%)	0 (0.0 %)	0 (0.0 %)
No response	25	25	41	42	29	232
Total	405	405	405	405	405	405
Total (excluding no responses)	380 (93.8 %)	380 (93.8 %)	364 (89.9%)	363 (89.6%)	376 (92.8%)	173 (42.7%)

did not respond to this further question about the number of hours they did housework after separation. The *Time Use* Studies in 1998–1999 by the Central Statistical Organisation also found that generally 'females spent about double the time as compared to males in activities relating to taking care of children, sick and elderly people'.[2]

[2] See http://www.mospi.nic.in/stat_act_t5_2.htm (last accessed on 16 November 2012).

The Central Statistical Organisation (CSO), Government of India, conducted a *Time Use* Survey in 1998–1999, which was a pilot survey and was conducted in six states, namely, Tamil Nadu, Meghalaya, Haryana, Madhya Pradesh, Orissa and Gujarat. In that survey, fairly detailed data was collected on time spent on non-market productive activities, particularly on the extended System of National Accounts (SNA) activities, and on purely non-economic activities, besides economic activities. All the activities were categorised into activities pertaining to SNA, Extended SNA and Non-SNA.

A new classification was developed for that survey. The activities were grouped into following categories:

- SNA (Productive and Economic) Activities
  - Primary production activities

Graph 4.7 and Table 4.1 highlight the number of hours that our surveyees typically had to spend in doing household work and in taking care of the children and the elderly. The surveyees reiterated the common experience that it is generally women who do the cooking and cleaning and taking care of children. Even women working outside the home bear the primary responsibility of looking after the house and caring for the children. Child care often requires a huge input of time, energy and supervision.[3] 'Working' women, thus, shoulder the double burden of both types of work. It has been pointed out,

> though the nature of the contribution differs between classes, with poor and working-class women putting in more direct physical labour, women of the middle and upper classes, who may have recourse to domestic help, nevertheless perform a range of activities to maintain the family or household in terms of supervision and responsibility.[4]

A total of 35.5 per cent of our surveyees reported that during their marriage they had to work for 8–12 hours in a day doing housework like cooking and cleaning and washing clothes. Many of them reported that they had to constantly supervise the children also. Quite a few reported that they had to get up in the night to look after the child and, thus, could not specify how many hours they had to work.

 - Secondary activities
 - Trade, business and services

- Extended SNA Activities
  - Household maintenance, management and shopping for own households
  - Care for children, the sick, elderly and disabled for own household
  - Community services and help to other households

- Non-SNA Activities
  - Learning
  - Social and cultural activities, mass media, etc.

- Personal care and self-maintenance

Out of 168 hours, on the average, males spent about 42 hours in SNA activities as compared to only about 19 hours by females. However, the situation completely changed when the extended SNA activities were compared. In these activities, a male spent only about 3.6 hours as compared to 34.6 hours by females. In non-SNA activities, which pertain to learning, leisure and personal care, males spent about 8 hours more as compared to females.

[3] 'Taking Care of Children Was Also Mainly the Women's Responsibility as They Spent about 3.16 Hours Per Week on These Activities as Compared to Only 0.32 Hours by Males.' Available at http://www.mospi.gov.in/stat_act_t5_2.htm (last accessed on 16 November 2012).

[4] Economic Research Foundation, *supra* note 1, pp. 127–132.

Graph 4.7 Contribution of the Surveyees to Household Work

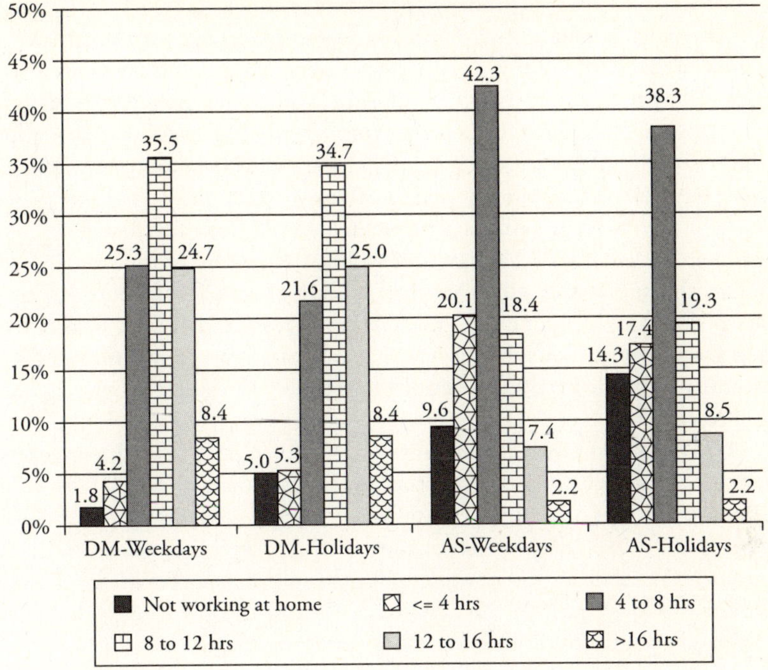

Notes: DM-Weekdays refers to the surveyees doing household work on weekdays during marriage.
DM-Holidays refers to the surveyees doing household work on weekends and holidays during marriage.
AS-Weekdays refers to the surveyees doing household work on weekdays after separation.
AS-Holidays refers to the surveyees doing household work on weekends and holidays after separation.
DM-Male Spouse refers to the male spouse of the surveyees doing household work during marriage.
AS-Male Spouse refers to the male spouse of the surveyees doing household work after separation.

During their marriage, in 24.7 per cent of the cases the surveyees reported that they had to work for even longer hours, that is, 12–16 hours a day while 8.4 per cent surveyees reported that they were involved in housework for 16 or more than 16 hours a day. A total of 25.3 per cent of the surveyees reported that they were working between 4 and 8 hours a day in the house. It was interesting that most of the surveyees reported that even on holidays they were forced to work a similar number of hours. The percentage of surveyees who worked between 4 and 8 hours a day however, decreased from 25.3 per cent to 21.6 per cent on holidays after their separation.

After their separation, a nominally higher percentage of the surveyees reported that they did not work at home. Whereas earlier 5 per cent of the surveyees had reported that they did not work at home, after separation 9.6 per cent of the surveyees reported this. The percentage of surveyees who did not do housework on holidays also increased to 14.6 per cent. Earlier, most of the surveyees had reported that they worked for 8–12 hours or more a day but after separation 42.3 per cent surveyees reported that they only worked for 4–8 hours. Though earlier only 4.2 per cent of the women had reported that they worked for less than 4 hours, a substantially more percentage of women (20.1 per cent) reported that after separation they worked for less than 4 hours. For surveyees who, after separation, worked for less than 4 hours a day or between 4 and 8 hours a day, the work became less on holidays.

Only 11.2 per cent of the spouses, that is, only in 42 cases the surveyees reported that their spouses did housework during marriage (see Graph 4.8). A total of 8.8 per cent of these spouses worked for considerably less than four hours a day. Thus, 88.8 per cent of the surveyees reported that their spouses did not do any housework during the subsistence of marriage. Three-hundred and seventy-six surveyees responded to this question about their husband's contribution to housework during marriage. Only 173 of these

Graph 4.8 Percentage Distribution of Male Spouses of the Surveyees by Number of Hours of Work Done at Home during Marriage and after Separation

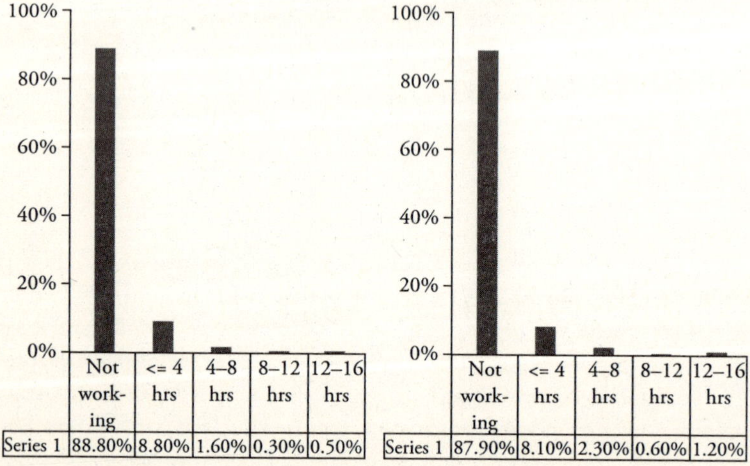

women knew about their husband's contribution to housework after their separation. These women reported that even after separation most of their spouses did not do housework. The percentage of spouses who did housework after separation was more or less similar to the percentage of spouses who worked during the marriage. It was reported that 12.1 per cent, that is, 21 male spouses did housework after separation. Naturally, an overwhelming majority of the surveyees did not know whether their spouses worked or did not work after separation. Therefore, 232 of our surveyees did not respond to this question. Even amongst the surveyees who responded, we felt that their knowledge of the facts was second-hand.

The seven surveyees (1.8 per cent of the reporting surveyees) who reported that while married they did not do housework during the weekdays increased five-fold to 35 (9.6 per cent of the reporting surveyees). This change implied that after separation almost 400 per cent more surveyees were not doing household work, especially during the weekdays. Nineteen surveyees (5 per cent of the reporting surveyees) reported that they did no household work during marriage on weekends or holidays. This number, after separation, increased to 52 which accounted for 14.3 per cent of the reporting surveyees. This change in number of surveyees not working during weekends implied an increase of 174 per cent (see Table 4.2).

The number of surveyees working more than 8 hours a day both during weekdays and the weekends during marriage decreased substantially after separation. The number of surveyees working less than 8 hours during

Table 4.2 Percentage Difference of Hours Spent on Housework by the Surveyees/ Their Spouses during Marriage and after Separation

	Wife (weekdays)	*Wife (holidays)*	*Male Spouse*
No housework	400.0	173.7	–54.5
Doing housework	–11.8	–13.9	–50.0
<= 4 hrs	356.3	215.0	–57.6
4 to 8 hrs	60.4	69.5	–33.3
8 to 12 hrs	–50.4	–47.0	0.0
12 to 16 hrs	–71.3	–67.4	0.0
> 16 hrs	–75.0	–75.0	
Total (excluding missing and no response cases)	–4.2	–4.5	–54.0

Note: In this table, we are trying to observe the percentage change in hours spent in housework by the surveyees and their spouses after separation, keeping the hours spent during the marriage as the basis. While considering the data for the women surveyees we have ignored the no-response cases, however, while considering the data of male spouses working at home we have considered the no-response cases.

weekdays or the weekends increased significantly after separation. *Thus, more surveyees were working for lesser hours after their separation.*

Moreover, the percentage of surveyees working 8–12 hours decreased by 50 per cent, and the percentage of those working 12–16 hours decreased by 71 per cent. Also, the number of surveyees 'working for more than 16 hours' decreased by a significant 75 per cent.

Percentage changes in the hours of housework were similar for the holidays as compared to weekdays after their separation.

After separation, 184 women (plus another 48 women who did not answer this question) did not know what housework, if any, their male spouses did. Another 173 of the surveyees provided us approximate information. During marriage 334 out of 405 (82.5 per cent) male spouses were not doing housework at all while after separation 152 out of 405 (37.5 per cent) did not seem to be doing any household work. During marriage, 33 out of 405 (8.1 per cent) male spouses were working for less than or up to 4 hours[5] and after separation the situation was the same. Six out of 405 (1.5 per cent) of the male spouses worked for 4 to 8 hours a day during their marriage while after separation 4 out of 405 (only 1 per cent) male spouses worked for similar hours. In only one of the cases, the male spouse, from Chennai, Tamil Nadu, worked for 8–12 hours a day during the marriage and also continued working for 12–16 hours after separation. Another surveyee, whose spouse worked for 12–16 hours after separation, was from Thiruvananthapuram, Kerala.

Types of Domestic Chores Performed by the Surveyees during Their Marriage

Three-hundred and sixty-seven surveyees answered the question about the nature of work they did in their marital households or at the place they were residing after separation. Most of the cooking was done by the women and 211 of our surveyees reported they cooked during weekdays in their marital homes. A total of 148 surveyees reported that they did household cleaning, 66 of these 367 surveyees took care of their children whereas 25 were taking care of the elderly, 117 surveyees did household chores whereas 34 had to fetch water and/or fuel for their day-to-day domestic needs and other

[5] Even this number is high as there is no separate table for weekdays and holidays; most of the male spouses worked on holidays/Sundays only, when they performed chores like cooking non-vegetarian food, or buying grocery items, etc.

activities in the household were also being performed by the surveyeees in 82 of these 367 cases. Almost all of these surveyees did similar work during weekends and/or holidays too during the subsistence of their marriage.

Graph 4.9 shows the average time spent by our surveyees on various household activities in their marital home during weekdays. Our surveyees reported that a considerable amount of time was spent on cooking (4 hours 6 minutes on an average) and household chores (4 hours 45 minutes on average). Household chores included serving meals, doing child related jobs, ironing clothes, helping family members in household work, nursing ill family members, etc. On an average another 4 hours approximately were spent on elderly care and approximately 3 hours on child care. Cleaning took 3 hours on an average. Some women also had to fetch water and/fuel for their household and they spent an average of one hour and 27 minutes on these activities.

Other household activities also took an average three hours of the surveyees. These included agriculture-based work of the household, attending to guests, paying household bills and supervising or taking care of maintenance of the house. Working women did additional jobs at home in comparison to their peers who were not employed gainfully. They spent time on preparing for the next day on the previous night, and similarly did various chores for the coming week on Sundays. Even when the surveyees had domestic workers they had to spend time in supervising the domestic work done by these domestic workers.

Graph 4.9 Average Time Put In by the Women in Different Household Activities during the Marriage (Weekdays)

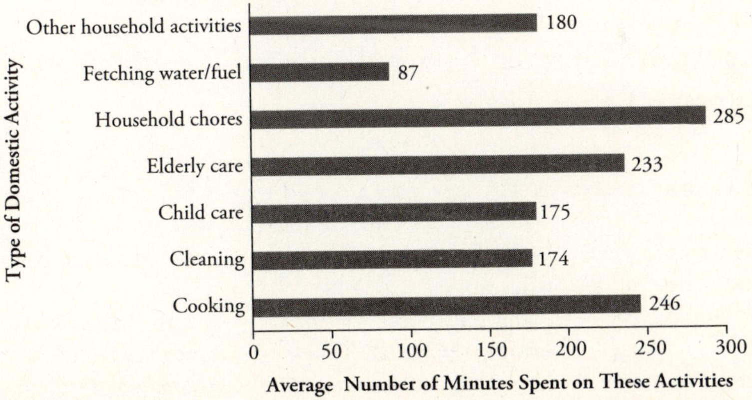

Note: The average time spent on the various works/activities has been calculated by dividing the total number of hours of work done by the surveyees, by the number of surveyees who were engaged in that particular work/activity.

Even on a weekend or holidays, our surveyees reported that they had to spend a considerable amount of time, in fact almost an equivalent amount of time, on various household activities. For instance, cooking and household chores took approximately 4 hours and 7 minutes and 4 hours and 40 minutes respectively. They spent approximately the same time in childcare (3 hours) and elderly care (4 hours). On an average, the other household activities also took 4 hours and 40 minutes while fetching water and/or fuel took 1 hour and 26 minutes (see Graph 4.10).

Graph 4.10 Average Time Put In by the Surveyees in Different Household Activities during the Marriage (Weekend and Holidays)

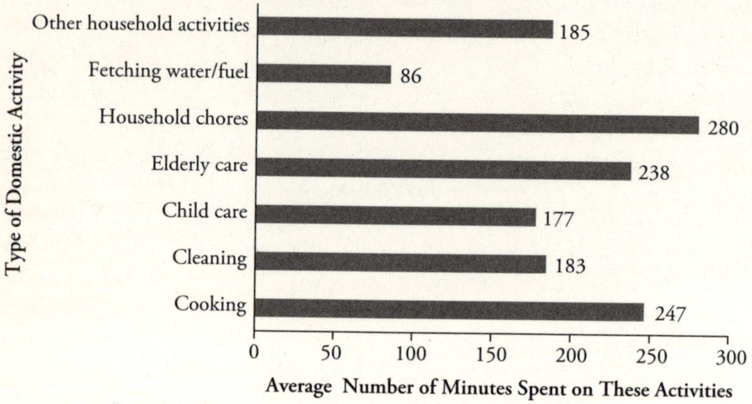

Types of Domestic Chores Performed by the Surveyees after Their Separation

After their separation, 318 surveyees reported that they were engaged in housework. However, 49 surveyees who were engaged in house work during their marriage were not performing any domestic chores after their separation. They felt liberated.

During weekdays, after separation, 167 of these 318 surveyees cooked, 82 were engaged in cleaning the house, 95 surveyees were engaged in child care, 13 surveyees were taking care of their elderly parents/grand-parents, 81 were engaged in household chores, 17 were fetching water/fuel whereas 44 surveyees were doing other household activities as well. During weekends/

holidays, the surveyees were again engaged in similar household work, except in cases of child care and household chores. Eight of the 95 surveyees were not taking care of their children during weekends/holidays and 11 more surveyees were doing household chores during weekends/holidays.

Graph 4.11 shows the average time spent by our surveyees on various household activities after separation during weekdays. Our surveyees reported that on an average they spent comparatively less time on these activities after their separation. On an average they spent 2 hours and 40 minutes on cooking and 3 hours and 19 minutes on household chores. Another 3 hours approximately were spent on elder care and a little over 3 hours on child care. Cleaning took approximately 2 hours. Women who had to fetch water and/ fuel for their household spent one hour and 16 minutes on these activities. Other household activities, took on an average 2 hours and 23 minutes.

If we compare the time spent on the various household activities during marriage and after separation, we find that the surveyees spent approximately one-and-a-half hours less on cooking, approximately one hour less on cleaning, approximately one hour less on elderly care, one hour and 26 minutes less on household chores, 11 minutes less on fetching water and/or fuel and 37 minutes less on other household activities. However, on child care they spent 10 more minutes.

Graph 4.12 shows time spent on various household activities by surveyees on weekends and holidays after separation. We found that there was not much difference in the time that the surveyees spent on household activities during weekdays and during holidays and weekends. In fact, the surveyees

Graph 4.11 Average Time Put In by the Surveyees in Different Household Activities after Separation (Weekdays)

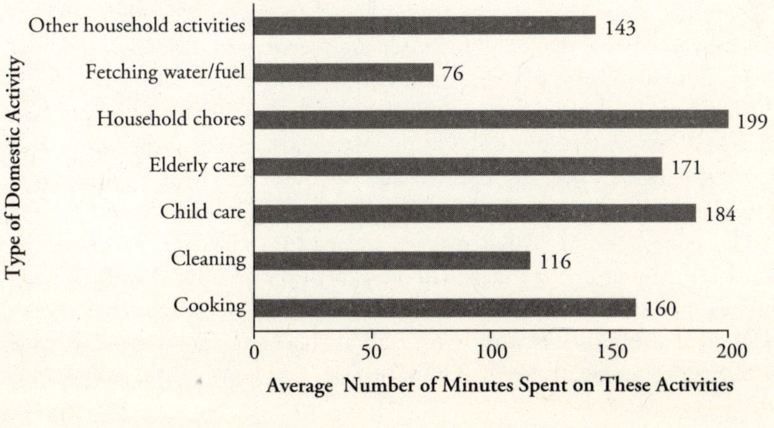

Graph 4.12 Average Time Put In by the Surveyees in Different Household Activities after Separation (Weekend and Holidays)

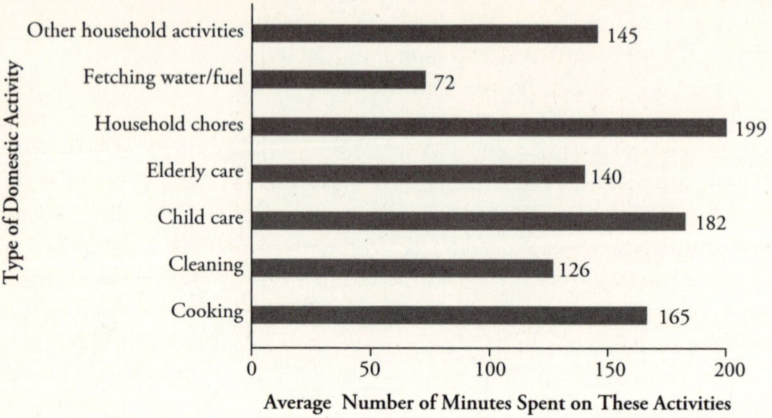

spent 10 more minutes, on average, on cleaning but spent half an hour less on elderly care on weekends and holidays.

After separation, however, the surveyees spent one hour and 20 minutes less on cooking, approximately one hour less on cleaning, one hour and 38 minutes less on elderly care, one hour and twenty minutes less on household chores, 15 minutes less on fetching water and/or fuel and 30 minutes less on other household activities during the weekend and holidays in comparison to what they had spent during their marriage. However, whether during marriage or on separation, the surveyees seem to spend the same amount of time on child care during weekends and holidays.

Another query that was put to the surveyees was whether they felt that the burden of their work had increased after separation. A total of 45.2 per cent of the surveyees in the north and 56.4 per cent in the east felt that the burden had decreased. However, in the south and in the west, 45.8 per cent and 44.1 per cent, respectively, of the surveyees felt that their burden had increased. Some surveyees reported that the burden of work had increased due to various reasons including having to do both household and outside work, taking care of the children alone, taking care of elderly parents, working outside the home and the increased pressure of the housework in their natal homes, etc. Almost half of the surveyees, however, reported that there was a decrease in the burden of work as they did not have to work for as many hours in their natal home as they had to in their marital home (see Graph 4.13).

Graph 4.13 Burden of Work of the Surveyees after Separation in Different Regions

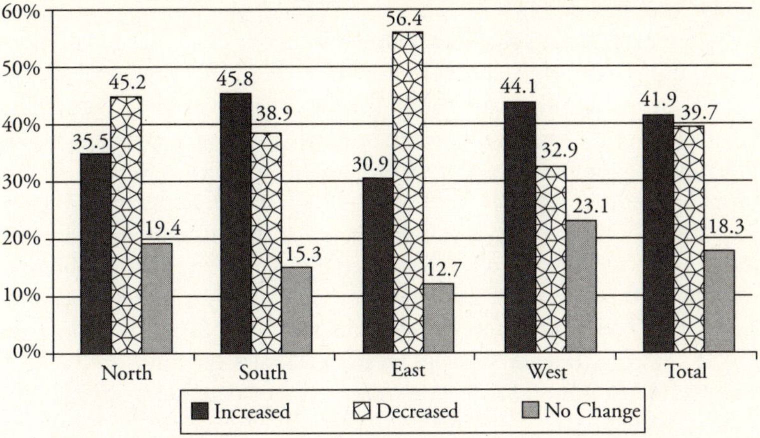

Note: A total of 360 surveyees have answered this question.

Twelve to twenty-three per cent of the surveyees from different regions reported that there had been no change in the burden of work that they had to do. If a percentage of the total number of responses is taken, 41 per cent of women reported that their burden had increased while 39.7 per cent of the women reported that it had decreased. Thus, almost an equal number of women felt that it had increased and decreased. The rest 18.3 per cent felt that there had been no change in their situation.

Post-Separation Pressures and Anxieties

Separation often results in acute feelings of anxiety and stress in most women. They are generally insecure about the future. They do not know how they will look after themselves both financially and in other ways. They feel upset and emotionally drained because of the trauma they have undergone in the marital home and after separation. Quite a few have no emotional support outside and many feel guilty about the break-up and the fact that they have to become dependent on their natal families. As children are often left with or go along with their mother, the responsibility for bringing them up also lies on them. So, the women constantly worry about their children's emotional and physical upbringing and their financial needs.

A large number of surveyees, therefore, reported feelings of stress or anxiety in all regions of the country. A sizable majority from the north (67.7 per cent) reported feeling stressed or anxious (see Graph 4.14). Fifty-five per cent from the south, 60 per cent from the east and 64.1 per cent from the west, all reported feelings of stress and anxiety after their separation. An average 60.5 per cent of the surveyees reported feelings of stress and anxiety. A heavy burden of responsibility was also felt by a sizable number of women. In the north 48.4 per cent women, in the south 58.4 per cent, in the east 55.4 per cent and in the west 57.9 per cent felt that their responsibility to deal with various issues had increased as they were now alone. They felt responsible for their children's future, they were worried about their elderly parents, felt that they had to somehow maintain the same lifestyle for their children but did not know how they would be able to obtain the funds to do so. A total of 53.4 per cent of the total surveyees reported that their responsibility had increased.

A total of 34.3 per cent of the surveyees also reported feeling emotionally burdened. They felt that they had been burdened with responsibility for their

Graph 4.14 Pressures Experienced after Separation by Surveyees in Different Regions

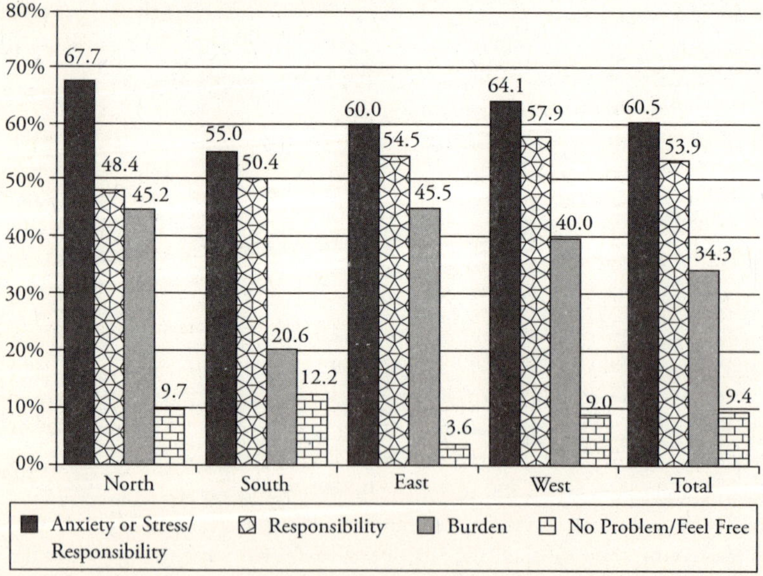

Note: A total of 362 surveyees responded to this question. As this question brought out multiple responses the total sum of percentages for each region is greater than 100 per cent.

children. Some said that they themselves were a burden on their parents and felt guilty about this. In the north and east 45.2 per cent and 45.5 per cent, respectively, of the surveyees respectively reported this.

A minority of the surveyees (9.4 per cent), however, said that getting out of their marital home was a positive experience for them and they felt free after the separation. A surveyee from Delhi reported that even though she had to take care of her children she felt mentally free. In another case, the surveyee said that she felt free as her parents and siblings were looking after her. A surveyee from Hyderabad felt free as she had a decent, stable, well-paying job and also a portion of a property willed by her mother. Another surveyee said that it would have been more stressful had she continued living in the marital home. The highest percentage of women who felt this came from the south and constituted 12.2 per cent of the surveyees from the south.

Earning Capacity of the Surveyees

One of the most contentious issues that arises on the breakdown of a marriage is the manner in which a wife should be compensated for the loss of earning capacity that she has suffered during the subsistence of marriage by not being able to earn, or spend enough time on her career or compete with her colleagues at work because of her responsibilities at home. Non-financial contributions, or what Frantz and Dagan classified as 'fungible assets', defined as assets which are substantially indistinguishable from one another, consist of 'earning capacity, pre-existing property, and gifts and inheritances'.[6] However, precisely because a wife takes on the part of a homemaker or primary care-giver for the children, a male spouse's potential to earn gets enhanced.

We, therefore, felt that it was necessary to ask our surveyees what they felt regarding their loss of earning capacity. We asked this question in spite of the fact that we knew that many surveyees may not have even thought about this issue. In fact a number of surveyees said that they had not conceived of working, so there was not any loss of earning capacity. However, the overwhelming majority felt that they had suffered a loss of earning capacity and many related the aspirations that they had to achieve certain goals as individuals.

---

[6] Carolyn J. Frantz and Hanoch Dagan, 'Properties of Marriage', 104 *COLUM. L. REV.* 75 (2004), 108.

A total of 75.6 per cent of our surveyees from the north, 67.5 per cent from the south, 59.3 per cent from the east and 54.9 per cent from the west said that they had suffered a loss of earning capacity. After they got married they had to leave their job, or they could not concentrate on their work, or work as long as they were required to get promotions, etc. Some surveyees reported that they could not study further and get the necessary degrees, etc., to make or further their career. One surveyee from Delhi reported that she had to work in the house as well as help her spouse and in-laws with their business. Another surveyee had to discontinue her partnership business. Others reported that their in-laws and spouses did not keep their promise to let them study. One surveyee said that due to household responsibilities she could not pursue her profession. Some surveyees reported that their spouses stopped them from working. One surveyee from UP, who was a national-level hockey player, had to stop playing hockey. Two surveyees from UP said that they stopped working after marriage due to fear of social stigma. The surveyees gave these and several other examples to show how their career opportunities were lost as they could not work after marriage or work in a very limited way.

However, 22 per cent in the north, 30.8 per cent in the south, 39 per cent in the east and 43.4 per cent in the west said that they had not felt any loss of earning capacity. Among these, a sizeable number said that they had in any case not planned to work. A total of 1.8 per cent of the surveyees said that they were not sure about their loss of earning capacity (See Graph 4.15).

The surveyees talked about the social norms and pressures, apart from their responsibilities at home, which had stopped them from earning or doing a job. They spoke of how first their fathers and brothers and later their male spouses stopped them from going out to work. Some spoke of how they had to leave their jobs when they got married or when their male spouses got transferred.

A total 50 per cent of our surveyees from the north who had been working prior to the marriage related how they had to give up their jobs when they got married. An almost similar number from the south (55.6 per cent) and from the east (47.8 per cent) reiterated this. From the west, however, the majority (63.6 per cent) said that they did not have to give up work. This was because many of them did not in any case work to begin with or were self-employed or had given up work before marriage. As per Graph 4.16(a), 69.3 per cent of the 405 surveyees were not working before their marriage.

In fact, 182 of the total number of surveyees answered that the question was not applicable to them as, in any case, they were not working at the time of marriage, or they had to leave the job due to other reasons like parents

Graph 4.15 Impact of Marriage on the Earning Capacity of the Surveyees in Different Regions

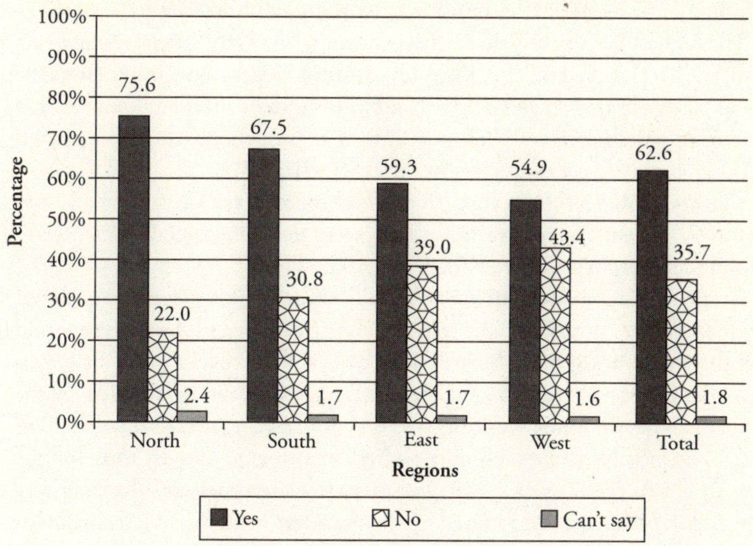

Note: A total of 342 surveyees responded to this question.

Graph 4.16(a) Percentage of Surveyees Who Had to Give Up Work or Aspirations to Work because of Their Marriage in Different Regions

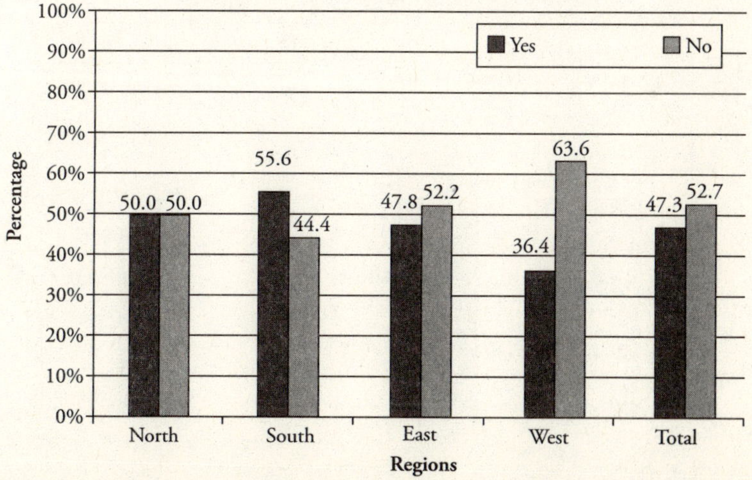

Note: A total of 182 surveyees answered this question as it was applicable to their situation.

asking them to resign before the marriage, or because of a child's poor health, or because she did not want to pursue a career, or because her job was not transferable while her male spouse was working in another city, etc.

The highest percentage, that is, 60 per cent of the OBC category surveyees reported that they had to leave their job. Around 54 per cent women from the SC/ST category had to give up their job during their marriage. However, a lesser number of surveyees (39.4 per cent) from the general category reported that they had to leave their job after their marriage.

Thus, Graph 4.16 (b) shows that a high percentage of women (40 per cent to 60 per cent) across various caste categories were forced to leave their employment/occupation after their marriage.

Graph 4.17 represents answers from all except 92 surveyees who said that the question was not applicable to them. Forty per cent of the surveyees said that their separation had affected their careers whereas 59 per cent of the surveyees felt it had not affected their careers. However, quite a few of the surveyees who were not working and did not have a career said that their career had not been affected and replied in the negative. In most of the cases in which the answer was in negative, the surveyees said that any way their career prospects were ruined by the marriage or they had left the job or studies due to the marriage, etc. Some gave a negative answer also because

Graph 4.16(b) The Percentage of Surveyees Who Had to Give Up Work after Marriage in Different Social Caste Groups

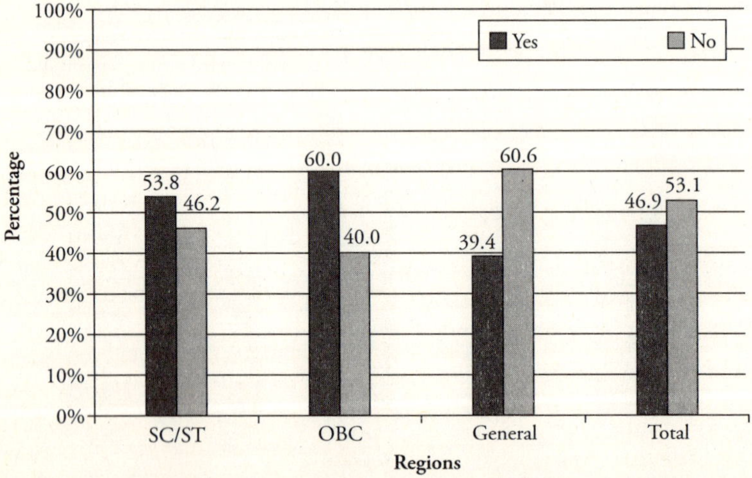

Note: 175 surveyees answered this question as it applied to their situation.

Graph 4.17 Impact of Separation or Divorce on the Career of Surveyees in Different Regions

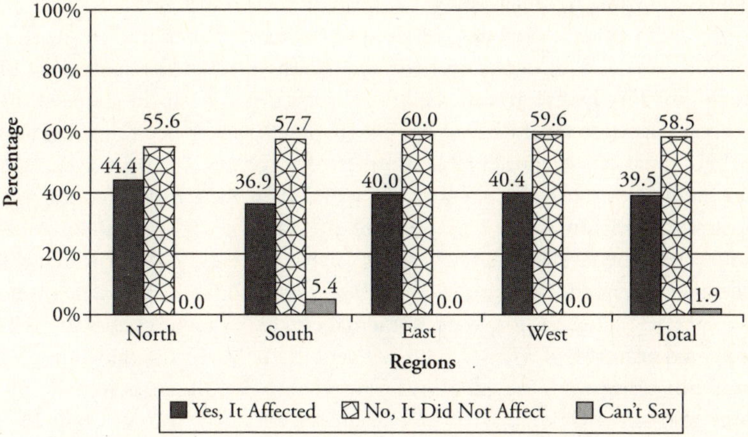

they started working after the marriage and the separation had no impact on their career. Others said that as they stopped working immediately after the marriage, the separation had no impact. Some said that they did not want to work, while others said that their parents did not want them to work.

Some of the reasons that the other surveyees gave regarding the impact of separation on their career were:

- they had to spend a lot of time on litigation;
- the separation resulted in so much stress and anxiety that they could not concentrate on their jobs; and
- they had to take on the burden of looking after and managing everything alone, within and outside the house.

Some surveyees, however, said that their separation had had a positive impact on their career and they were now able to concentrate on their work as they felt free and were in a better emotional state after their separation.

According to the SOPPECOM study on deserted women in Pune, for women life changed drastically after separation. The women felt that they belonged neither to the marital home nor to the natal one and their situation became even more vulnerable than that of widows. It was found that most of these women had to work hard in the natal home when they returned to it. They also had to work outside and give their entire income to their brothers if they lived with them. They felt that life for men after desertion was business as usual and most men simply got remarried.[7]

The surveyees were also asked to compare their status at work and their income with other colleagues (married or unmarried men and unmarried women) who also belonged to their age group and had the same level of education. This question was asked to try to ascertain what the status of the surveyees at work would have been like if they had not been married and in their situation. A considerable number of surveyees (47.7 per cent) said that their work status and income was worse than their friends/colleagues. However, surprisingly 10.2 per cent of the women said that their status was at the same level as their colleagues. 'Same' here did not mean that the colleagues/friends were doing well in their work, but that the friends were also similarly situated and were homemakers, or in some cases were self-employed at home. A total of 30.6 per cent of the surveyees said that they could not compare as they did not know what their colleagues were doing. Some also said that their friends/colleagues were not working. Only 11.4 per cent of the surveyees said that they were doing better than their colleagues (see Graph 4.18).

Some of the surveyees who said that they were worse off than their colleagues further expressed that their friends/colleagues were earning much more than them and were either financially independent or far more independent than them. Some surveyees regretted that they had spent their valuable years in doing household work and, therefore, lacked the experience and/or the expertise that their colleagues had. Some said that even after separation they could not work for as many hours as some of their colleagues did since they had to look after their children. Two of the surveyees from UP reported that working for lesser hours resulted in lower wages as they were unskilled and semi-skilled workers. Some said that they could not give their best to their jobs as they had too many household responsibilities. This resulted in them losing opportunities for promotions.

It is generally acknowledged that the contribution of the wife/female-partner in the home allows the husband/male-partner to pursue his career. In India most men are fed, their house and clothes are cleaned and their children and often their parents are looked after by their wives, leaving them free to work outside the house. This is true of both urban and rural India and also involves subsistence work—such as collection of fuel, wood and

---

[7] SOPPECOM, Hindola, *Assessing the Extent and Nature of Desertion in Daund Taluka and Ghole Road Ward of Pune City* (Pune: SOPPECOM, December 2008), 79.

Graph 4.18 Comparison of Work Status of Surveyees with Other Colleagues of Same Age in Different Regions

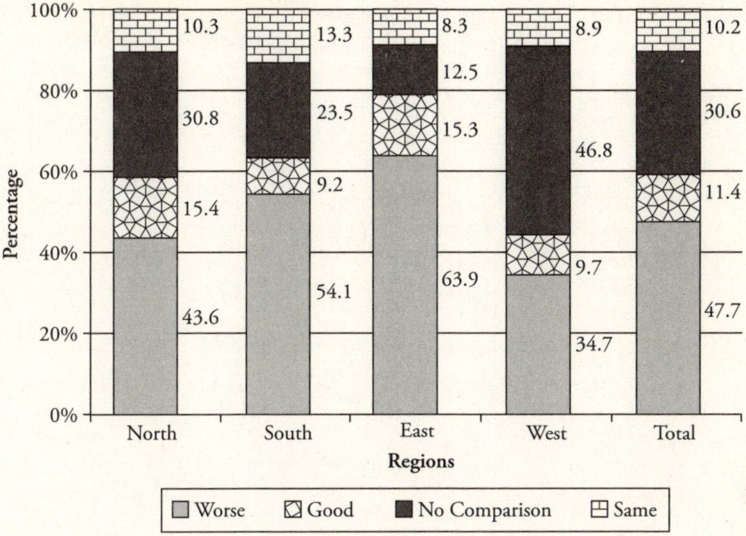

Note: A total of 333 surveyees answered this question.

water for the household—apart from household work and care-work.[8] Very few of the male spouses of the surveyees perform household tasks as shown in the Graph 4.19.

An overwhelming number of surveyees felt that their male spouses had benefited both directly and indirectly because they were looking after the household and taking care of the children and other household affairs. Eighty per cent of the women felt that their male spouses had benefited because of their contribution to the household and only 10.4 per cent, that is, 41 surveyees said that their male spouses had not benefited while 9.6 per cent of the surveyees were unsure whether their male spouses had benefited or not. Strangely enough eight surveyees reported that their spouses and in-laws constantly complained about their housework and hence their spouses did not benefit from the household work they performed.

---

[8] *Supra* note 2. Also see Indira Hirway, *Estimating Work Force Using Time Use Statistics in India and Its Implications for Employment Policies* (Ahmedabad: Centre For Development Alternatives, 1999). Available at http://www.unescap.org/stat/meet/timeuse/conceptual_ses1.pdf.

Graph 4.19 Did the Male Spouse Benefit because of Wife's Household Work or Talent or Skills in Different Regions?

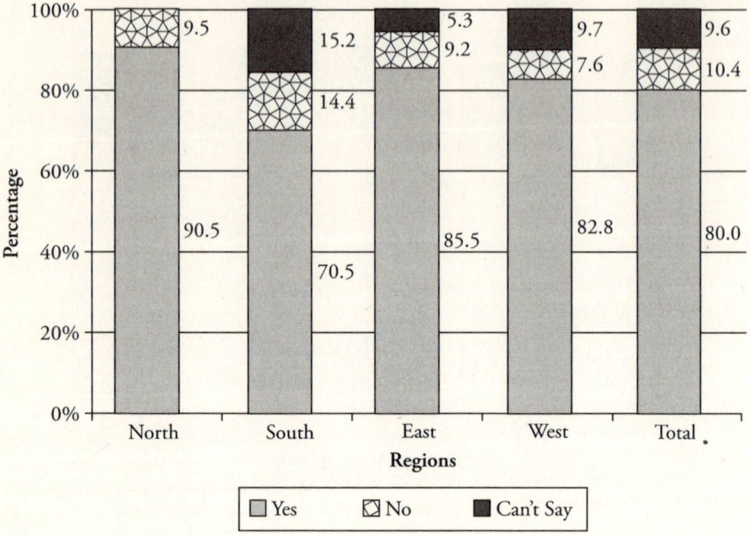

Note: A total of 395 surveyees have answered this question.

5

Family Status and Lifestyle

It has been widely reported across the world that the female partner and any children with her experience a sharp decrease in their lifestyle after separation and divorce. Some studies from North America in particular validate this.[1] This is true in spite of the fact that laws for sharing of marital property exist. This reality has been the basis for further demands to strengthen child and spousal support laws and for a more just and equitable division of marital property. It has also led to the criticism that division of property by itself cannot lead to an improved status of women which is also impacted by other policies and discriminatory practices of the state like its employment policy, rules for social security, etc.[2]

In India, the situation is even worse in the absence of any laws regarding division of marital property. When a separation or divorce takes place in India, the female spouse normally has to leave her marital home and her lifestyle plummets sharply. However, the male spouse/husband on separation becomes entitled to all the movable and immovable assets of the household. Separation, therefore, results in a completely unfair and discriminatory situation for the wife who has no legal rights to any of the assets of the household which she has helped to acquire. She is only entitled to an asset that has been acquired in her name (see Box 5.1).

Graph 5.1 shows that the majority of surveyees were living in extended families. A total of 59.8 per cent, that is, nearly three-fifth of the surveyees

---

1 Libertad González and Tarja K. Viitanen, 'The Effect of Divorce Laws on Divorce Rates in Europe', *Sheffield Economic Research Paper Series*, No. 2006003, March 2006. Available at http://www.shef.ac.uk/content/1/c6/05/30/15/SERP2006003.pdf (last accessed on 21 September 2010). Also, see National Commission on Children, *Beyond Rhetoric: A New American Agenda for Children and Families* (Washington DC: National Commission on Children, 1992), 253; David J. Eggebeen and Daniel T. Lichter, Race, 'Family Structure, and Changing Poverty Among American Children', *American Sociological Review* 801, no. 806 (1991), 56.

2 Brenda Cossman, 'Contesting Conservatisms, Family Feuds and the Privatization of Dependency', *American Journal of Gender Social Policy and the Law* 13, no. 3 (2005), 415.

Box 5.1: Fighting for Her Share

Mary D'Sousa, age 62, lives alone. She had French citizenship but had married an Indian and settled in Goa. She works during the tourist season, baking and marketing cakes and bakery goods. Her husband is a well-known musician. She had filed cases against him for divorce, maintenance, residence and separation of property and also filed a police complaint for cruelty. She did not file for custody as the children were already eighteen and there was not much issue about custody. Mary was married under Goa's unique civil code and is therefore entitled to a share in matrimonial property, unlike most women in India.

Mary could not prove her husband's income exactly. During the divorce proceedings he started hiding his income. He used to put all the assets in the company's name since 1995 onwards. Only he, his sisters and mother held the shares of the company. She had to sue the company. The Chartered Accountant put the marital house and office in the company's name. This could not have been done without her signature, hence it was done illegally. Her husband transferred two of the houses but he could not transfer whole of the company in someone else's name during the court proceedings as she got a stay on the transfer. She feels that her husband should have been asked to disclose his income and assets instead of her proving it. She feels that the court should be proactive and it should not be required to act as she has had to 'be like a spy' to get her due.

Mary says that the reason for separation was adultery by her husband. After about ten years of marriage her husband began to see other women. When she confronted him he became angry and violent. During arguments he used to throw things around and hit the dog. He even threw some furniture down from the first floor. After separation she faced a big problem in continuing to live in India, where she has been for 25 years and where her children live. She could push the divorce case only after getting Person of Indian Origin status.

Mary worked before marriage as a stewardess and continued to work until the birth of their first son. For another four years she ran a shop but did not earn much from it. As a stewardess she earned ₹2 lakh. From her catering business she now earns around ₹260,000 per year. Her husband is a self-employed professional. His husband's income was around ₹100,000 per month during their marriage. She does not know the exact amount. He has income from the rent of three houses and a shop. Mary finds it difficult to live alone. Post divorce her burden of work has increased. She does all the shopping and all the work in the house; she gets less help in the house. She takes the dogs to the veterinary doctor too. She feels the responsibility and the burden of work. She is also getting her house built. It is expensive and she has exhausted her savings. However, she now feels less stress, tension and depression. She says that her marriage affected her career as she had to resign from her permanent job. Later, she agreed to her husband's suggestion that she close down her shop and help him with his accounts. She feels that this

(Continued)

(Continued)

was a big mistake. She feels that her friends who continued to work did better as they retired well with a nice package.

Her husband benefitted from her household work and care of children. He was free to work as she was a good manager. She also entertained for him. She used to wake up by 6.30 am, make breakfast and then take the children to school in Panjim. After leaving the children at school she would go to the shop. At 1 pm she would pick up the children up from school and give them lunch. At 4 pm she would take the children for tuition and then bring them back. On Sundays she used to rest or go to the beach, supervise the garden, the maid, etc. Her husband did not do any work in the home.

Mary's matrimonial home was her father-in-law's house. The in-laws did not live there but in Panjim. During the marriage, the household expenses were ₹50,000 per month, apart from the husband's travelling expenses. She feels that post separation her husband's lifestyle has improved as he has to spend less on his wife and children. During the marriage, they had two inherited houses and a shop, two vehicles, jewellery, TV, fridge and other electronic goods. They also had cash, deposits, mutual funds/shares and life insurance. Her husband is in the possession of the houses and the shop. He also has two vehicles.

Mary was able to get a lump sum amount in lieu of maintenance, i.e., ₹8,500,000 and a car, that too through negotiations and settlement. She feels this is not adequate, given her husband's income and assets. The matter was being delayed and no positive order was being issued, either due to the delaying tactics of the opposite party's counsel or adjournment by the judge.

were living with their spouses in houses that were owned by their in-laws. Only 15.3 per cent of the surveyees lived in a house which was owned by either their spouses or themselves. Fifty-six or 13.8 per cent of the surveyees either lived in rented accommodation or in houses owned by other relatives. The fact that such a vast majority of surveyees from the lower and lower-middle income groups in urban areas live in houses belonging to the male spouse's parents, will have an impact on any law for division of marital property.

The lower and middle income group surveyees include 41.7 per cent who had no income, 27.6 per cent who earned less than ₹2,000 per month and 16.6 per cent who earned between ₹2,000 and ₹6,000 per month. Thus, 86 per cent of the women were in a vulnerable position financially. Only in 1 per cent of the cases the surveyees reported that they were living in their parents' home during their marriage. At least 10 per cent of the surveyees—which accounted for 41 surveyees—did not respond to this question.

Graph 5.1 Distribution of Surveyees in Different Regions by the Type of Marital Home

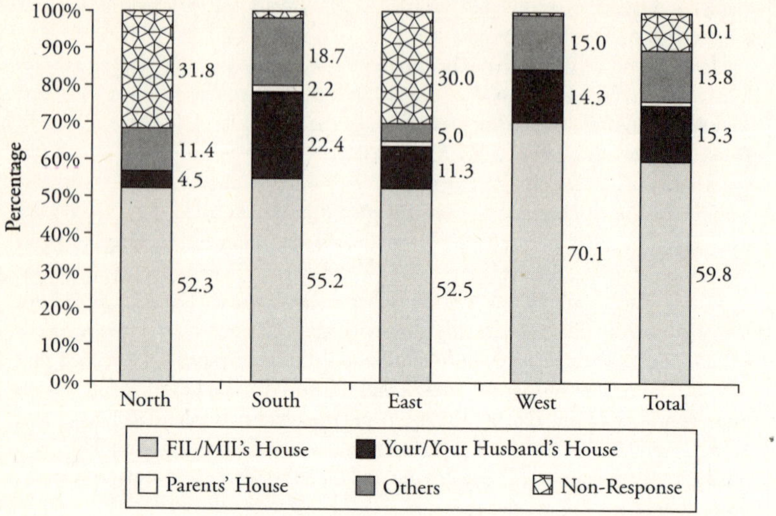

Note: A total of 364 surveyees have responded to this question. The non-responses in the north and the east are high as the early questionnaires did not have this question as a part of this survey.

To assess the manner in which the surveyees' male spouses were living, they were asked to specify if there had been any change in their husbands' lifestyles. A substantial number of the surveyees said that they did not know about their husband's lifestyle post separation as they were not in touch with them. However, 29.1 per cent of the surveyees said that their male spouses had a better lifestyle after the separation/divorce. Twenty-one per cent of the surveyees reported that their male spouses had the same lifestyle as before. Thus, 87.9 per cent—203 of the 231 surveyees, excluding the non-responses/not known cases—of the surveyees who knew about their male spouses' lifestyle said that they lived better than they had earlier or maintained the same lifestyle. Only 6.9 per cent of the surveyees said that their male spouses' financial situation was worse than it had been before (see Graph 5.2). Six of the surveyees said that their male spouses had started drinking a lot and also developed 'wrong habits' after separation. Three surveyees said that their male spouses had nobody to look after them; three said that they were not socialising with people outside their homes. One surveyee said that her male spouse missed her a lot after separation. Among the reasons ascribed for this worsening of lifestyle were that their husbands were drinking too much alcohol and were now squandering money and had got into 'bad'

Graph 5.2 Change in the Husband's Lifestyle Post Separation or Divorce

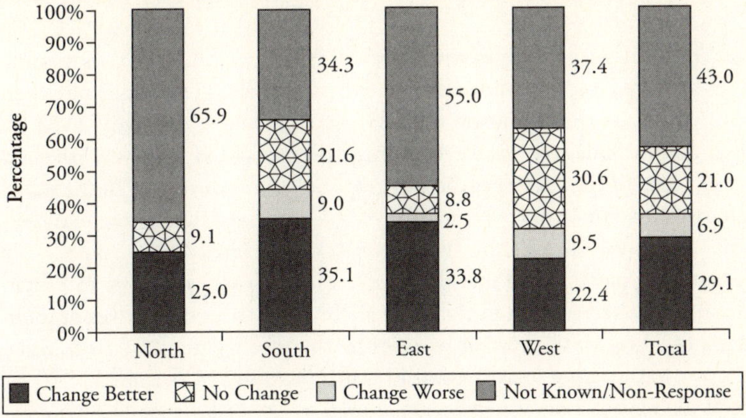

Note: A total of 174 surveyees, that is, 43 per cent did not respond to this question. Thus, the question was answered only by 231 surveyees.

company or had nobody to look after them, etc. As seen earlier in Table 3.3 (Chapter 3), some of the women were financially better off than their male spouses, in terms of earning.

Assets Owned by the Surveyees or Their Spouses

Table 5.1 is the first of the tables meant to enumerate the assets—both immovable and movable—that the surveyees and their spouses owned or were in possession of during the marriage and after the separation. The tables, thus, seek to find out the assets that the surveyees have retained on separation. The tables in this chapter show some key assets that the surveyees and their spouses and, in some cases in-laws, had when the surveyees were living in their marital homes and what they have been able to retain. The tables also provide information on who had acquired the assets to begin with, as this will decide whether the marital home should be divided or not. For instance, if the marital home has been acquired by the surveyee's in-laws or parents it cannot obviously be divided between the surveyee and her male spouse. If, however, the marital home has been acquired by either the surveyee or her spouse during the subsistence of marriage then, perhaps, it should be equally divided or given to the surveyee along with her children.

Information on Household Assets: Immovable Asset—House

Table 5.1 shows that most of the surveyees (60.5 per cent) lived in marital homes acquired and, thus, owned either by themselves or parents of either the surveyees or their spouses. Only 5 per cent of the surveyees lived in rented accommodation. However, a large percentage of surveyees, that is, 34.5 per cent of the surveyees did not respond to this question. In the west, the maximum, almost 80 per cent of the surveyees, lived in their own houses. In the south, only 44 per cent lived in their own houses.

Surprisingly, we found that the homes in which the surveyees and their male spouses lived were acquired not only by the parties themselves or their in-laws but in a small number of cases by the wife's parents. This finding perhaps needs further examination in a future study. In the north, 32 per cent of the marital homes had been acquired by the in-laws while 2 per cent of the homes had been acquired by the surveyees' parents; in the south, 18.6 per cent of the marital homes had been acquired by the in-laws while 18.6 per cent of the homes had been acquired by the surveyees' parents; in the east 25.6 per cent of the marital homes had been acquired by the in-laws while 16.3 per cent of the homes had been acquired by the surveyees' parents; in the west, 27.1 per cent of the marital homes had been acquired by the in-laws while 11 per cent of the homes had been acquired by the surveyees' parents. In total, 25.3 per cent of marital homes had been acquired by the in-laws while 15.5 per cent of the marital homes had been acquired by the surveyees' parents. The surveyees or their spouses or both of them together had acquired 36 per cent marital homes in the north; 22 per cent

Table 5.1 Information on Household Assets: Immovable Asset—House

	During Marriage	*Sources of Acquisition of the House*						
	Own House	*Male Spouse*	*Wife*	*Both*	*In-laws*	*Wife's Parents*	*Others*	*No Response*
North	56.8	28.0	8.0	0.0	32.0	28.0	4.0	0.0
South	44.0	18.6	1.7	1.7	18.6	18.6	3.4	37.3
East	53.8	9.3	7.0	0.0	25.6	16.3	9.3	32.6
West	80.3	28.8	5.9	1.7	27.1	11.0	2.5	22.9
Total	60.5	22.9	5.3	1.2	25.3	15.5	4.1	25.7

Note: The 60.5% of surveyees who reported that the marital house was 'own house' said that the house was acquired either by themselves or parents of either of them. These 60.5% houses have been distributed in the second column of this table, 'Sources of acquisition of the house'. In Table 5.3, only those 60.5% of the houses have been distributed among the current owners.

in the south; 16.3 per cent in the east and 36.4 per cent in the west. The overall average showed that 29.4 per cent of the marital homes had been bought either by the surveyees or their male spouses or by both of them (see Table 5.1 and Box 5.3).

The fact that 22.9 per cent—i.e. 77.8 per cent out of the total of 72 of the surveyees, who themselves or their husbands or both of them acquired the marital homes which is little more than one-third of the 206 responses given to the concerned question—of the total number of marital homes had been bought by the surveyees' male spouses out of these 29.4 per cent of the marital homes bought by either or both of the couple, reemphasises what those working with family law and women's issues have said about the ownership of assets being mostly in the name of the male spouse. Thus, in the north 77.8 per cent, in the south 91.6 per cent, in the east 57.05 per cent and in the west 83 per cent of the total number of houses bought by either of the parties were in the male spouses' names. Only in one case in the south and in two cases in the west, the house was bought by the surveyee and her spouse together.

Table 5.2 shows the current possession of only those marital homes of the surveyees which were not rented. If Table 5.2 is compared with Table 5.1 it will be seen that the male spouse has retained not only the house/property bought by him but also the house/property which had been acquired by his in-laws/wife. Both tables show that though the surveyees' in-laws had bought marital homes in 25.3 per cent of the cases they managed to retain more homes than the number they acquired (28.6 per cent). This was true across all regions where the survey was conducted.

Table 5.2 further shows that male spouses have retained 40.8 per cent of the houses and together with their parents have retained 69.4 per cent of the house/property. Thus, the wife has not only not got an equal share

Table 5.2 Immovable Assets: Current Possession of the House

	Male Spouse	*Wife*	*Both*	*In-laws*	*Wife's Parents*	*Others*	*Non-Response*	*Total*
North	20.0	4.0	4.0	56.0	4.0	4.0	8.0	100.0
South	37.3	32.2	1.7	18.6	1.7	3.4	5.1	100.0
East	37.2	9.3	0.0	20.9	7.0	2.3	23.3	100.0
West	48.3	6.8	2.5	30.5	3.4	1.7	6.8	100.0
Total	40.8	13.1	2.0	28.6	3.7	2.4	9.4	100.0

Note: A total of 9.4% of the surveyees whose marital home was their own could not respond about the current possession of these houses. This percentage was highest in the eastern region (23.3%).

in the house/property acquired in the name of her male spouse but has also lost property which was acquired by her parents. The legal system, therefore, allows the male spouse and his family to be the gainers when a separation takes place. Only in a minuscule percentage of cases (2 per cent) did the wives also manage to retain the possession of the marital home jointly with their spouses while in another small percentage (13.1 per cent) of the cases the surveyees managed to retain sole possession of the marital home.

Immovable Asset—Land

Table 5.3 shows that 23 per cent of the surveyees owned land during the subsistence of their marriage. A very large percentage, approximately 85 per cent, of the surveyees was unable to give information on the sources of the acquisition of the land. In most cases either the women did not have information about the land held by the family or they simply did not have land as many of them were comparatively poor. Table 5.3 again shows that the surveyees' parents had acquired the land in 3.2 per cent of the cases, as had the surveyees' in-laws. In 2.7 per cent of the cases the surveyees and in another 2.7 per cent of the cases their male spouses had acquired the land. Acquisition by both spouses of a piece of land occurred in less than 1 per cent of the cases. During the marriage, 93 surveyees either partially or fully owned the land. However, these numbers decreased to 24 post separation.

Table 5.4 highlights that in the vast majority of cases the male spouse and his family managed to retain the possession of the land. While the male spouses and the surveyees' in-laws had only bought land/property in 25.8 per cent of the cases, they managed to retain land in another 24.8 per cent of the cases. Thus, not only did the surveyees not get an equitable

Table 5.3 Information on Household Assets: Immovable Asset—Land (per cent)

	During Marriage	*Sources of Acquisition of the Land*						
	Had Land	*Spouse*	*Wife*	*Both*	*In-laws*	*Wife-Parents*	*Others*	*Non-Response*
North	20.5	22.2	33.3	0.0	33.3	0.0	0.0	11.1
South	20.1	7.4	7.4	0.0	11.1	18.5	25.9	29.6
East	28.8	4.3	17.4	0.0	4.3	21.7	17.4	34.8
West	23.1	17.6	5.9	2.9	17.6	8.8	2.9	44.1
Total	23.0	11.8	11.8	1.1	14.0	14.0	12.9	34.4

Table 5.4 Immovable Assets: Current Possession of the Land (per cent)

	Spouse	*Wife*	*In-laws*	*Wife's Parents*	*Others*	*Non-Response*	*Total*
North	11.1	22.2	33.3	11.1	11.1	11.1	100.0
South	25.9	44.4	22.2	0.0	0.0	7.4	100.0
East	34.8	8.7	4.3	4.3	0.0	47.8	100.0
West	52.9	2.9	8.8	0.0	2.9	32.4	100.0
Total	36.6	18.3	14.0	2.2	2.2	26.9	100.0

share in the property acquired by them and their male spouses, but they also managed to lose property (5.3 per cent out of 25.8 per cent) which had been given to them by their parents or had been acquired in their names. In 2.9 per cent of the cases, the surveyees' parents also seem to have taken possession of the land/property which was earlier with the surveyees. In around 3 per cent of the cases, the property was in the possession of others. In one case from Delhi, the land had been sold off by the male spouse while in another case from Jaipur the land had been sold off by the surveyee. One interesting thing that is evident from Tables 5.3 and 5.4 is that the wife's parents had acquired the land in 14 per cent of the cases but they could get the possession only in 2.2 per cent of these cases (see Box 5.2).

Land is a customary part of dowry in some communities. It has been reported:

> A special practice in the southern part of Kerala is that if some property is given to the daughter before the marriage, it will be settled in the joint name of husband and wife. If the marriage is strained, you will have to go to court to realize that property. Before entering into the marriage, the parents settle property in the joint name of husband and wife. The property given to the wife cannot be handled by the wife; it is handled and enjoyed by the husband.[3]

The woman's lack of control over property that may be owned by her is also an issue that will have to be addressed. Women, even if they are earning often do not control how their earnings are spent. Similarly women, even if they own property, often allow the male members of their family to deal with this.[4]

---

[3] Economic Research Foundation, *Economic Rights and Entitlements of Separated and Divorced Women*, Report of Regional Seminar Proceedings (2008–2009) (New Delhi: ERF, 2010), 219.

[4] Ibid., 145.

Box 5.2: She Lost Her Land and House

Dowry, in cash and kind, is sometimes used to buy substantial assets, such as land or a house. Despite this a woman may be thrown out of the marital home with nothing, as the case of Sheema (name changed for privacy) illustrates.

Sheema from Thiruvananthapuram, aged about 28 at the time of this survey, lives with her parents and her three small daughters. She works as a domestic help and earns ₹1,000 monthly. She separated from her husband in March 2008 after he had an extra-marital affair and began living with another woman. Her parents filed a police complaint against her husband stating that he had abandoned her and the children. The police questioned him and asked him to give her some expenses but he did not give anything.

Sheema is ashamed that she had to return to her parents after all the money they spent on her wedding. Although they had little income they gave her husband a gold chain, gold ring and ₹50,000 in cash besides a TV set. Her relatives gave some jewellery. The total value of *stridhan* including jewellery from her parents was ₹300,000. The total value of dowry from her parents was ₹350,000. Her parents borrowed ₹150,000 for these expenses and her marriage was a great financial burden on them.

Sheema says that her in-laws used the dowry money to buy the land and house in which the couple lived during the marriage. It was jointly in her and her husband's name. He now retains possession. However, she has some stridhan/*dowry gift items which are kept with her grandparents.*

Sheema's husband is a head-load worker. She does not know his income. During the marriage, they spent ₹5,000 per month on household expenses. She worked hard in the house starting from 6 am, cooking, cleaning and looking after the children till late at night. He did no domestic work. Now, she starts her day at 5 am, goes to work from 6 am to 6 pm and struggles to bring up the children, with help from her parents. Her three daughters are aged seven, four and half, and two years, respectively.

Her husband has filed for divorce against her while she has filed for maintenance, recovery of dowry and dowry harassment under Section 498A against him. She feels that her husband should be asked to disclose his income instead of her proving it in the court. She also feels that she is entitled to share the household assets equally with her husband because she gave birth to his three children and is bringing them up on her own.

Immovable Assets: Other Immovable Property

Other immovable properties included flats, compensation in form of other land/flat/plots, etc., that was given by the government in lieu of land, and any interest in a particular immovable property like leasehold, tenancy, etc.

Other immovable properties which were owned by some surveyees (33) had been acquired by them or their parents in 42.4 per cent of the cases while the surveyees' male spouses/in-laws had acquired 30.3 per cent of the properties which were in possession of the surveyees. Table 5.5 again reemphasises the truth regarding the lack of resources and assets that separated women have or are left with in India and underscores the need to address the situation. The non-response of the vast majority of surveyees to this question perhaps shows how few of our surveyees owned any immovable property.

Table 5.6 shows the percentage of cases in which the surveyees had possession of the other immovable properties after the separation. Only 17 surveyees responded to this question. An obvious deduction would be that the other surveyees did not have any other immovable properties. Again, most of the immovable properties seem to be in the possession of the male spouses/in-laws (39.4 per cent of the 33 surveyees) while the wife and her parents only retained possession in 12.1 per cent of the cases. Table 5.6 reemphasises the truth regarding the lack of resources and assets that separated women have or are left with in India and underscores the need to address the situation.

Table 5.5 Information on Immovable Assets: Other Immovable Properties (per cent)

	During Marriage	*Sources of Acquisition of the other Immovable Property*				
	Had Other Immovable Properties	*Spouse*	*Wife*	*In-laws*	*Wife's Parents*	*Non-Responses*
North	18.2	0.0	75.0	0.0	12.5	12.5
South	2.2	0.0	0.0	33.3	0.0	66.7
East	11.3	11.1	55.6	0.0	22.2	0.0
West	8.8	46.2	0.0	7.7	0.0	46.2
Total	8.1	24.2	33.3	6.1	9.1	24.2

Table 5.6 Current Possession of the Other Immovable Property

	Spouse	*Wife*	*In-laws*	*Wife's Parents*	*Non-Response*	*Total*
North	12.5	25.0	12.5	0.0	50.0	100.0
South	0.0	0.0	33.3	0.0	66.7	100.0
East	33.3	11.1	0.0	0.0	55.6	100.0
West	38.5	0.0	15.4	7.7	38.5	100.0
Total	27.3	9.1	12.1	3.0	48.5	100.0

Movable Assets: Vehicles

Out of the 161 surveyees who said that they owned vehicles—cars, scooters/ motor-cycles, bi-cycles—we found that in 42.8 per cent of the cases either the surveyees or their parents had bought the vehicles (see Table 5.7). Here, vehicle did not mean only automobiles, as some surveyees (23) mentioned that they had a cycle or rickshaw during their marriage and in seven cases after their separation. The buying of immovable and movable properties, especially vehicles, in 24.8 per cent of the cases by the parents of the surveyees, shows the extent to which dowry is flourishing even today. Table 5.8, however, again shows that most of the vehicles (65.3 per cent) remain with the in-laws and male spouses while the wives retain possession only in 18 per cent of the cases and her parents in 1.2 per cent of the cases. Table 5.8 again highlights the relative 'assetlessness' of the surveyees.

Table 5.7 Sources of Acquisition of the Movable Assets—Vehicles

	During Marriage	*Sources of Acquisition of the Movable Assets—Vehicles*						
	Had Vehicle(s)	*Spouse*	*Wife*	*Both*	*In-laws*	*Wife's Parents*	*Others*	*Non-Responses*
North	40.9	11.1	38.9	0.0	0.0	50.0	0.0	0.0
South	24.6	27.3	6.1	0.0	6.1	24.2	9.1	27.3
East	42.5	41.2	26.5	0.0	0.0	29.4	2.9	0.0
West	51.7	52.6	7.9	2.6	7.9	18.4	0.0	10.5
Total	39.8	41.6	18.0	1.2	5.0	24.8	2.5	6.8

Table 5.8 Movable Assets: Current Possession of the Vehicles Bought/Gifted during the Marriage

	Spouse	*Wife*	*Both*	*In-laws*	*Wife's Parents*	*Non-Response*	*Total*
North	44.4	44.4	0.0	5.6	5.6	0.0	100.0
South	48.5	33.3	0.0	9.1	0.0	9.1	100.0
East	64.7	0.0	0.0	0.0	0.0	35.3	100.0
West	61.8	11.8	1.3	10.5	1.3	13.2	100.0
Total	57.8	17.4	0.6	7.5	1.2	15.5	100.0

Movable Assets: Jewellery

Jewellery was one kind of movable property which was owned by most of the surveyees, that is, 60 per cent of the 405 surveyees (see Table 5.9). This point has also been reinforced by other data. In a general survey[5] about asset ownership amongst women it was pointed out:

> Jewellery was the only asset where individual ownership by women dominated individual ownership by men. Women individually owned 69 percent of all pieces of jewellery in rural areas, 66 percent of the same in urban areas and similarly, 46 percent in Bengaluru.

The jewellery had been acquired by the surveyees (9.1 per cent) or their parents (49.8 per cent) in 58.9 per cent of the cases while the surveyees' male spouses/in-laws had given them jewellery only in 9.9 per cent of the cases. However, even jewellery, which is the *stridhan* of a woman and should not be taken away from her without her will, was retained by the surveyees in only one-fourth of the cases as shown in Table 5.10.

Table 5.9 Information on Movable Assets: Jewellery

	During Marriage	*Sources of Acquisition of the Movable Assets—Jewellery*					
	Had Jewellery	*Spouse*	*Wife*	*In-laws*	*Wife's Parents*	*Others*	*Non-Responses*
North	63.6	0.0	35.7	0.0	46.4	0.0	17.9
South	56.0	6.7	5.3	1.3	48.0	1.3	37.3
East	57.5	2.2	10.9	8.7	43.5	0.0	34.8
West	63.9	2.1	3.2	11.7	55.3	0.0	27.7
Total	60.0	3.3	9.1	6.6	49.8	0.4	30.9

Table 5.10 Movable Assets: Current Possession of the Jewellery

	Spouse	*Wife*	*Both*	*In-laws*	*Wife's Parents*	*Others*	*Non-Response*	*Total*
North	17.9	17.9	0.0	25.0	3.6	0.0	35.7	100.0
South	32.0	32.0	0.0	4.0	1.3	1.3	29.3	100.0
East	21.7	30.4	0.0	0.0	0.0	0.0	47.8	100.0
West	42.6	19.1	1.1	13.8	2.1	0.0	21.3	100.0
Total	32.5	25.1	0.4	9.5	1.6	0.4	30.5	100.0

Table 5.10 shows the percentage of surveyees (25.1 per cent) who had current possession of the jewellery after the separation. Only 169 surveyees responded to the specific query regarding possession of jewellery. Again, a

[5] Hema Swaminathan, Suchitra J.Y. and Rahul Lahoti, *KHAS: Measuring the Gender Asset Gap* (Bangalore: Indian Institute of Management Bangalore, 2011).

Box 5.3: A Fight for Her House and Maintenance even though Deserted by Her Husband and Shunned by Her Relatives

Rose Rebello (name changed), from Hyderabad, is 57 and lives alone in a rented house. She is unemployed while her husband is a practising lawyer. Her husband's income is ₹50,000 per month approximately. She is surviving on a small income from fixed deposits saved while she was working. She has three grown up sons and a daughter who are all married and busy with their own families. She got married at the age of 14 in the year 1967. *She told us that her husband had raped her, and so she was forced by her family to marry him.* They got married under the Indian Christian Marriage Act 1872. In her marital home she and her husband lived with her sons, their wives and children.

She separated from her husband in 1992. Her cases were pending at the time of this survey. She has filed for divorce on grounds of desertion, and has claimed for maintenance and residence against her husband. She stated she was earning and her husband was unemployed. She acquired the property, the house where he is living. He wanted all the money and gold that she earned in his name. When she did not do so, he threw her out of the house. As she is caught up with court proceedings, she does some work but not on a regular basis. Her separation has affected her interaction with relatives, as nobody talks to her.

Rose worked as an office assistant during marriage, earning more than ₹10,000 monthly. Her husband worked as a clerk typist before marriage and during marriage started practising law. Currently, he is a practising lawyer in Hyderabad. His earnings are not known to her. She states that the house he now lives in was acquired from her earnings. He wanted all the money and gold that she earned to be put in his name. When she did not do so, he threw her out of the house. She feels that her marriage affected her career as she was a good student and would have done well had she not got married. She studied during the marriage and even managed to do her Masters in computers, alongside her full-time job. On separation, she wanted to study further but was unable to do so as nobody was supporting her and she was engrossed in court cases.

She feels that her husband benefited because of her household work and skills. After her marriage, she was the only person who was working at her husband's place. Because of her, his sisters were at ease. Rose's day began at 4 am. She left for work by 6.30 am and returned by 7.30 pm to cook dinner and feed the children. On Sundays she would go to church and do some of the week's housework in advance, shopping, washing clothes, readying the children's uniforms, school bags, etc. After separation the domestic work burden has decreased, she has only herself to look after.

She feels that the lifestyle of her husband post separation is worse as he is 'into drinking and all bad habits'. During the marriage she had a house, jewellery (was with her, sold now), TV, fridge, all acquired by her. After separation, her

(Continued)

(Continued)

husband kept all the household goods. She thinks he has wasted it all because of his drinking habit.

Rose gets only ₹1,500 per month as maintenance. The quantum is not enough as her house rent alone is ₹5,000 per month for a one-bedroom house. Her expenses come to ₹10,000 per month. She filed for maintenance in 2006 but her husband has put many obstructions to delay it. The matter took three years. No appeal was filed against the maintenance order. She gets the maintenance irregularly. He tried to conceal his income and said he is retiring and not earning. She feels her husband would be happy to see her 'on the footpath' and does not want to give her anything. She believes that she is entitled to an equal share in the household assets, as a husband and wife should share everything. At the time of her marriage she was given a dowry of ₹3,000, a bicycle, and a gold chain and watch by her parents, while her relatives gave gifts and cash.

sizeable percentage of the jewellery seems to be in the possession of the male spouses/in-laws (42 per cent) while the wife and her parents only retained the possession in 26.7 per cent of the cases. In a few cases (0.4 per cent), the jewellery had got divided and was in the possession of both the parties. It is pertinent to mention that jewellery forms a part of the wife's *stridhan* according to Hindu law and all *stridhan*, that is, whatever is given to the bride personally, is her sole and absolute property.[6]

Movable Asset: Television

Table 5.11 shows that during the marriage the surveyees had TVs in 58 per cent of the 405 cases. The total number of surveyees who answered this question was 250. The TVs had been acquired by their male spouses and

[6] In modern Hindu law, the term 'Stridhana' denotes not only the specific kinds of property enumerated in the Smritis, but also other species of property acquired or owned by a woman over which she has absolute control; and she forms the stock of descent in respect of such property, which accordingly devolves on her own heirs. Properties gifted to a girl before the marriage, at the time of marriage or at the time of giving fare-well or thereafter are her Stridhan properties. It is her absolute property with all rights to dispose at her own pleasure. Husband or other members of his family have no control over the Stridhan property. Husband may use it during the time of his distress but nevertheless he has a moral obligation to restore the same or its value to his wife.

John D. Mayne, *Hindu Law and Usage* (New Delhi: Bharat Law House, 2006, 15th edition), 1028.

Table 5.11 Information on Movable Property: Television Set (per cent)

	During Marriage	*Sources of Acquisition of the Movable Assets—Television Set*						
	Had TV	*Spouse*	*Wife*	*Both*	*In-laws*	*Wife's Parents*	*Others*	*Non-Responses*
North	70.5	6.5	22.6	0.0	9.7	12.9	3.2	45.2
South	47.0	17.5	20.6	1.6	6.3	14.3	6.3	33.3
East	57.5	10.9	10.9	2.2	17.4	15.2	13.0	30.4
West	64.6	25.3	9.5	1.1	11.6	25.3	11.6	15.8
Total	58.0	17.9	14.5	1.3	11.1	18.7	9.4	27.2

their in-laws in 29 per cent of the 235 cases in which the surveyees had a TV during the time of their marriage. In 33.2 per cent of the cases the TVs had been acquired by the surveyees and their parents. In a minuscule number of cases (1.3 per cent), they were acquired by both of the parties.

Table 5.12 shows that even though the TVs were acquired in 33.2 per cent of the cases by the surveyees or their parents, these were grabbed by their male spouses/in-laws. The wife and her parents had its possession only in 25.5 per cent of the cases. The male spouses/in-laws had bought the TV sets in 29 per cent cases, but were in possession in 43.4 per cent of the cases. In a marginal number of cases, that is, 1.7 per cent of the cases, the surveyees said that the television was with others like their daughter or brother-in-law or sister-in-law or a buyer, to whom the surveyee sold it.

Table 5.12 Movable Assets: Current Possession of the Television Set

	Spouse	*Wife*	*In-laws*	*Wife's Parents*	*Others*	*Non-Response*	*Total*
North	12.9	12.9	9.7	6.5	0.0	58.1	100.0
South	30.2	34.9	4.8	3.2	3.2	23.8	100.0
East	30.4	13.0	10.9	2.2	0.0	43.5	100.0
West	46.3	16.8	10.5	7.4	2.1	16.8	100.0
Total	34.5	20.4	8.9	5.1	1.7	29.4	100.0

Movable Asset: Fridge

Table 5.13 is based on replies by 174 surveyees to this question. One hundred and fifty-nine, that is, 39.3 per cent of the 405 surveyees reported that they had a fridge in the marital home, while 231 surveyees did not respond to

Table 5.13 Information on Movable Assets: Fridge

	During Marriage	*Sources of Acquisition of the Movable Assets: Fridge*						
	Had Fridge	*Male Spouse*	*Wife*	*Both*	*In-laws*	*Wife's Parents*	*Others*	*Non-Responses*
North	52.3	17.4	17.4	0.0	8.7	21.7	0.0	34.8
South	35.1	10.6	19.1	4.3	8.5	19.1	6.4	31.9
East	38.8	19.4	6.5	3.2	0.0	35.5	6.5	29.0
West	39.5	25.9	6.9	1.7	13.8	22.4	5.2	24.1
Total	39.3	18.9	11.9	2.5	8.8	23.9	5.0	28.9

this question. The fridges were acquired obviously as dowry by the parents in 23.9 per cent (38) cases and by the wife, perhaps also as dowry, in 19, that is, 11.9 per cent of the cases, whereas both the spouses together contributed to the acquisition of a fridge in 2.5 per cent of the cases. In 44, that is, 27.7 per cent of the cases, however, the surveyees' male spouses and in-laws had acquired the fridge. About 29 per cent of the 159 surveyees did not specify the source of the fridge.

Out of the 112 surveyees who answered this question, only 15.7 per cent of the surveyees reported that the possession of the fridge was with them. In an overwhelming majority of cases (47.6 per cent), the possession of the fridge was with their male spouses/in-laws, whereas the male-spouse and the in-laws had acquired fridges in only 27.7 per cent of the cases (as shown in Table 5.14). In some cases (3.1 per cent), the parents were in possession of the fridge which had earlier been in the marital home.

Table 5.14 Movable Assets: Current Possession of the Fridge

	Spouse	*Wife*	*In-laws*	*Wife's Parents*	*Others*	*Non-Response*	*Total*
North	17.4	17.4	17.4	4.3	8.7	34.8	100.0
South	25.5	29.8	6.4	2.1	2.1	34.0	100.0
East	45.2	0.0	9.7	0.0	3.2	41.9	100.0
West	51.7	12.1	8.6	5.2	5.2	17.2	100.0
Total	37.7	15.7	9.4	3.1	4.4	29.6	100.0

Movable Assets: Other Electronic Goods

One hundred and thirty-one of the surveyees responded to this question and 109, that is, 26.9 per cent of the 405 surveyees reported that they had electronic items in their marital homes. These items had been bought by the surveyees in 11.9 per cent of the cases or their parents in 13.8 per cent of the cases. The electronic items had been bought by their spouses in 23.9 per cent of the cases or their in-laws in 7.3 per cent of the cases, that is, in 31.2 per cent cases the electronic items had been bought by the spouse/his family. Both the spouses bought these items together in 1.8 per cent of the cases (see Table 5.15).

Table 5.15 Information on Movable Assets: Other Electronic Goods

	During Marriage	*Sources of Acquisition of the Movable Assets—Other Electronic Goods*						
	Had Other Electronic Goods	*Spouse*	*Wife*	*Both*	*In-laws*	*Wife's Parents*	*Others*	*Non-Response*
North	40.9	16.7	16.7	0.0	5.6	22.2	5.6	33.3
South	23.1	16.1	19.4	6.5	3.2	0.0	3.2	51.6
East	31.3	8.0	12.0	0.0	16.0	28.0	8.0	28.0
West	23.8	45.7	2.9	0.0	5.7	11.4	5.7	28.6
Total	26.9	23.9	11.9	1.8	7.3	13.8	5.5	35.8

However, when we asked the surveyees about who had the current possession of the electronic items, they replied that the items were with the spouse and his parents in 43.2 per cent of the cases and with the wife and her parents in 19.3 per cent of the cases. In 1.8 per cent of the cases, the surveyees reported that the goods were with others, like a brother-in-law or sister-in-law. Eighty per cent of the surveyees, therefore, no longer had the possession of the electronic goods which they had in the marital home, while spouses of 34.9 per cent of the surveyees were in current possession of these goods and in 8.3 per cent of the cases the in-laws were in current possession (see Table 5.16).

Table 5.16 Movable Assets: Current Possession of Other Electronic Goods

	Spouse	*Wife*	*In-laws*	*Wife's Parents*	*Others*	*Non-Responses*	*Total*
North	16.7	11.1	16.7	0.0	0.0	55.6	100.0
South	29.0	35.5	6.5	0.0	3.2	25.8	100.0
East	28.0	8.0	12.0	0.0	0.0	52.0	100.0
West	54.3	8.6	2.9	8.6	2.9	22.9	100.0
Total	34.9	16.5	8.3	2.8	1.8	35.8	100.0

Note: Seventy out of 109 surveyees who had answered the earlier question in Table 5.15 have answered this question.

Financial Assets: Cash in Bank or Other Sources

Seventy-seven (19 per cent of the 405) surveyees stated that they had some cash in the bank during the marriage, while the other 29 surveyees responded in the negative. Eighteen (23.4 per cent) of the 77 surveyees did not disclose the source of the cash in their bank account. The sources of cash in the remaining cases were the surveyees (36.4 per cent of the cases), their parents (20.8 per cent of the cases), their spouses (15.6 per cent of the cases) and the in-laws (2.6 per cent of the cases) or both of the parties (1.3 per cent). Thus, we can say that in 57.2 per cent of the cases the surveyees or their parents had provided the cash, while only in 18.2 per cent of the cases the spouses or the in-laws were the sources of the cash. In very few cases, that is, 1.3 per cent both the spouses had acquired the money. In most of these cases, the money had been provided/given by the parents of the surveyees or was their own income as is reflected in Table 5.17.

In almost 58.4 per cent of the cases, the cash was either with the surveyees (57.1 per cent) or with their parents (see Table 5.18). The source of this money was the wife's own earnings or had been given by her parents.

Table 5.17 Information on Financial Assets: Cash in Bank

	During Marriage	*Sources of Acquisition of the Financial Assets—Cash in Bank/Elsewhere*					
	Had the Cash	*Spouse*	*Wife*	*Both*	*In-laws*	*Wife's Parents*	*Non-Response*
North	29.5	7.7	30.8	0.0	0.0	0.0	61.5
South	18.7	8.0	28.0	0.0	4.0	24.0	36.0
East	15.0	16.7	41.7	0.0	0.0	41.7	0.0
West	18.4	25.9	44.4	3.7	0.0	14.8	11.1
Total	19.0	15.6	36.4	1.3	2.6	20.8	23.4

Note: 106 surveyees had responded to the question, whether they had cash or not.

Table 5.18 Financial Assets: Current Possession of Cash in Bank or Elsewhere

	Spouse	*Wife*	*In-laws*	*Wife's Parents*	*Non-Response*	*Total*
North	7.7	46.2	0.0	0.0	46.2	100.0
South	32.0	56.0	12.0	0.0	0.0	100.0
East	8.3	66.7	0.0	0.0	25.0	100.0
West	33.3	59.3	3.7	3.7	0.0	100.0
Total	24.7	57.1	5.2	1.3	11.7	100.0

Note: 9 out of the 77 surveyees who had earlier responded to Table 5.17 did not respond to this question.

Financial Assets: Deposits

Of the 72 surveyees, who responded to this question, only 22 (30.6 per cent of the 405 surveyees) had deposits during the subsistence of marriage. In 31.8 per cent of these 22 cases, the surveyees (27.3 per cent) or their parents (4.5 per cent) were the source of the deposits. In all, 22 surveyees had deposits during the marriage. An astounding 50 per cent of the 22, that is, 11 surveyees did not or could not respond to the further query about who had acquired the deposits (see Table 5.19).

Table 5.20 shows that out of the 22 surveyees, who had deposits during their marriage, only 16 answered the query about the current possession of the same. The deposits were with the surveyees in 36.4 per cent of these 22 cases or were in their children's name in another two (9.1 per cent) cases. The deposits had been acquired by the wife or her parents in nine of the cases; and they remained with them in all of these cases (see Table 5.20).

Table 5.19 Information on Financial Assets: Deposits

	During Marriage	*Sources of Acquisition of the Financial Assets—Deposits*				
	Had Deposits	*Wife*	*Wife's Parents*	*Both*	*Others*	*Non-Responses*
North	9.1	75.0	0.0	25.0	0.0	0.0
South	6.0	12.5	0.0	0.0	12.5	75.0
East	6.3	40.0	20.0	20.0	20.0	0.0
West	4.1	0.0	0.0	0.0	0.0	100.0
Total	5.4	27.3	4.5	9.1	9.1	50.0

Table 5.20 Financial Assets: Current Possession of Deposits

	Spouse	*Wife*	*Both*	*Wife's Parents*	*Others*	*Non-Response*	*Total*
North	0.0	75.0	0.0	0.0	25.0	0.0	100.0
South	37.5	25.0	0.0	0.0	12.5	25.0	100.0
East	0.0	20.0	0.0	0.0	0.0	80.0	100.0
West	16.7	33.3	16.7	16.7	0.0	16.7	100.0
Total	18.2	36.4	4.5	4.5	9.1	27.3	100.0

Financial Asset—Mutual Funds and/or Shares

During their marriage, 3.7 per cent (15 out of 61 who responded to this query) of the 405 surveyees had mutual funds and/or shares with them. Responses about the source of acquisition of mutual funds/shares and current possession of these are given in very few cases, that is, 5 and 10, respectively (see Tables 5.21 and 5.22). It may be a probability that the husband continued to have the possession of the shares which the couple possessed during the subsistence of their marriage. Out of the 15 women who had fixed deposits at the time of marriage, 5 surveyees were not working whereas two had low-paying jobs. Another eight had comparatively well-to-do jobs. One of these eight surveyees was earning a substantial income of ₹55,000 per month. In one case, the surveyee had received shares from the company with which she was working.

Table 5.21 Information on Financial Assets: Mutual Funds and/or Shares

	During Marriage	*Sources of Acquisition of the Financial Assets—Mutual Funds*			
	Had Mutual Funds	*Wife*	*Wife's Parents*	*Others*	*Non-Responses*
North	6.8	0.0	0.0	33.3	66.7
South	4.5	33.3	0.0	0.0	66.7
East	3.8	0.0	33.3	33.3	33.3
West	2.0	0.0	0.0	0.0	100.0
Total	3.7	13.3	6.7	13.3	66.7

Table 5.22 Financial Assets: Current Possession of Mutual Funds

	Spouse	*Wife*	*Non-Response*	*Total*
North	0.0	33.3	66.7	100.0
South	16.7	50.0	33.3	100.0
East	0.0	33.3	66.7	100.0
West	33.3	66.7	0.0	100.0
Total	13.3	53.3	33.3	100.0

Financial Assets: Insurance Policy

Only 103 surveyees answered this question. Forty out of these 103 surveyees had an Insurance Policy during the marriage. The policies were acquired by the surveyees and her parents in 50 per cent of these 40 cases whereas they were acquired by the male spouse of the surveyee in 7.5 per cent of the cases (see Table 5.23). In 13 cases, the surveyees did not respond to this query.

As per Table 5.24, the wife had the possession of the insurance policy only in 22.5 per cent, that is, 9 of the 40 cases after the separation, whereas in the other 25 per cent, that is, 10 cases the spouses or the in-laws of the surveyees had the policies. Thus, in more of the cases the husband or in-laws did not hand over the Insurance Policy bought or possessed by the

Table 5.23 Information on Financial Assets: Insurance Policy

	During Marriage	*Sources of Acquisition of the Financial Assets—Insurance*				
	Had Insurance	*Spouse*	*Wife*	*Wife's Parents*	*Others*	*Non-Response*
North	15.9	0.0	71.4	14.3	14.3	0.0
South	11.9	6.3	18.8	6.3	0.0	68.8
East	7.5	0.0	50.0	0.0	50.0	0.0
West	7.5	18.2	9.1	9.1	0.0	63.6
Total	9.9	7.5	42.5	7.5	10.0	32.5

Table 5.24 Financial Assets: Current Possession of Insurance Policy

	Spouse	*Wife*	*In-laws*	*Non-Response*	*Total*
North	14.3	14.3	0.0	71.4	100.0
South	25.0	43.8	6.3	25.0	100.0
East	0.0	33.3	0.0	66.7	100.0
West	36.4	36.4	0.0	27.3	100.0
Total	22.5	35.0	2.5	40.0	100.0

surveyee during the subsistence of her marriage. Here too 16 surveyees did not respond to this query.

Financial Assets: Other Savings

Table 5.25 shows that during the marriage 24 (5.9 per cent of the 405) surveyees had other kinds of savings with them. The responses for source of acquisition and current possession were very low, that is, 18 and 8, respectively (see Table 5.26). The wife and her parents were the source for these savings in 6 cases but she had possession of these savings in four cases only.

The response on cash in the bank suggests that this form of property may be easier for many women to retain even after separation, compared to other forms of property. Possibly because withdrawing it requires the woman's signature and assent. Assets like jewellery are often retained by the mother-in-law or spouse on the pretext of keeping them safe. Other assets are 'managed' by the husband. Physical assets like the papers of an insurance policy or shares held in physical form are frequently retained by the spouse/in-laws. Cash in the bank may, therefore, be one of the best ways to give a daughter a little money at the time of marriage. However, this finding is not conclusive and further research is required in this matter.

Table 5.25 Financial Assets: Information on Other Savings

	During Marriage	*Sources of Acquisition of the Financial Assets—Other Savings*				
	Had Other Savings	*Spouse*	*Wife*	*Wife's Parents*	*Others*	*Non-Responses*
North	11.4	0.0	20.0	0.0	60.0	20.0
South	5.2	14.3	28.6	0.0	0.0	57.1
East	10.0	0.0	12.5	12.5	75.0	0.0
West	2.7	25.0	0.0	0.0	0.0	75.0
Total	5.9	8.3	20.8	4.2	41.7	25.0

Table 5.26 Financial Assets: Current Possession of Other Savings

	Spouse	*Wife*	*Wife's Parents*	*Others*	*Non-Response*	*Total*
North	0.0	0.0	0.0	0.0	100.0	100.0
South	14.3	28.6	0.0	0.0	57.1	100.0
East	0.0	12.5	0.0	12.5	75.0	100.0
West	50.0	0.0	25.0	0.0	25.0	100.0
Total	12.5	12.5	4.2	4.2	66.7	100.0

6

Spousal and Child Support and the Dowry System

One of the most critical issues in the payment of maintenance is the amount of maintenance that is awarded by the courts. The courts have discretion to decide what the maintenance should be. The Supreme Court of India and various high courts have laid down guidelines which should govern the grant of maintenance by all courts. These guidelines stipulate that the maintenance amount should be such that it allows a woman and any children staying with her to live a lifestyle which is similar to the one she and the children were used to during their stay in the marital home.[1] It has further been stated by the courts that the maintenance amount should be in tandem with the salary/income of the male spouse, and the wife's salary, if any, may be also taken into account.[2] Some courts have even said that half the husband's salary should be awarded as maintenance.[3] Under the PWDVA 2005, it is also laid down that the 'monetary relief granted under this section shall be adequate, fair and reasonable and consistent with the standard of living to which the aggrieved person is accustomed.' However, the amount of maintenance that is granted by the courts is often meagre.

The total number of cases in which our surveyees asked for maintenance was 213. This showed that 47.4 per cent of the surveyees, that is, almost half of our surveyees had not even asked for maintenance. The reasons for these were varied and ranged from not knowing that they were entitled to maintenance to not having the money to approach the courts or the time to follow up their cases. Further, a few women felt that they were not 'entitled' while others felt that they would not like to be dependent on their former spouse and would like to sever all connections with him.

---

[1] *Komalam Amma v Kumara Pillai Raghavan Pillai and Ors.* AIR 2009 SC 636; *Radhika Narang and Ors.v Karun Raj Narang and Anr.* 159 (2009) DLT 158.

[2] *Eveneet Singh v Prashant Chaudhri and Ors.* MANU/DE/3497/2010.

[3] *Joginder Singh v NCT of Delhi* MANU/DE/2448/2010.

Out of the total number of cases which were filed, 48.8 per cent of cases were pending, in 41.8 per cent of the cases maintenance had been allowed while in 9.4 per cent of the cases their applications had been dismissed (see Table 6.1).

Out of the 213 maintenance cases, maintenance for the child/children was also claimed in 140 cases. In another 10 cases, maintenance was claimed only for the child living with the surveyee and no financial support was claimed by the surveyee for herself. In one of these cases, the woman was a divorced Muslim woman who was not even earning. She filed a petition claiming maintenance for her child on the day we interviewed her. In another four cases, the surveyees were earning but their salaries were far lesser than the salaries that their husbands earned. In 3 of these 10 cases, the surveyees did not even know their husbands' income—one from Bangalore, one from Guwahati and another from Darjeeling. Thus, a total of 223 cases were filed for maintenance out of which in 213 cases maintenance was claimed either for the surveyee or for her as well as her child, and in another 10 cases maintenance was claimed only for the child.

Even in the 89 cases where maintenance was allowed, only 12 women reported that they had received a satisfactory amount. Three of these women had received lump sum amounts while another three were receiving the monthly payments regularly. However, four women reported that though they had been awarded an adequate amount of maintenance, this was not actually being given to them. In two cases, the surveyees were not getting the maintenance allowance regularly. As shown in the other tables in the chapter, not getting the maintenance allowance regularly or at all, in spite of it being awarded to them, is a major issue faced by the surveyees and underscores the need to evolve mechanisms for enforcement.

Table 6.1 Whether the Surveyee Was Awarded Spousal Support/Maintenance for Herself and Her Children and Whether She Was Satisfied with the Quantum

Did you get any spousal support or maintenance for yourself?			*Were you satisfied with the quantum of maintenance?*					
			Numbers			*Percentage*		
	Number	*Percentage*	Yes	No	Non-response	Yes	No	Non-response
Yes	89	41.8						
No	20	9.4	12	72	5	13.5	80.9	5.6
Case pending	104	48.8						
Total	213	100.0						

Table 6.2 shows that out of the 60 surveyees who answered the question on the quantum of maintenance awarded to them, those with no income at all received an average of merely 13 per cent of their spouses' salary[4] and accounted for 55 per cent of the 60 surveyees. Those surveyees whose male spouses earned between ₹5,000 and ₹56,000—and they earned less than ₹1,000—were awarded an average of 11 per cent of their male spouse's salary. Those surveyees who earned between ₹1,000 and ₹5,000 per month while their male spouses earned between ₹5,000 and ₹100,000 per month, were awarded only an average of 16.9 per cent of their spouses' income as maintenance. Where the surveyees earned between ₹5,000 and ₹10,000 per month and their spouses between ₹40,000 and ₹100,000 per month, the average percentage of maintenance awarded was only 7.5 per cent. For surveyees who earned more than ₹10,000 per month where their spouses earned between ₹100,000 and ₹250,000 per month, the average percentage of maintenance awarded was 4.5 per cent.

Table 6.2 Average Maintenance Awarded to the Surveyees

Income of wife	*Number of female respondents*	*Average income of male spouses*	*Maximum income of male spouse*	*Minimum income of male spouse*	*Average maintenance as percentage of male spouse's salary*
<= 1,000	7	26,143	56,000	5,000	11.0
1,000–5,000	16	17,906	100,000	5,000	16.9
5,000–10,000	2	70,000	100,000	40,000	7.5
> 10,000	2	175,000	250,000	100,000	4.5
No income	33	76,212	700,000	6,000	13.0

Annexure A2 contains the detailed list of surveyees who were awarded maintenance by the courts. It highlights that across the country, maintenance amounts paid to the surveyees and any children with them are pitiable. For instance, at serial number 1 and 2 though the surveyees only had an income of ₹500 per month while their spouses had incomes of ₹25,000 per month each, surveyee 1 received a sum of ₹4,000 per month through a settlement outside the court while surveyee 2 only received a sum of ₹1,000 per month after fighting in the courts for six years. In one case from Kerala, the surveyee

[4] The surveyees who were not earning anything were mostly from the east (12) and the south (11) and five from the north and west each. Out of these surveyees, 13 had one child, 9 had two children, 8 did not have any child, and 1 had three, 1 had four and another had five children.

fought for 17 years to be awarded a maintenance of ₹900 per month even though her male spouse was earning ₹56,000 per month and she was merely earning ₹1,000 per month. Delays in maintenance awards compounded the problem. Only a small number of surveyees (31 out of 213, i.e. 14.55 per cent) managed to get maintenance awarded to them within a year.

One hundred and fifty surveyees reported to us that they had asked for maintenance for the children living with them. However, maintenance for the child was awarded only in 42.7 per cent cases, while it was rejected in 16.7 per cent of the cases. A large number, that is, 40.7 per cent of the cases were still pending. Again, there was widespread dissatisfaction with the amount of maintenance that was awarded with 79.7 per cent of the women reporting that the maintenance amount was not satisfactory and was not enough for them to be able to support their children. However, 14.1 per cent of the surveyees said that they were satisfied with the maintenance award (see Table 6.3). In 2 of these 9 cases, maintenance had still not been given even though it was awarded and in another five it was not being given regularly. Two women had received lump sum maintenance.

Table 6.3 Support or Maintenance for the Child/Children

Did you get any spousal support or maintenance for yourself?			*Were you satisfied with the quantum of maintenance? (In the cases where maintenance was awarded.)*					
			Frequency			*Percentage*		
	Frequency	*Percentage*	*Yes*	*No*	*No Response*	*Yes*	*No*	*No Response*
Yes	64	42.7	9	51	4	14.1	79.7	6.2
No	25	16.7						
Case pending	61	40.7						
Total	150	100.0						

Another problem that often arises in these cases and several others is the amount of time that the courts take to award the maintenance. The lawyer for the male spouse tries to take frequent adjournments to delay the granting of maintenance by the court, as this benefits his client and results in harassment of the wife and children along with her. Our surveyees complained about the frequent adjournments in their cases, due to a variety of frivolous reasons, like the absence of the opposite party, failure on the part of the counsel of the respondent to file the reply within a reasonable time, frequent dates sought by the counsel of the opposite party on various other pretexts. The court also shows its patriarchal bend of mind and perhaps its inefficiency by agreeing to these adjournments. Delay was, thus, a critical issue for the surveyees who asked for maintenance for themselves and their children. Lawyers and activists have recounted stories of how adjournments are given in these cases. While giving an account of one such incident, a researcher recalled how the judge had refused to even look at a woman claimant while adjourning her interim maintenance application. Other stories of the patriarchal mindset, apathy and sometimes callousness shown by judicial functionaries have been reported from the trial and other courts in India.[5]

A Delhi-based advocate reported in a seminar:[6]

> as lawyers we often feel helpless in court. The wife files the maintenance application and the husband files the reply ... a round of litigation keeps going on. One application, then reply to it. One affidavit, then counter affidavit. After so many rounds of litigation, the woman who is already financially constrained gets demoralized. Most women quit the fight for their rights because they get so exhausted.

An activist[7] from a women's organisation in UP reported:

> We sought information from the Lucknow Family Court and we got to know that more than 10,000 cases are pending in the court. There are supposed to be four courts but only two courts are functional. Only eight or ten districts in UP have family courts. The family courts are also very crowded now as compared to five–six years ago.

Another activist[8] added:

> Due to the prolonged litigation or because of the threats of their husband, the women finally give up. If during the court proceedings, the judge gets transferred, then for months the courts remain empty. Nobody cares about appointing a new judge for the speedy disposal of cases.

The problem, of course, is not restricted to north India. Women from every region, whether they are advocates, activists or plaintiffs, complain of too few family courts and inordinate delays in awarding maintenance and resolving other matrimonial issues.

---

[5] Economic Research Foundation, *Economic Rights and Entitlements of Separated and Divorced Women,* Report of Regional Seminar Proceedings (2008–2009) (New Delhi: ERF, 2010), 158.

[6] Ibid., 93.

[7] Madhu Garg of the Janwadi Mahila Samiti; see Economic Research Foundation, *supra* note 5, pp. 83–85.

[8] Zarina Khursheed; see Economic Research Foundation, *supra* note 5, pp. 85–86.

Table 6.4 seeks to detail the length of time that the cases in which maintenance was granted took. In 35.6 per cent of the 87 cases, maintenance was granted within a year. An almost similar percentage of cases took between 1 and 3 years and 16.1 per cent of the cases took between 3 and 5 years, while 11.5 per cent of the cases took more than 5 years. Through the conciliation process 18 cases were solved and 55.6 per cent of these cases got solved within a year. However, 27.8 per cent of the cases took between 1 and 3 years to be settled. Surprisingly, 5.6 per cent of the cases and 11.1 per cent of the cases took between 3 and 5 years and more than 5 years, respectively, to be settled. Table 6.4 also details the length of time in which cases have remained pending. Out of the total of 98 pending cases, 46.9 per cent cases had been pending for less than one year and 32.7 per cent cases had been pending for up to 3 years. In another two cases in which the surveyees managed to get an extra-judicial settlement, the cases took between 1 and 3 years.

Table 6.4 How Long Did the Court or Other Process Take (in Years)?

	< 1 year	*1–3 years*	*3–5 years*	*5–10 years*	*> 10 years*	*Total*	*No. of cases*
From court	35.6	32.2	16.1	11.5	4.6	100.0	87
Through conciliation/ family discussion	55.6	27.8	5.6	11.1	0.0	100.0	18
Other process	0.0	100.0	0.0	0.0	0.0	100.0	2
Case pending	46.9	32.7	12.2	8.2	0.0	100.0	98
Total	42.4	32.7	13.2	9.8	2.0	100.0	205

Note: In this table, only those cases have been taken into account in which the kind of legal process and the time taken in the process had been reported by the surveyees.

Most of our surveyees did not file an appeal even though they were dissatisfied with the quantum of maintenance. Appeals were only filed in 25, that is, 11.21 per cent of the cases in which maintenance were claimed (see Table 6.5).

Only 15 out of 72 surveyees who said that they were not satisfied by the amount filed the appeal while others did not. While 8 of the 72 surveyees were not asked this question as it was not included in an earlier pilot questionnaire, 23 women for some undisclosed reasons said that the question was not applicable to them.

Table 6.6 shows the length of time that our surveyees have had to fight appeals. Our surveyees reported that in two cases and in one case in which appeal was filed in the western region and in the eastern region, respectively, the time taken was between 5 and 10 years. In north India, it was reported

Table 6.5 Frequency of Cases in Which Appeal Was Filed Against the Order of Maintenance

	Was an appeal filed against the maintenance order?				
	Yes	*No*	*NA*	*Question not asked*	*No. of cases (excluding missing cases)*
North	3	3	14	11	30
South	11	23	29	0	63
East	7	14	38	3	62
West	4	23	40	0	67
Total	25	63	121	14	223

Table 6.6 Time Taken by the Courts for the Appeal Filed

	Process and time taken for appeal					
	< 1 year	*1–3 years*	*3–5 years*	*5–10 years*	*No response*	*Total*
North	0	1	0	0	2	3
South	6	2	0	0	3	11
East	6	0	0	1	0	7
West	1	0	0	2	1	4
Total	13	3	0	3	6	25

that two appeals took less than 3 years while in the south six appeals took about one year, around three took between 1 and 3 years and two took between 3 and 5 years.

Graph 6.1 shows that a marginal 3.4 per cent of the surveyees reported that the question was not applicable to them but the overwhelming majority reported a complete lack of support from their in-laws and husband after separation, apart from what they were forced to give by the order of courts or other settlement or negotiations, etc. (see Box 6.1). This is in spite of the fact that 429 (85.6 per cent) out of 501 children were living with their mother, that is, the surveyees (see Graph 3.12 [d]). Graph 6.1 highlights the fact that hardly any women get support from their spouses or in-laws if they do not approach the courts or ask for financial support with the help of other processes. Only in 4 per cent of the cases did the surveyees say that they were receiving financial support from their husband/in-laws or anybody else. However, we found that 14 out of these 16 surveyees had misunderstood the question and talked of the support that they were getting from their own natal family.

Our surveyees had reported that maintenance had been granted to them in 101 cases. Most of the maintenance, that is, in 87 cases, was granted on a monthly basis. The 302 surveyees who said that the query was not applicable to them had either not applied for maintenance or their cases were pending (in 106 cases) (see Table 6.7).

Graph 6.1 Whether the Surveyees Were Getting Any Further Support from Their Male Spouses or In-laws?

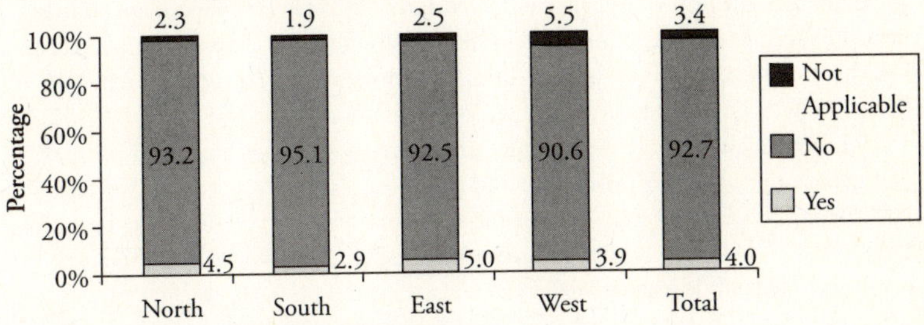

Note: 354 surveyees have answered this question.

Box 6.1: From Plentiful to Restricted Means and Lifestyle

Meenakshi Anand (name changed for the reason of privacy) from Delhi, aged about 43 years, is separated and lives with her mother. Her husband is a businessman based in Delhi. Meenakshi's is a classic case of a sharp fall in living standards and lifestyle because of a broken marriage. Her case also shows how women have to struggle with the law and the courts for a number of years to achieve any results.

Meenakshi states that the main cause of separation was mental cruelty. After 16 years of marriage (married in 1987, separated in 2003), her husband threw her out after taking away all the money in her name and making her sign away all her shares. She had to call the police to ensure that the children could come with her. She wanted to go back subsequently on several occasions but the husband refused.

She has filed for maintenance under Sections 18 and 20, Hindu Adoption and Maintenance Act 1956, recovery of dowry under Section 406 IPC and guardianship and custody of children.

Meenakshi belongs to a well to do family but married into a far richer family. During her married years she became accustomed to an affluent lifestyle, with plenty of money to spend. She has an MA in Communications and before marriage worked for a short while in an advertising agency, earning ₹3,500 per month. During marriage, she was a director in the companies of her husband's family and earned ₹125,000 per month. Presently, she is not employed. Her husband earns between ₹500,000 to ₹1,000,000 per month from the business.

Meenakshi's marriage affected her career as she could not continue working. Her former colleagues are earning well in their own business and employment.

(Continued)

(Continued)

Several of them earn between ₹150,000 to about ₹500,000 per month. Instead of building her own career, Meenakshi had participated fully in her in-laws' household which was joint and also in her husband's and in-laws' business.

She says that because of her support, her husband had an incremental increase in his income and property. It is reflected in his lifestyle and expansion of business. He started four factories in Gurgaon and added assets to his name. One indicator of his income is the fact that he owns several luxury cars including a BMW, a Mercedes Benz sports car and three Honda Accords.

Her monthly household expenditure during marriage was as high as ₹1,100,000. She spent huge amounts on clothes and toiletries and various luxuries for herself and the family. Post separation, her monthly household expenditure is between ₹51,000 to ₹56,000. Her expenses are borne by her mother whose monthly income is around ₹150,000. The expenses are reduced to 20 per cent of what they were when she was residing with her husband, although she is also bringing up two of the children. The third child is with the husband.

She was granted ₹45,000, besides a car and a flat, for the three of them. She is not satisfied with the quantum at all because she feels that it is too meagre considering that her husband earns ₹1,000,000 per month.

Meenakshi stated that her in-laws did not return her jewellery and the police filed a charge sheet in the court. The proceedings in the CAW cell are still pending. She feels that the legal system is unfair and there are too many loopholes in it. The judges do not take into account the expensive lifestyle of people of her background and think that an average lifestyle should be the benchmark. The break-up of the family and the fall in lifestyle has affected her children's esteem and self-image in their growing up years.

Meenakshi had married by choice so her dowry was limited to clothes and personal items. She has possession of most of these but the police still have to recover some items. She complains of experiencing hostility and prejudice on account of her separation at the CAW Cell and in her interaction with the police.

Table 6.7 Frequency of Surveyees Getting Either Lump Sum or Monthly Maintenance

	Frequency	*Per cent*
Lump sum	14	3.5
Monthly	87	21.6
Not applicable	302	74.9
No response	2	
Total	405	
Total (excluding No response)	403	100.0

Table 6.8 contains the answer of the surveyees to the further query whether the 101 surveyees to whom the maintenance had been granted actually received the maintenance in hand. A total of 55.4 per cent of the surveyees said that they had received the payment. However, 43.6 per cent said that they had not. Thus, a huge percentage of the surveyees who had been awarded maintenance by the court or other processes, said that they had not received the maintenance awarded to them (see Box 6.2). Out of the 14 surveyees who had been awarded lump sum payment through court after a mutual settlement or otherwise, 12 had received the payment whereas one of the surveyees replied that the question was not applicable to her as she had just entered into a compromise and the payment had still not become due. In another case where only ₹25,000 was awarded as lump sum payment, the husband offered to take the surveyee back and she agreed to go with him, so the amount was not actually paid.

Table 6.8 Whether the Surveyees Got the Maintenance Payments

	Frequency	*Per cent*
Yes	55	54.4
No	44	43.6
Not applicable	2	2.0
Total	101	100.0

Note: This table reflects the answers provided by all those (14 + 87 = 101) surveyees who got the maintenance award whether as lump sum or monthly.

The surveyees who were receiving the monthly maintenance were further asked whether they received these payments regularly and on time. Only in 17 cases (39.5 per cent) these surveyees answered 'Yes'. However, 60.5 per cent of the surveyees said that they were not receiving the payment regularly (see Tables 6.9 and 6.10).

When the surveyees were asked whether their male spouses should also have the right to ask for maintenance almost all of them said no (see Graph 6.2). Only 9.2 per cent gave the answer in the affirmative, saying that they believed in equality between husband and wife. However, 98.1 per cent of the surveyees in the east, 90.5 per cent in the north, 87.2 per cent in the west and 84.8 per cent in the south said that their spouses should not be entitled to maintenance. A marginal percentage (2.3 per cent) of the surveyees was not sure whether their spouses should be allowed to ask for maintenance or not.

The above questions and their responses reveal the dispossession that women experience when a marriage breaks down. This is compounded by

Box 6.2: Not a Paisa Paid

Praveen (name changed for privacy purposes), aged about 24, from Bhavnagar lives with her parents and children and does stitching work for a living. Her husband is a rickshaw puller and also does paint work. She is separated and has filed for maintenance from her husband. She separated as her husband had an extra-marital affair. He used to give whatever he earned to his girlfriend. He would not give money for household expenditure. He used to fight with her and beat her.

Praveen started working post separation and earns ₹3,000 per month. Her husband earns ₹8,000 per month. Post separation, she spends eight hours on stitching work and another eight hours on household work. Although she works hard, she says she does not feel the burden of work. She is happy that she does not need to listen to any abuses. However, she feels responsible for her children and burdened because her husband does not pay maintenance for them. Praveen's matrimonial house was rented. During marriage, her father bore her household expenses so that she could feed herself and her children. Post separation, he continues to give her money. She lives in her parents' rented house and they have electronic goods like a TV, DVD player, iron and mixer. Her husband has a rickshaw bought from his own earnings and a TV given by her father.

Praveen was ordered a sum of ₹2,000 per month for herself and ₹1,500 per month for the children. She is satisfied with the quantum of maintenance but she has not received any money from her husband. The interim maintenance proceedings in the court took two years. It took so long because her husband was not appearing in court. Her husband has not paid a single penny even after the passing of the maintenance order. She filed an execution application but her husband never came to court. She feels that she is entitled to share the household assets equally with her husband and that he should pay maintenance and be responsible for her and her children.

At her wedding, her parents gave household articles and furniture; the in-laws gave her jewellery. The total value of *stridhan*/dowry gift items from her parents is ₹20,000 and from her in-laws is ₹500. Her father earns ₹6,000 as a daily labourer. Her parents did not borrow any money to acquire her *stridhan*/dowry gift items, so she does not feel that her marriage was a great financial burden. *She has some of her stridhan/dowry gift items while her husband has sold the rest.* She complained to the police that her husband used to torture her and was refusing to return her belongings. *The police helped her to get her things back.*

the denial of adequate maintenance to them and their children. Clearly, the attitude of the courts to maintenance is that it is charity rather than the right of the women and children to a life similar to that which they had during the marriage. This attitude needs to be challenged. It is obvious that to enable women and children to lead a decent life, they need more substantial assets than the uncertain charity of small monthly payments which are often

Table 6.9 Whether the Maintenance Awarded as Lump Sum/Monthly Was Received by the Surveyees?

Did you get a lump sum payment or monthly maintenance payment? (Number of cases)	*Do you get these payments? (Number of cases)*			
	Yes	*No*	*Not Applicable*	*Total*
Lump sum	12	0	2	14
Monthly	43	44	0	87
Total	55	44	2	101

Table 6.10 Whether the Surveyees Got the Monthly Payments Regularly

Payment received regularly	*Frequency*	*Percentage*
Yes	17	39.5
No	26	60.5
Total	43	100.0

Graph 6.2 Perception of Surveyees in Different Regions regarding Their Husbands' Right to Maintenance

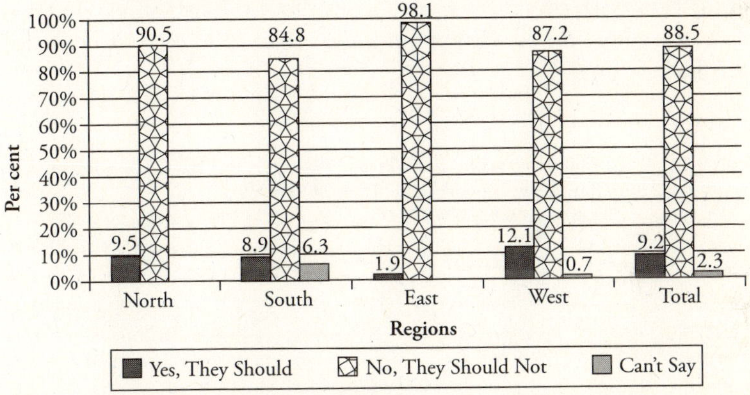

Note: 347 surveyees have answered this question.

delayed or denied and may be stopped at any time at the whim of the male spouse. A woman cannot be expected to run to court every month when the payment does not come in. The obvious solution to the problem is not only a stronger maintenance law coupled with women-sensitive procedures and proper enforcement mechanisms but also a law for division of marital assets when the marriage breaks down. Many countries already follow legal regimes that require the sharing of marital assets by both spouses. It is time for a review of matrimonial property laws in India. Our survey indicates that the vast majority of separated and divorced favour this proposition.

We asked the surveyees whether in their opinion they were entitled to share the household assets equally with their husbands. In other words we were asking the surveyees whether they should have received a half/equal share of the assets that the parties had accumulated during the subsistence of their marriage. An overwhelming percentage (79.3 per cent) of the surveyees answered in the affirmative (see Graph 6.3).

In the north 93.2 per cent of the surveyees replied that on separation all household assets should be divided while in the east 80.6 per cent said the same. The eastern region was closely followed by the south and then the west in which 77 per cent and 76.2 per cent, respectively, said that the assets should be divided. However, some 3 per cent stated that they were uncertain about how the assets should be divided. In 17.7 per cent cases they said that it should not happen, as they did not need it, or there were no household assets. When we asked the surveyees to give reasons as to why they were so entitled to a share, they gave a variety of replies. Some surveyees claimed that their marriage gave them an entitlement to the assets while others said they had acquired the assets along with their male spouses, or they needed it for their children, etc.

Graph 6.3 Perception of Surveyees in Different Regions regarding the Sharing of Household Assets Equally with Their Husbands

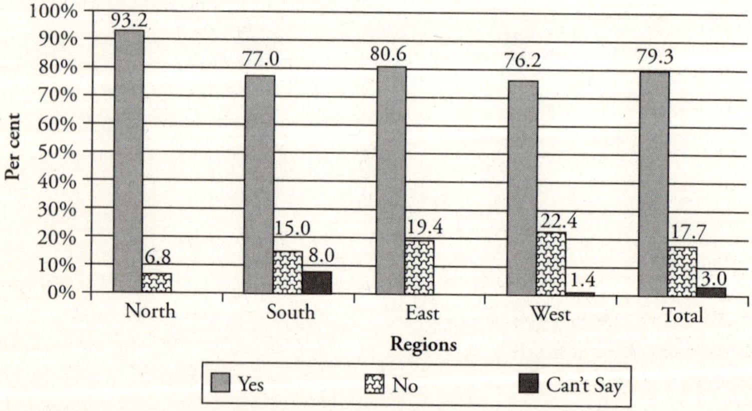

Note: 372 surveyees have answered this question.

Some Aspects of Burden of Proof

Graphs 6.4, 6.5, 6.6 and 6.7 highlight some of the difficulties that women litigants face in proving the income of their husbands in court and some tactics that some male spouses employ to defeat the claims of their wives and children. One common tactic is to transfer their assets during the proceedings in the court or prior to the proceedings when they want to separate or in fact separate from or desert their wives.

Graph 6.4 Percentage of Surveyees Who Could Not Prove Their Husbands' Income in Court or Outside in Different Regions

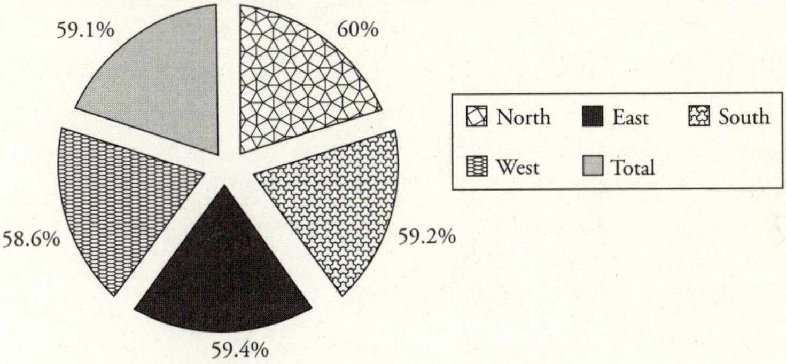

Note: 186 surveyees replied to this question, whereas 223 petitions were filed for maintenance of surveyees or their children or both.

Graph 6.5 Percentage of Surveyees Whose Spouses Tried to Conceal Their Income in Different Regions (as Percentage of the Responding Cases in Each Region)

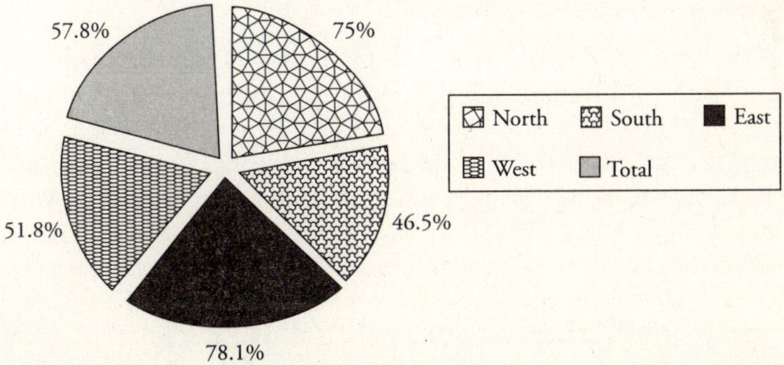

Note: 187 surveyees answered this question whereas in all 223 petitions were filed for maintenance of surveyees or their children or both of them.

Graph 6.6 Percentage of Surveyees Whose Spouses Transferred Assets to Others during Court Proceedings in Different Regions

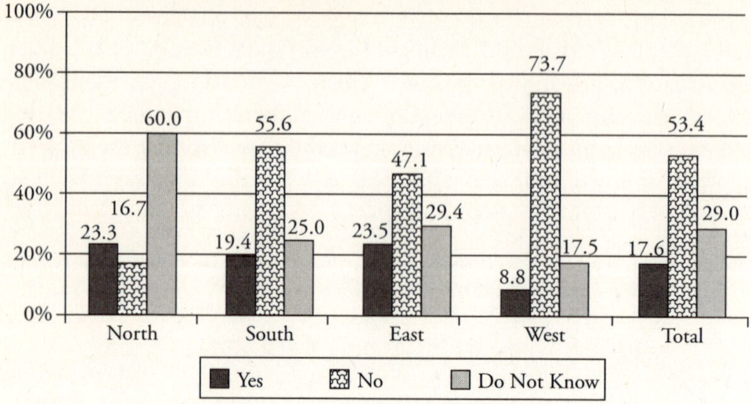

Graph 6.7 Percentage of Surveyees Who Wanted Their Spouses to Disclose Their Income instead of Proving It (in Different Regions)

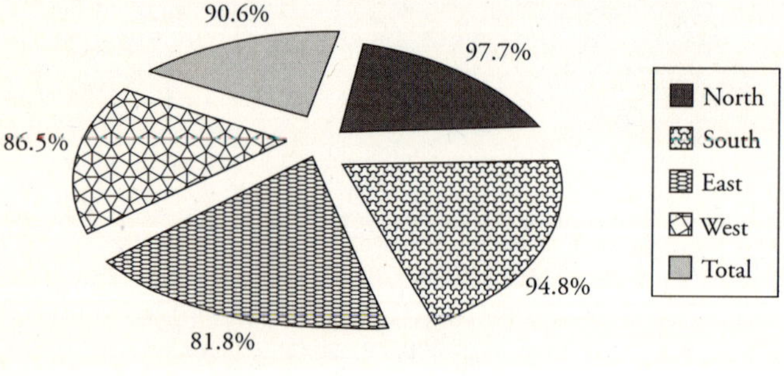

Note: 276 surveyees responded to this question.

It is strange that the law, as it presently exists, expects the wife to prove the income of their husbands when in fact the wives are not in possession of even the documents of income which are normally and obviously with the husband. Many of our surveyees reported that they did not either know what the incomes and savings of their husbands were, nor were they in a position to procure the documents to prove this income. Recently, a couple of positive judgments[9] state that an adverse inference can be drawn against the husband if he does not produce documents of income which are in his possession but

[9] *Radhika v Vineet Rungta* AIR 2004 Del 324; *Rishi Kumar v Suman I* (2008) DMC 355.

this is not enough and statutory law should compel the husband to disclose his income and assets instead of the wife having to prove these.

In total, in 59.1 per cent of the 186 cases the wife could not prove the income of the husband either in or outside the court. This problem was prevalent in all the regions equally and 60 per cent of women in the north, 59.4 per cent in the east, 59.2 per cent in the south and 58.6 per cent in the west stated how difficult it had been for them to prove the income of their spouses for a variety of reasons including not knowing the income, not having access to their spouses' income documents and because their spouses tried to hide/conceal their income (see Graph 6.4). Only 37 surveyees out of the total 223 surveyees could not/did not respond to this question.

Graph 6.5 shows that more than half (57.8 per cent) of the spouses tried to conceal their income so that the surveyees could not to ask for an appropriate amount of maintenance in the courts. This trend of concealing income by the husband of the surveyee was the least in the southern region (46.5 per cent) and was the most prevalent in the eastern (78.1 per cent) and western regions (75 per cent).

Graph 6.6 shows the percentage of surveyees who reported that their spouses transferred assets to others during the court proceedings. Surprisingly, 73.7 per cent of the surveyees in the west said that this had not happened. A total of 53.4 per cent said that this had not taken place. The reasons for this were varied. Either there were no assets to be transferred or the assets were bought in someone else's name. About 30 per cent of the surveyees said that they did not know whether assets had been transferred or not. Surprisingly this percentage rose to 60 per cent in the north. In 17.6 per cent cases, the surveyees responded that their spouses tried to transfer assets in the name of either their parents, siblings or even their girlfriends or second wives.

Graph 6.7 contains the answer to the question whether the husbands/male spouses should be asked to disclose their income instead of the wife having to prove it. It is pertinent to mention that at present the onus of proving the income of her spouse is on the woman and this is one of the most difficult tasks that she has to perform. Often, she does not have access to the income documents and cannot get these; she does not have the documents relating to the title of other assets; in many cases she does not have information regarding either the income of her spouse or his savings, bank accounts, etc. However, the court expects her to somehow prove the income of the male spouse and this often entails filing applications to ask the court to direct her spouse to produce relevant documents and disclose his income. Sometimes, when the spouse refuses to do this the woman is left helpless and tries to prove the income by stating the details of the lifestyle led by the parties. The court then has to surmise what the income must be and the conclusion it reaches is often an approximate income that is much less than the actual income.

When the surveyees were asked whether their male spouses should be asked to disclose their income instead of them proving it, they unequivocally answered 'Yes' in all regions in more than 90 per cent of the cases.

Dowry and *Stridhan*

Statistics of the National Crime Records Bureau show that dowry remains one of the biggest causes of violence against Indian women. A total of 48.5 per cent of the crimes against women are related to dowry (4.2 per cent dowry deaths, 2.8 per cent cases registered under the Dowry Prohibition Act and 41.5 per cent cases of cruelty by husband and his relatives).[10] One of the major causes for subjecting women to domestic violence is dissatisfaction with the amount of dowry which a wife may have brought or demands for further dowry by her spouse and in-laws. It is interesting that when we interviewed women in the south, we found that even the poorest of them had some gold jewellery.

The value of *stridhan*[11] given to the surveyees was reported to be between ₹100,000 and ₹500,000 in 23.5 per cent cases, less than ₹100,000 but over ₹50,000 in 15 per cent of the cases and more than ₹500,000 in 9.8 per cent of the cases. In approximately 26 per cent of the cases, the surveyees did not know the value of the jewellery and household goods given by their parents and other relatives. It was therefore difficult to assess the value of the *stridhan* in these cases (see Graph 6.8[a]).

---

[10] Government of India, *Crime in India 2008* (New Delhi: National Crime Records Bureau (NCRB), Ministry of Home Affairs, 2010). See http://ncrb.nic.in/cii2008/cii-2008/Chapter%205.pdf (last accessed on 16 July 2010).

[11] In modern Hindu law, the term 'Stridhana' denotes not only the specific kinds of property enumerated in the Smritis, but also other species of property acquired or owned by a woman over which she has absolute control; and she forms the stock of descent in respect of such property, which accordingly devolves on her own heirs. Properties gifted to a girl before the marriage, at the time of marriage or at the time of giving fare-well or thereafter are her Stridhan properties. It is her absolute property with all rights to dispose at her own pleasure. Husband or other members of his family have no control over the Stridhan property. Husband may use it during the time of his distress but nevertheless he has a moral obligation to restore the same or its value to his wife.

John D. Mayne, *Hindu Law and Usage* (New Delhi: Bharat Law House, 2006, 15th edition), 1028.

Graph 6.8(a) Total Value of *Stridhan* including Jewellery

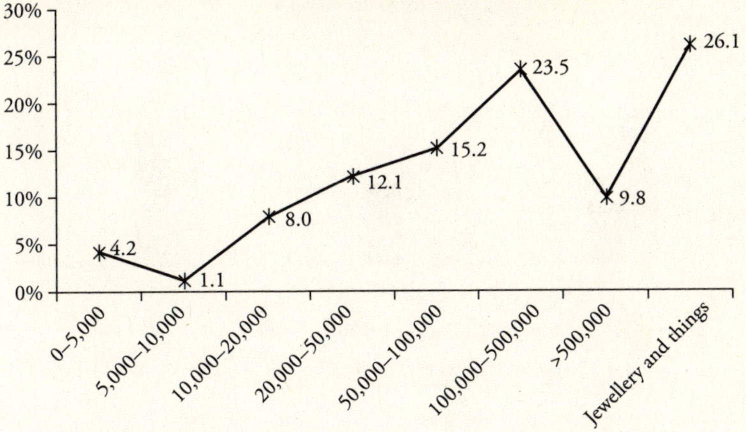

Note: 264 surveyees replied to this query.

Graph 6.10 indicates that the income of the parents of the surveyees was in most of the cases (42.7 per cent) as low as ₹1,000 to ₹5,000 per month while in another 19.6 per cent cases it was between ₹5,000 and ₹10,000 per month. In 5 per cent cases they earned barely ₹1,000 per month and in 20.5 per cent cases they did not earn at the time of survey. Thus, the parents were poor and earning very little. Despite their poverty, parents managed to pay substantial dowries. Table 6.11 shows that out of 82 cases in which the parents were earning below ₹5,000 per month as many as 27 daughters had been given dowry worth between ₹100,000 and ₹500,000. In another 22 of these cases, dowry worth between ₹50,000 and ₹100,000 was given. Despite this, these marriages could not be saved.

As per Graph 6.8(b), among our surveyees who reported that they belonged to the SC/ST category, 30 per cent reported that their parents gave them *stridhan* valued between ₹20,000 and ₹100,000. In 2 out of 37 cases, the *stridhan* was valued at over ₹500,000. In 32.4 per cent of these cases, the surveyees had been given jewellery and other household goods worth less than ₹20,000 by their parents, relatives, etc.

Among 106 who reported that they belonged to the OBC category, 22 per cent had received *stridhan* valued between ₹20,000 and ₹100,000. In 17.8 per cent OBC cases, the *stridhan* was valued at between ₹100,000 and ₹500,000. In another 15 per cent of these cases, the *stridhan* was worth more than ₹500,000. In 30 per cent of the cases they could not respond

Graph 6.8(b) Distribution of the Surveyees by the Total Value of *Stridhan* Including Jewellery among Different Caste Groups

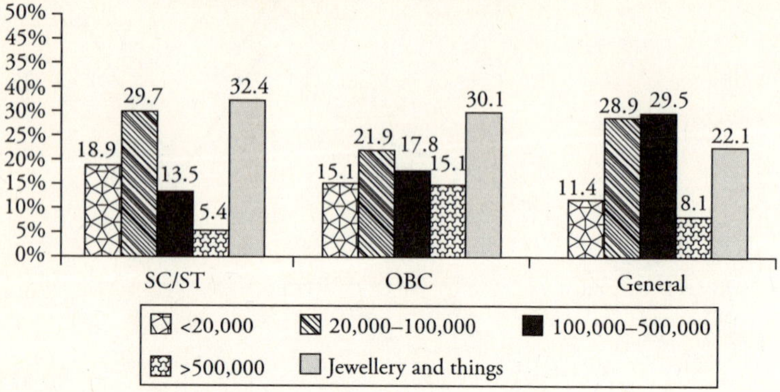

Note: 370 surveyees responded to this question.

about the value of the *stridhan* but gave details of the items they had been given as *stridhan*.

Among the 227 general category surveyees, the *stridhan* was valued between ₹20,000 and ₹100,000 in about 30 per cent cases and between ₹100,000 and 500,000 in 29.5 per cent cases. Only 8 per cent of the surveyees received *stridhan* valued at more than ₹500,000. Besides the *stridhan*, the majority of the women surveyed reported that dowry had been given in their marriage.

In a fairly high number of cases, that is, 222, our surveyees reported that dowry had been given. From the north, the surveyees reported that in 57.1 per cent of the cases dowry between ₹100,000 and ₹500,000 had been given. This was closely followed by the east and south in which 42.9 per cent and 34.7 per cent of the parents had given similar dowries. The least percentage was also a high at 28.6 per cent from the west. Surprisingly, surveyees in the south reported that in more than 25 per cent of the cases, a dowry of more than ₹500,000 had been given. Thus, in 60 per cent of the cases from the south, dowries of more than ₹100,000 had been given (see Graph 6.9).

When we see the data on income of the parents of the surveyees, we find that in most of the cases (42.7 per cent) their income was between ₹1,000 and ₹5,000 per month. In another 19.6 per cent cases, it was between ₹5,000 and ₹10,000 per month. In 10 per cent of the cases, they were earning between ₹10,000 and ₹20,000 per month while in 0.9 per cent of the cases the parents had an income over ₹100,000 per month and in 0.8 per cent of the cases the income of the parents was between ₹50,000 and ₹100,000 per month.

Graph 6.9 Total Value of Dowry from Parents in Terms of Rupees

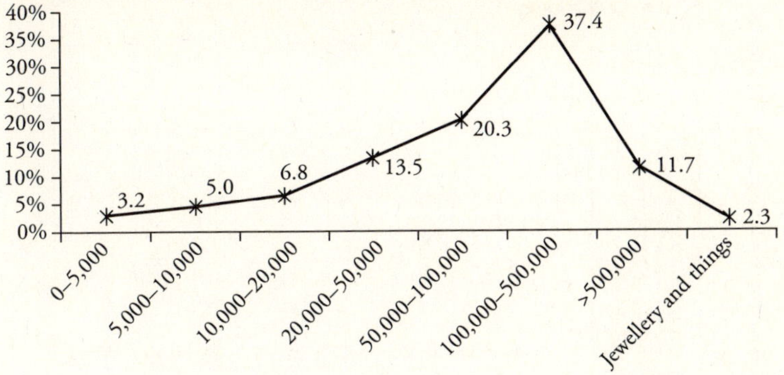

Note: 222 surveyees responded to this question.

Graph 6.10 Percentage Distribution of the Surveyees' Parents' Income

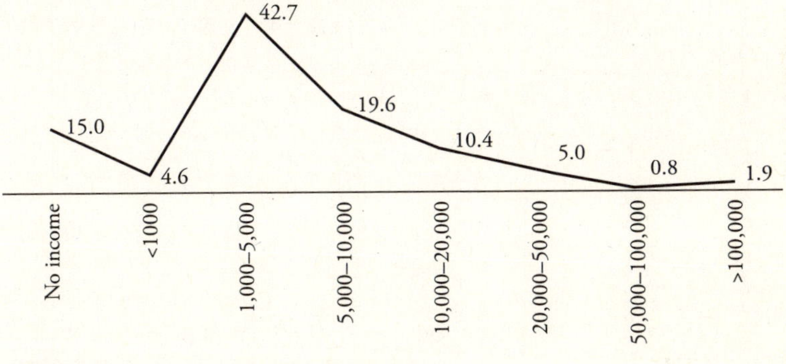

Note: 260 surveyees have responded to this question.

However, in 15 per cent of the cases the parents were not earning at all. In another 4.6 per cent cases it was less than ₹1,000 per month (see Graph 6.10).

Table 6.11 details the value and extent of dowry given by the parents of the surveyees belonging to different caste groups. It highlights the pervasive nature of dowry and the fact that it is practised in all classes and caste groups. The Joint Select Committee of Parliament on Dowry had noted as far back as 1982 that the system of dowry had 'permeated' into all strata, communities and regions of the country.[12]

[12] Lok Sabha, *Joint Committee of the Houses to Examine the Question of the Working of the Dowry Prohibition Act, 1961*, Lok Sabha Report (New Delhi: Lok Sabha, 1982), 24.

Table 6.11 Correlation between Parent's Income and Dowry Given at the Time of Marriage of the Surveyees by Their Parents, as Distributed between Given Caste Groups

		Total Value of Dowry Given at the Time of Marriage					
Caste category	*Parents income*	*<10,000*	*10,000 to 50,000*	*50,000 to 100,000*	*100,000 to 500,000*	*>500,000*	*Total*
SC/ST	<5,000	4	4	5	8	0	21
	5,000–20,000	0	2	1	2	0	5
	20,000–100,000			0	0	1	1
	Total	4	6	6	10	1	27
OBC	< 5,000	1	6	4	3	2	16
	5,000–20,000	0	3	1	4	4	12
	20,000–100,000			0	0	1	1
	> 100,000	1	1			0	2
	Total	2	10	5	7	7	31
General and others	< 5,000	3	9	13	16	2	43
	5,000–20,000	1	6	6	19	5	37
	20,000–100,000			1	7	1	9
	> 100,000	0	0			1	1
	Total	4	15	20	42	9	90
Total (excluding missing cases)	< 5,000	8	19	22	27	4	80
	5,000–20,000	1	11	8	25	9	54
	20,000–100,000	0	0	1	7	3	11
	> 100,000	1	1	0	0	1	3
	Total	10	31	31	59	17	148

If we look at the caste categories, we see that amongst the surveyees' parents who were earning less than ₹5,000 a month, a substantial number gave dowries which were well beyond their means. Thus, among the SC/ST category, only four women were given dowry worth less than ₹10,000 at the time of marriage. In another four cases, the dowry given was of a value between ₹10,000 and ₹50,000. In the rest of the cases, the dowries were between ₹50,000 and ₹500,000. Amongst the OBC surveyees whose parents earned less than ₹5,000 per month, we again see that half of the parents gave dowries worth between ₹50,000 and ₹500,000. Two OBC surveyees reported that their parents had given dowries over ₹500,000. Similarly in the general category while nine surveyees with parents earning under ₹5,000 per month reported that dowries between ₹10,000 and ₹50,000 had been given, 29 surveyees reported that their parents had given dowries between ₹50,000 and ₹500,000, while two reported that their parents had given dowries over ₹500,000.

In the SC/ST category, only one woman's parents earned between ₹20,000 and ₹100,000. Five parents who earned between ₹5,000 and ₹20,000, gave dowries ranging from ₹35,000 and ₹500,000. In the one case in which the parents were earning between ₹20,000 and ₹100,000, a dowry of more than ₹500,000 was given.

In the OBC category, in the 12 cases where the parents earned between ₹5,000 and ₹20,000 they gave dowry valued between ₹100,000 and ₹500,000 in four cases, in another four cases the parents gave dowry worth more than ₹500,000. In the other four cases, the dowry was valued between ₹10,000 and ₹100,000.

In one case of the OBC category where the parent's income was between ₹20,000 and ₹100,000 per month, the dowry was worth more than ₹500,000. However, in two other cases where the parents were earning more than ₹100,000 per month they surprisingly gave a lesser dowry of ₹50,000.

In our general category, there were 43 cases of parents who earned less than ₹5,000 per month. However, even these parents gave dowry far beyond their means. For instance, 16 parents gave dowries ranging from ₹100,000 to ₹500,000; while 13 parents gave a dowry ranging from ₹50,000 to ₹100,000. Two parents of this income group gave a dowry of more than ₹500,000 while nine sets of parents gave a comparatively less dowry ranging from ₹10,000 to ₹50,000 and only three sets of parents gave less than ₹10,000. In the income group of ₹5,000–₹20,000 per month in the general category, five parents gave a dowry of more than ₹500,000 while 19 dowries ranging from ₹100,000 to ₹500,000 were given.

If we look at the total figures of all the categories, parents of 82 surveyees who earned less than ₹5,000 per month gave dowry far beyond their means to their daughters' husband and in-laws at the time of marriage. In about 33 per cent of such cases, the parents gave dowry valued between ₹100,000 and ₹500,000. In another 5 per cent of these cases, the parents gave dowry worth more than ₹500,000. In another 27 per cent of these cases, the parents gave dowry valued between ₹50,000 and ₹100,000. In only one-third of these 82 cases did the parents give dowry worth less than ₹10,000.

In 55 cases the parents of the surveyees earned between ₹5,000 and ₹20,000 per month. In another 16.4 per cent of such cases the parents gave dowry of worth more than ₹500,000. In another 36 per cent of such cases the value of the dowry was comparatively less, being below ₹100,000.

Graph 6.11(a) and Table 6.12 show that over half of the surveyees' parents, that is, 53.8 per cent had to borrow money to pay for their dowry and *stridhan*. Here, we can see a regional disparity. In the northern region while a sizeable 54.8 per cent parents had to borrow, in the southern region even more parents had to borrow, that is, 60.2 per cent. Dowry seems to have a greater presence in the south.

In the western region in 55.7 per cent of the cases, parents borrowed to acquire dowry, while the least percentage was reported from the eastern region, where in 34.6 per cent of the cases parents had to borrow money.

Graph 6.11(b) shows us in how many cases the parents of the surveyees belonging to different social caste categories had to borrow money for giving dowry to their daughter or for marriage expenses. Among the SC/ST category, 60.4 per cent of the surveyees reported that their parents had to borrow money for giving dowry, etc. There was not much difference between

Graph 6.11(a) Whether the Parents/Family of the Surveyees Had to Borrow Money to Acquire Dowry, *Stridhan* or Gifts for Them

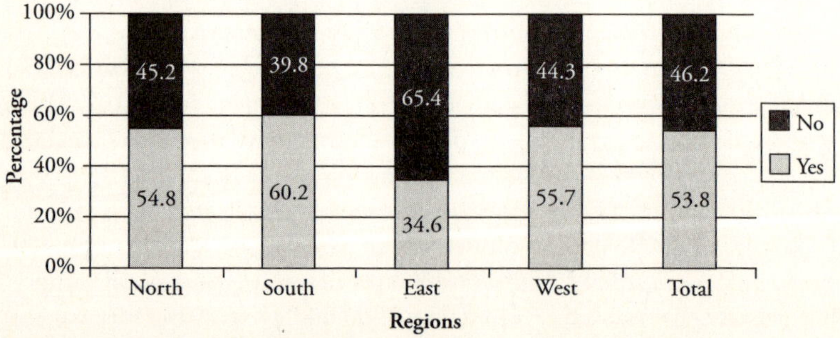

Note: 338 surveyees have answered this question.

Table 6.12 Dowry as a Financial Burden on the Parents

	Percentage Distribution										
	Did your parents family borrow money to acquire the dowry, stridhan *or gifts*			*Was your marriage a great financial burden on your family?*			*With whom are these dowry and* stridhan *and the gift item now?*				
	Yes	*No*	*Total*	*Yes*	*No*	*Total*	*Wife*	*FIL/ MIL (1)*	*Male spouse (2)*	*In-laws and male spouse (1+2)*	*Total*
North	54.8	45.2	100	63.3	36.7	100	25	38.6	36.4	75	100
South	60.2	39.8	100	63.2	36.8	100	28.9	20.6	50.5	71.1	100
East	34.6	65.4	100	35.5	64.5	100	52.3	11.4	36.4	47.7	100
West	55.7	44.3	100	43.3	56.7	100	26.6	48.4	25	73.4	100
Total	53.8	46.2	100	52	48	100	30.7	36.2	69.3	33	100

Graph 6.11(b) Percentage of Parents of the Surveyees Belonging to Different Social Groups Who Had to Borrow for Giving Dowry to Their Daughter

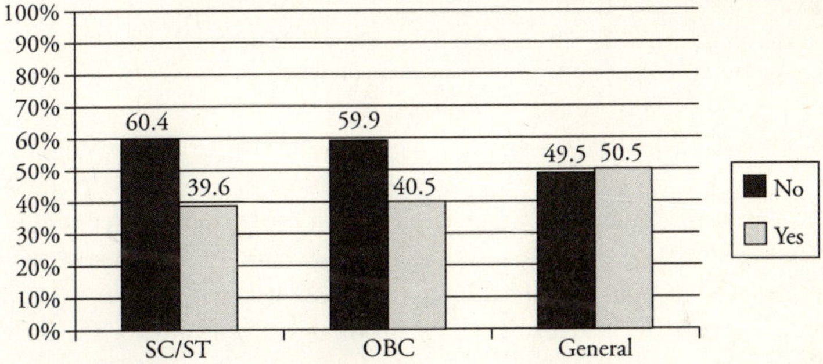

Note: 320 surveyees replied to this question.

the SC/ST category and the OBC category as far as money was concerned. Even in the general category, though a lesser percentage of the surveyees reported that their parents had to borrow money to get them dowry, gifts, etc., the percentage of parents who borrowed was just around 10 per cent lesser than the other categories.

In 52 per cent of the cases, the surveyees felt that their marriage was a financial burden for their parents, while in 48 per cent of the cases the surveyees did not feel so. In the northern and southern region, approximately, 63 per cent of the surveyees reported that the giving of dowry had been a burden on their parents while in the western region a somewhat less percentage of surveyees, that is, 43.3 per cent reported that it was a burden. In the eastern region 35.5 per cent surveyees, however, reported that it was a burden (see Graph 6.12). The marriage had been considered as a burden in the cases where the surveyees' parents did not have much income or assets to get them married or the expenses to be incurred in the marriage were so huge or the demand of dowry that it was more like a burden for them. In some cases, the parents spent about ₹5,00,000 for the marriage of the surveyees but even then it was not burden for the parents as they had the financial capacity to incur the expense.

Graph 6.12 Whether the Marriage of the Surveyees Was a Financial Burden on Their Families

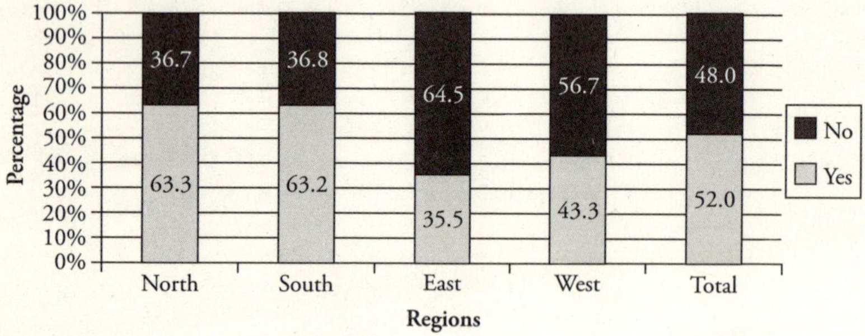

Note: 327 surveyees replied to this question.

The Graphs 6.13(a) and 6.13(b) show that in more than 69 per cent of the cases, the dowry and *stridhan* was in the possession of the male spouse and in-laws and only in around 30 per cent cases it is with the surveyees. In quite a few cases it had also been sold off by the in-laws and/or the male spouse (see Box 6.4).

It was with the surveyee in 52.3 per cent of the cases in eastern India and in 25 per cent of the cases in northern India. In southern India, it was with surveyees in 28.9 per cent of the cases whereas in western India it was with them in 26.6 per cent of the cases.

Here, we see that only 40.1 per cent of the surveyees went to the police for recovery of dowry, *stridhan* or gift items and their experience was not positive (see Graph 6.14). The initial hitch was to get the case registered as the police did not file the complaint (see Box 6.3). The women had to take the help of women's groups or organisations or State Commissions for Women for just getting their cases registered. One woman said that it took a year to get the case registered due to the non-cooperation of the police and no recovery had been made by them. The court, too, had proved equally

Graph 6.13(a) Whether the Dowry, *Stridhan*, Gift Items Post Separation or Divorce Are with Surveyees or In-laws

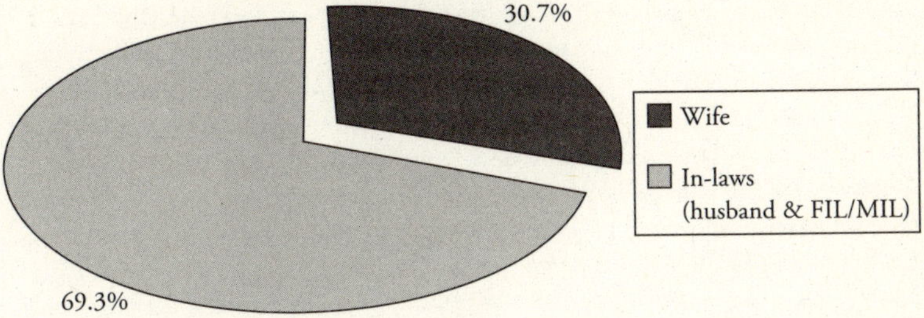

Graph 6.13(b) Whether the Dowry, *Stridhan*, Gift Items Post Separation or Divorce Are with Surveyees

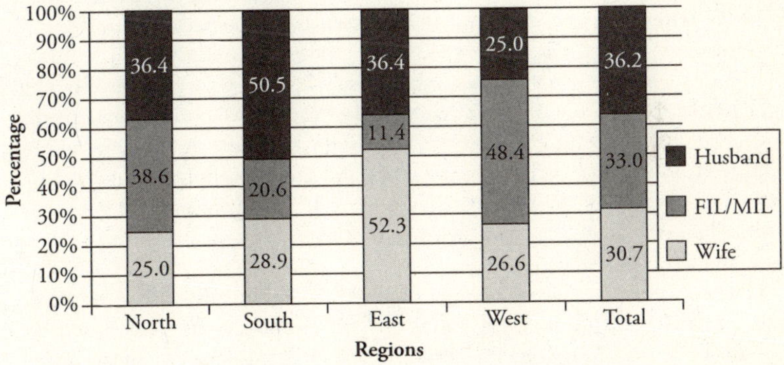

Note: 309 surveyees answered this question.

Graph 6.14 Surveyees Who Had to Approach the Police to Get Back the *Stridhan*/Dowry/Gift Items and Other Personal Items

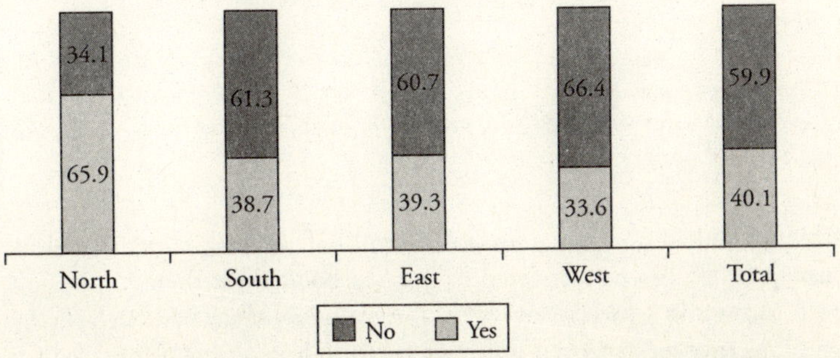

Note: 367 surveyees have answered this question.

Box 6.3: Police Refuses to File complaint, Court Denies Maintenance

Santoshi (name changed for privacy), aged about 24 years at the time of this survey, is a separated Hindu woman from Bhopal who lives with her parents, along with her son and daughter. Santoshi's first marriage took place in 2000. In 2005 divorce took place between her and her first husband, and she remarried in hope of a better future with her second husband. It was the man's third marriage and her second. *Her dream turned into a nightmare when her second husband turned out to be violent and would beat her a lot. Her mother-in-law would complain about her to her husband and then he would fight with her. Once, she tried to file a police complaint but the police did not listen to her. She even had to bear the taunts of her neighbours and relatives that her marriage would have worked had she been a nicer wife.*

Santoshi is uneducated and did not work before marriage. After marriage she started doing labour work to fend for herself. During marriage she earned ₹3,000 per month but post separation she could not earn that much and earned only ₹1,000 per month. Her husband is a farmer, so she has no knowledge of his income.

During marriage, she did most of the household chores like cooking, cleaning the house, filling water and washing utensils. Post separation she performs the same household chores. Her husband did not do any domestic work. Santoshi's burden has increased as now she has to earn and also look after her two children. Yet, she says that she does not experience stress or feel any responsibility or burden. She is able to work more efficiently after the separation and earns the same amount as her colleagues.

Santoshi does not know what the household expenditure was during marriage, except that ₹2,000 per month was spent on food, etc. Post separation her monthly household expenditure comes to around ₹4,700 which is incurred jointly by her and her parents.

During marriage Santoshi had a house (owned by husband), bike, scooter, TV and fridge (bought by husband with his own income before marriage and presently in his possession). Her husband has cash in the bank (acquired before marriage, amount not known). Post separation, Santoshi lives in her parents' home. She has no asset of her own.

Santoshi lost her maintenance case after two-and-a-half years of litigation. In the court her husband said that she had her own income. Unlike her husband she did not have a good lawyer and she lost her petition for maintenance of her and her child from the second marriage.

indifferent and had not passed an order despite several requests that at least the surveyees' clothes be recovered so that she could wear them.

Even in cases in which recovery of dowry and *stridhan* had been filed, a very tedious process had been followed by the police/court. Only in a few cases was it returned in 1–2 months' time. In one case, the surveyee said

Box 6.4: Disabled and Dumped: A Case of Dowry Harassment

Kavita Sharma (name changed for privacy purposes) from Lucknow, who was in her late twenties at the time of this survey, was a young educated working woman when she met and married her husband. They came from different backgrounds and her family was more educated. The couple lived in the husband's joint family household. His family was dissatisfied with her dowry. Her parents had given jewellery, clothes, furniture, TV and a fridge. Her relatives also gave her jewellery. Her in-laws gave her only one saree. The stridhan was worth ₹25,000 and the dowry cost ₹150,000. Her father had borrowed ₹100,000 from his office for the marriage. The dowry and stridhan items are now with her husband. She has filed cases for recovery of dowry and dowry harassment.

Kavita was working as a sales executive and earned ₹12,500 per month during the marriage. *Unfortunately, she met with an accident and became disabled.* After she lost her job, her husband started abusing her physically and verbally as she had lost both her looks and her capacity to earn.

Kavita went to the police station to file a complaint under Section 498A but the police refused to register the complaint. Then she approached the All India Democratic Women's Association (AIDWA) at whose initiative her husband was arrested. It could not work as a deterrent though, as he was released on bail after only 12 days.

Kavita now lives in her parents' home with her one-year-old daughter. She is disabled and unable to earn. Her father, who earns only ₹8,000 per month, is supporting them. Her businessman husband, who earns ₹20,000 per month, is paying no maintenance.

During marriage the couple lived in a rented house, she had a car of her own, jewellery given by her parents, TV and fridge given by her parents, cash (₹5,000) in her bank account and insurance. Post separation she stays in her parents' house. The only asset she has is her car. Her husband on the other hand has his parental house, 4–5 bighas of land and a bike besides the jewellery, TV, fridge and mixer-grinder from her parents and cash (₹25,000 approximately) in the bank.

Kavita is worried about her future as she is not fit to work. Her father supports her now but she does not know what will happen after her parents are gone. She is studying for a diploma in business management and hopes that later she will be able to work. She feels that she is entitled to share the household assets equally with her husband because her marriage has ruined her life. Moreover, her daughter, she feels, should have full rights to the property of the father.

that it took almost a year and repeated visits to the police cell to recover her belongings, that is, *stridhan*. Her husband eventually agreed that she could take back her clothes and jewellery. The in-laws and the husband brought it to the cell. However, a case was still pending.

The functioning of the police cells set up to ostensibly resolve issues concerning dowry and *stridhan* have been repeatedly criticised by women and women activists who have visited these cells. Some of the problems that have been highlighted are that these cells rarely manage to bring about a settlement between the parties in favour of the wife. It has been reported that instead of helping the woman to recover her dowry and *stridhan* jewellery by the ordinary police procedures, or by pressurising the husband to return the dowry, etc., the police keep on calling the parties to the cell to discuss settlement over a long period of time. During this period, the husbands get an opportunity to hide/dispose of the dowry items and *stridhan*, particularly jewellery which can provide some financial security to the women. Eventually, only some items of the dowry which are not valuable like tables, beds, etc., are recovered. Women have also complained that they are extremely scared of going to the police station as the police harass them and make them feel insecure. Many women have reported that the police personnel expect to be bribed and often side with the party who can bribe them more.[13]

[13] Economic Research Foundation, *supra* note 5, pp. 79–80 and 156.

7

Social Status, Mobility, Skills and Decision Making

In 54.4 per cent of the cases, our surveyees reported that they had to face hostility or prejudice on account of their separation. The hostility or prejudice was most prevalent in northern India and least in eastern India. However, the surveyees also reported that in 54 per cent of the 370 cases, women had to face hostility or prejudice on account of their separation or divorce, for no fault of theirs. In northern India 72.1 per cent of the surveyees faced hostility, in western India 51 per cent of the surveyees reported that they had to face hostility, in southern India 57 per cent of the surveyees reported hostility on account of their divorce/separation whereas in eastern India 42.9 per cent of the surveyees had to face hostility on account of their divorce/separation (see Box 7.1).

In the cases where they did not have to face hostility they said that as their parents and other relatives and neighbours, etc., knew about the ill-behaviour of their in-laws and husbands so they were not taunted and were warmly received when they returned to their natal homes.

Graph 7.1 Percentage of Surveyees Who Had to Face Hostility or Prejudice on Account of Their Separation

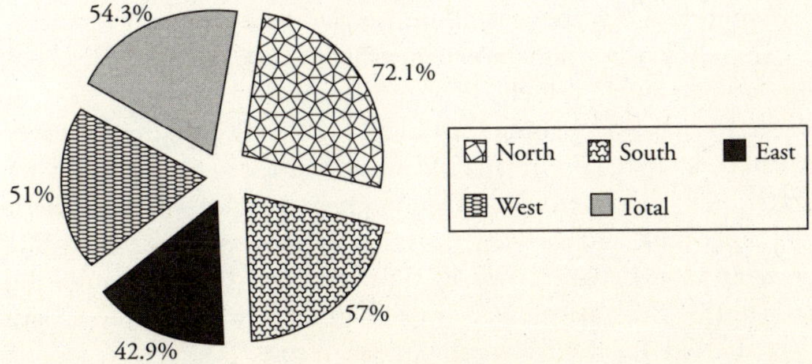

Note: 370 surveyees have responded to this question.

Box 7.1: A Hostile Natal Family

The social status of separated women falls sharply and some natal families resent their return. M. Kaveri (name changed for privacy) from Chennai who is aged about 30 years, has been separated since 2002. She has a minor son and is not working presently. She says that her husband filed for divorce as her family did not pay the balance of dowry promised. The case was dismissed in 2004 in Devakottai Court for want of evidence.

She has filed a criminal complaint against her husband. She had also filed for maintenance two years before this interview. She had not been granted maintenance so far. Her husband earns ₹7,000 per month and also owns ancestral land. She states that she could not prove her husband's income in court as he is self employed. He also transferred his assets after they separated.

Kaveri's parents had given 15 gold sovereigns (coins) during her marriage, besides household vessels and ₹100,000 in cash. The total value of *stridhan* including jewellery/dowry was ₹200,000. Her dowry/*stridhan* gift items are now with her grandparents.

Kaveri's natal family has been riven by conflicts. She alleges that her own brother murdered their father with the help of the Madavaram police. Her brother- and sister-in-law are abusive towards her since her separation, as they fear that the family property will have to be shared with her. They complained to police that she is immoral. She says they torture her mentally and even threaten to murder her. Her mother, however, is supportive.

With regard to the social impact of separation or divorce on the surveyees, we found that the daily interaction of the surveyees was affected in a majority of the cases. A total of 35.2 per cent of the surveyees reported that their interaction with relatives had been affected while 30.7 per cent of the surveyees reported that their interaction with others including authorities had been affected. Similarly, the surveyees were equally affected in terms of their interaction with landlords (15.2 per cent), employers (16.8 per cent) and other authorities (16 per cent). Surprisingly, there were very few cases (0.3 per cent, all in the west), in which their interaction with the school authorities of their children's schools were affected.

However, in a fairly large number of cases (42.3 per cent), the surveyees reported that their separation/divorce did not affect their interaction with the various authorities, people, etc. This trend was most prevalent in the southern region (64.3 per cent) and the western region (49 per cent) of India, while in the north and south, respectively, 27.3 per cent and 30.6 per cent of the surveyees reported that their interaction with other members of the society did not get affected due to their separation (see Table 7.1).

Table 7.1 Percentage of Surveyees Whose Interaction with Others Got Affected Due to Their Separation

	Relatives	*Landlords*	*School authorities*	*Employers*	*Other authorities*	*Other persons*	*No effect*	*No response*
North	50.0	20.5	0.0	20.5	18.2	38.6	27.3	2.3
South	44.0	20.9	0.0	23.9	23.9	33.6	30.6	9.0
East	28.6	7.1	0.0	7.1	7.1	14.3	64.3	42.9
West	25.2	11.6	0.7	12.9	11.6	32.0	49.0	4.1
Total	35.2	15.2	0.3	16.8	16.0	30.7	42.3	11.3

Note: As this is a multiple-response answer, the sum of percentages of each row will be more than 100 per cent.

Decision Making in the Home

During the subsistence of their marriage our surveyees made some household decisions but not in most of the cases, as we can see from the analysis made in Table 7.2.

Matters regarding children's education were decided by the surveyees in about 40 per cent cases but decisions regarding their children's marriage were made by them in an abysmal 8.2 per cent cases; in most of the cases the decision was that of the male spouse or in-laws.

Decisions regarding expenditure inside the house and outside the house were made by the surveyees in 20.5 per cent and 18.2 per cent of the cases, respectively.

Decisions regarding expenditure on investment and applying for loans were made by the surveyees in 17.1 per cent and 18.5 per cent cases, respectively, whereas decisions regarding applying for jobs were taken by them in 24.4 per cent cases. Even decisions regarding buying jewellery were taken by the surveyees only in 21 per cent of the cases, while their male spouses decided it in about 48 per cent of the cases. In many of the cases, the surveyees said that they could not afford to buy jewellery and so the question about decision making regarding buying of jewellery never arose.

Decisions regarding choosing a place of residence were made by the surveyees only in 16.7 per cent cases whereas decisions regarding health related matters were made by the surveyees in 24 per cent cases.

Decisions regarding entertainment and holidays were made by the surveyees in 26.7 per cent and 26.2 per cent cases, respectively, while the rest of the time the decision was taken by the male spouses though in some

Table 7.2 Who Were the Decision-makers during Marriage in the Marital Home regarding Various Tasks

	Percentage of the Decision-makers during Marriage					
Nature of tasks	*Both*	*Wife*	*Husband*	*FIL/MIL*	*Others*	*Total*
Education of child	9.6	30.1	38.4	18.5	3.4	100.0
Expenditure in house	6.9	13.6	41.0	33.7	4.8	100.0
Expenditure outside the house	6.6	11.6	43.6	33.2	5.0	100.0
Expenditure on investment	3.7	13.4	56.1	23.2	3.7	100.0
Applying for loans	5.1	13.4	58.6	19.7	3.2	100.0
Applying for jobs	4.5	19.9	55.8	16.7	3.2	100.0
Buying jewellery	4.4	12.8	47.2	30.6	5.0	100.0
Choosing place of residence	5.2	11.5	43.1	21.2	19.1	100.0
Health-related decisions	7.3	16.7	41.0	29.0	6.0	100.0
Children's marriage	4.1	4.1	38.8	51.0	2.0	100.0
Entertainment	14.1	12.6	34.6	13.1	25.7	100.0
Holidays	11.0	15.2	54.5	15.9	3.4	100.0
Whom to meet	7.0	15.7	47.9	25.9	3.5	100.0
Where to go	7.3	14.6	47.2	27.5	3.5	100.0
What to cook	7.0	22.1	35.8	30.9	4.2	100.0
What to wear	3.3	39.9	33.3	20.7	2.7	100.0

regions it was taken by others, like relatives of the husbands, children in the household, etc.

In about 22 per cent cases, decisions about where she wanted to go or whom she wanted to meet were taken by the surveyee. She also decided what to cook in approximately 29 per cent of the cases. In more than 43 per cent cases, surveyee at least had the choice to decide what to wear.

After Separation Who Took Decision regarding Various Household Tasks

After separation, however, the picture changed and more than 75 per cent of the surveyees told us that they were taking decisions regarding their children's education and 70.4 per cent on their children's marriage. Decisions regarding expenses in the house and outside the house were being made by the surveyees in 59.7 per cent and 60.1 per cent cases, respectively.

Decisions regarding investment and applying for loans were taken by her in 67.1 per cent and 70.6 per cent cases respectively after separation. The surveyees had also started taking decisions in 76.8 per cent cases regarding applying for jobs, buying jewellery in 64.3 per cent cases.

Surveyees were also taking decisions regarding choosing of place of residence in 63.8 per cent cases, health-related matters in 63.5 per cent cases, entertainment in 77.5 per cent cases and holidays in 76.9 per cent cases after separation. With regard to matters relating to their mobility, the majority of surveyees now took decisions, like where to go (76.1 per cent), whom to meet (74.5 per cent), what to cook (75.9 per cent) and what to wear (92.2 per cent) (see Table 7.3 and Box 7.2).

Table 7.3 Who Is the Decision-Maker regarding Various Tasks after Separation

Percentage Distribution of the Decision-makers after Separation Distribution across Various Tasks

Nature of tasks	*Jointly with parents*	*Surveyee*	*Children (daughter/son)*	*Parents*	*Others*	*Total*
Education of child	2.4	73.5	4.2	19.3	0.6	100.0
Expenditure in house	4.5	54.2	0.9	35.9	4.5	100.0
Expenditure outside the house	4.5	55.6	0.3	35.4	4.2	100.0
Expenditure on investment	2.6	64.5	1.3	29.6	2.0	100.0
Applying for loans	4.4	66.2	1.5	26.5	1.5	100.0
Applying for jobs	3.5	73.3	1.2	20.3	1.7	100.0
Buying jewellery	3.3	61.0	1.1	32.4	2.2	100.0
Choosing place of residence	2.9	57.9	0.8	35.8	2.5	100.0
Health related decisions	4.2	59.3	0.6	32.7	3.2	100.0
Children's marriage	1.9	68.5	3.7	25.9	0.0	100.0
Entertainment	4.4	73.1	1.3	19.4	1.9	100.0
Holidays	3.9	73.0	1.3	20.4	1.3	100.0
Whom to meet	3.4	71.1	0.6	24.8	0.0	100.0
Where to go	3.4	72.7	0.6	23.3	0.0	100.0
What to cook	5.1	70.8	2.4	21.7	0.0	100.0
What to wear	0.9	86.3	0.6	11.6	0.6	100.0

Box 7.2: Struggling to Survive without Support

G. Maithili (name changed for privacy purposes) from Hyderabad got married at the age of 13. Now 28, she lives with her two children. She works as a domestic help and earns ₹4,000 monthly. She is Hindu by religion and SC by caste. She got married in 1992 and separated in 2000. She filed for divorce but as the husband could not be located, she gave up the case. She got no maintenance for herself or her children. She had an arranged marriage under the Hindu law and lived in a rented house with her husband, mother-in-law and sister-in-law. She had studied till the secondary level and after marriage sat for exams to qualify for a constable's job. However, housework and child care left little time for studies and she failed in the exams.

(Continued)

(Continued)

Maithili complains:

> My husband did not work. He never gave me any money. He drank and beat me and the children. He went around with different women. I caught him with another woman in our house. We separated ten years ago but he still comes to taunt me.

Maithili did not work before her marriage, but took up domestic work later. During the marriage, she earned ₹2,500 per month, now she earns ₹4,000 per month. Her husband was a peon in an office and earned ₹2,500 per month. She has no knowledge of her husband's present salary. Maithili used to get up by 4 a.m., do housework for an hour, then go out for domestic work in other people's homes from 5 a.m. to 7 a.m. and later work in a school. After coming home she used to do housework, wash clothes, cook and feed the children. She used to take the younger child with her to work while the elder boy would go to school on his own. After separation, her work routine hardly changed. She feels that her husband benefited from both her household work and outside work in terms of money and leisure.

Her parents are day-labourers and earn ₹2,000 each per month. Nevertheless, they gave ₹80,000 in dowry, five *tola* gold, silver anklets, bed, almirah, fan and utensils. Her elder brother gave a gold ring to her husband as well as clothes and money. The total value of *stridhan* from her parents (₹1,50,000) and other relatives (₹50,000) was ₹200,000. Her parents borrowed ₹60,000 for her marriage. Her husband finished using up all the money and sold the gold. He also took ₹50,000 on loan and ran away. Her burden of work increased post separation as she had to repay the loan. She also had to earn to bring up her two sons who are now aged 15 and 10 years. She still has some household goods but her in-laws have the rest. She did not complain to the police to get her *stridhan* back. She complained once that he was living with another woman but the police did not do anything about it.

Maithili faced hostility on account of her separation; people used to comment and ridicule her. Her in-laws would send people to disturb her. The landlord was suspicious that she would not be able to pay the rent. But she got help from her employers and the school authorities. During her marriage her husband objected to her going out and even meeting her parents. Now she decides all household matters. She wants to acquire some technical or educational skills and use a computer but she does not have time to learn. She uses a bicycle. She has a life insurance policy in her child's name but no other savings.

New Skills Learnt or New Tasks Performed by the Surveyees after Their Separation

The percentage of surveyees who learnt new skills or performed new tasks had increased in all the cases. The surveyees had, however, stopped meeting or socialising with their husband's relatives. In the task of paying of bills the percentage had increased from 14.5 per cent to 35.4 per cent (Table 7.4).

About 50 per cent surveyees had started shopping for household goods, and little less than 50 per cent had started keeping household accounts, whereas about 40 per cent of the women were repairing household items.

Table 7.4 New Skills Learnt or New Tasks Performed by the Surveyees after Their Separation (in Percentage)

	During marriage			*After separation*		
New skills learnt or tasks performed	*Yes*	*No*	*Total*	*Yes*	*No*	*Total*
Paying of bills	14.5	85.5	100.0	35.4	64.6	100.0
Shopping for household goods	27.6	72.4	100.0	49.3	50.7	100.0
Keeping household accounts	21.0	79.0	100.0	43.3	56.7	100.0
Operating bank account	9.7	90.3	100.0	26.0	74.0	100.0
Repairing household items	22.6	77.4	100.0	38.6	61.4	100.0
Going to children's school	19.4	80.6	100.0	37.3	62.7	100.0
Driving a car or a two wheeler	11.0	89.0	100.0	18.4	81.6	100.0
Acquiring assets	7.1	92.9	100.0	17.6	82.4	100.0
Travelling inside the city	24.7	75.3	100.0	49.1	50.9	100.0
Travelling out of town for work or other purposes	9.2	90.8	100.0	21.3	78.7	100.0
Booking rail or air tickets	13.1	86.9	100.0	32.5	67.5	100.0
Meeting socialising with own friends	15.0	85.0	100.0	34.1	65.9	100.0
Meeting socialising with common friends	16.5	83.5	100.0	31.2	68.8	100.0
Meeting socialising with own relatives	34.6	65.4	100.0	38.6	61.4	100.0
Meeting socialising with husband's relatives	31.0	69.0	100.0	18.9	81.1	100.0
Acquiring new friends	8.7	91.3	100.0	21.8	78.2	100.0
Daily hours of leisure time or time for yourself	32.8	67.2	100.0	45.4	54.6	100.0
Do you read newspapers	19.7	80.3	100.0	39.9	60.1	100.0
Additional technical educational skills	10.0	90.0	100.0	13.6	86.4	100.0
Operating computer or accessing internet	8.4	91.6	100.0	16.5	83.5	100.0

More than one-fourth of the women were operating their bank accounts and more than one-third of them went to their children's school. About 18 per cent now drove a car/two wheeler, 17 per cent were acquiring assets, etc.

About 50 per cent of them were travelling inside the city and 21 per cent were travelling out of town for work or other purposes, whereas about one-third were booking rail or air tickets.

More than one-third of the surveyees were often meeting and socialising with their friends, while a bit less than one-third were meeting and socialising with common friends.

Also, more of the surveyees (approximately 40 per cent) were meeting and socialising with their own relatives. It was interesting to note that 18.9 per cent of the surveyees were still meeting/socialising with their husband's relatives.

More surveyees have started acquiring new friends (21.8 per cent) and more of them (45.4 per cent) now had daily hours of leisure time for themselves and read newspapers (40 per cent), etc.

Though more of the surveyees were acquiring additional technical or educational skills, the percentage was not very significant and was only 13.6 per cent of the surveyees. A total of 16.5 per cent of the surveyees were learning, operating computers and accessing internet (16.5 per cent). It is important to remember that 17 per cent of the surveyees were not literate at all and 52 per cent of them had not studied beyond the higher secondary level.

Kind of Identity Cards Held by Surveyees

A majority of the surveyees had a Voter ID card (69.88 per cent) while 63.7 per cent women had a Ration Card (Table 7.5). However, only 14.1 per cent of the surveyees had a Driving License and only 12.6 per cent of them had Passports.

Table 7.5 Identity Cards Held by Surveyees

	Number of surveyees			*Percentage of surveyees holding the cards*
	Yes	*No*	*Total*	
Ration Card	258	147	405	63.70
Voter ID Card	283	122	405	69.88
Driving License	57	348	405	14.07
Passport	51	354	405	12.59

8

Findings from Different Cities

As we conducted the survey in different cities, certain trends began to emerge. These trends highlighted both similarities and differences amongst separated and divorced women across India.

The pilot survey of 15 separated women in Delhi, from different income groups, highlighted the fact that most of the women had been forced to leave their marital home due to domestic violence. This included both verbal and physical violence. In a large number of cases, dowry had been demanded. In two of the cases, violence was associated with extramarital affairs of the husband. In another two of the cases, the women had been illtreated for not giving birth to a son. In almost all the cases, women, often along with their children, started living with their parents or relatives and were financially dependent on them post separation. As we realised soon, this seemed to be the norm in India as opposed to certain other countries where women and children often live alone.

In almost all the cases, women earned far less than their husbands during the marriage and post separation. In the lower income group, women often worked during the marriage and still spent lengthy hours doing domestic work (10–18 hours). Domestic work was characterised as domestic chores in the house that included cooking and cleaning, as well as child care and elder care. The men spent hardly any time doing domestic work, though some participated with elder care. Quite a few women reported that after separation they spent fewer hours doing domestic work.

Almost all the women reported a drop in their financial status and style of living post separation. All these women were dependant on their natal families after separation. Those who were awarded maintenance from the court complained that the amount of maintenance was extremely inadequate. Even though some of these women worked, they reported that the money was not enough for them to manage their households on their own.

Many of the women interviewed reported that most of the household assets were with their husbands including their jewellery and other dowry items though some had managed to retrieve these. In a number of cases, women reported very bitter experiences while interacting with the police. They said that the police refused to lodge complaints and sought pecuniary benefits (bribes) to take the case forward. They also reported that their experience with the courts was not good. Even to get interim maintenance awards, women had to wait for long periods. They complained of procedural hurdles and of the courts giving repeated and long adjournments for no valid reasons. They said that it was very difficult for them to prove the income of their husbands since they had no evidence. Some of them detailed how their husbands had devised various means to conceal their income and transfer assets during the proceedings.

In the eastern and northern parts of India, 159 women took part in the survey. A majority of the women surveyed belonged to the lower income group followed by the middle income group. Most of the women surveyed had approached women's groups or institutions like the State Commission for Women in Kolkata or had filed cases in family/matrimonial courts. The major cause for separation was domestic violence. However, the separation had usually been initiated by the male spouse. Almost all these women were in an extremely insecure financial situation. Most of them had hardly any immovable assets including a home to live in or adequate finances and were dependant post separation on their natal families particularly their parents with whom they mostly lived. We came across very few women who lived alone, though this may be because a lot of these single women do not approach either women's groups or the courts. Almost all the women complained of the extremely inadequate support they received from the courts, the length of time that the court proceedings took and their lack of knowledge about their spouses' income and their inability to prove this. Most of the women surveyed said that they should be given a half share in the marital property at the time of separation because of their contribution in building up the home and in looking after the children.

Both in the eastern and the northern regions, we found that an alleged lack of dowry and dowry demands were a major cause for domestic violence. In most of the cases dowry had been given in the form of cash, household goods like furniture, electronic goods like TV, gifts of clothes and jewellery for the husband and his family, etc. The female spouses' *stridhan* mostly consisted of some jewellery. In a number of cases, the dowry given was far beyond the financial capacity of the parents and they had taken loans to give dowry. The physical and mental cruelty or violence towards the women often occurred over demands of dowry; as a result of the woman not acting according to the stereotypical role expected of her; because of the male spouse being under the influence of alcohol; and over trivial issues to subjugate the woman. Some of the women complained of being sexually abused by the husband and sometimes by his family or being ill-treated because of the birth of a daughter.

Survey Reports in the Eastern Region

Kolkata, West Bengal

Twenty-three women were interviewed in Kolkata. They were women who had come to the Women's Commission or the Parivarik Mahila Lok Adalat—a one-day court set up for speedy settlement of family law cases—or NGOs like the Human Rights Law Network. Each interview took two to three hours. The women interviewed belonged mostly to the lower income group and the middle income group. Some of the main findings were:

- Most of these women had to live with their parents or other relatives after separation.
- Most of the women worked for inordinately long hours doing both domestic and care work, sometimes coupled with employment outside the house as well.
- The main causes of separation in most cases were dowry harassment and domestic violence/physical and mental cruelty due to various reasons.
- Out of the nine women who had been working before marriage outside the house, five stopped working post marriage. This had affected their careers. They lacked experience to rejoin the work market at the same level as their colleagues who were all earning much better than them.
- Most of the women said that marriage had adversely affected their possible careers. Some of these women had got married before they could finish their education and therefore had no job prospects.
- Post separation, none of these women had the same lifestyle that they had during the marriage.
- Though dowry had been given in almost all the cases, it was very difficult if not impossible to retrieve this. Cash, which had been spent at the marriage or given to the in laws, or the *stridhan* jewellery which had been given, were almost never returned.

- Almost all women complained of harassment by the police when they went to lodge their complaints or resist being thrown out of the marital house.
- Almost all women complained of the lack of proper maintenance being given or awarded to them and the procedural obstacles that they faced.
- Quite a few women complained of social ostracism and hostility.

Guwahati, Assam

Almost all the separated and divorced women interviewed in Guwahati stayed with their parents and belonged to the lower income group. The main causes of separation or divorce amongst these women were physical and mental violence by the husband and in-laws. In only two cases, women complained of harassment over dowry demands. An activist from Assam who spoke at the ERF Kolkata Seminar[1] said that dowry was less of an issue in Assam than in other states. These women also related how their marriages had adversely affected their career. They related the trauma that they had suffered prior to and post separation and how this also affected their career. Again, most of the women spoke of the long hours of domestic and care work during the marriage. Some, however, spoke of greater freedom in their parental home post separation and less hours of domestic work. Their experiences with the courts and the procedural obstacles that they faced were dismal and women complained of the meagre amount of maintenance awarded to them. They also complained of the delays in the courts and the fact that the courts made no efforts to get to know the correct income of their husbands who were concealing it.

Orissa

The survey of 25 women conducted in Orissa was mostly at the State Commission for Women at Bhubaneshwar and the Family Court at Cuttack. The researcher also went to the Mahila Police Thana at Bhubaneshwar and

[1] The seminar, titled 'Economic Rights and Entitlements of Separated and Divorced Women in India including Child Support and Right to Marital Property', was held in Kolkata at National University of Juridical Sciences, Conference Hall, Salt Lake, Kolkata on 5 December 2008. The organisers were the Economic Research Foundation, New Delhi, in association with The State Commission for Women, West Bengal.

Cuttack for some cases. In the Family Court at Cuttack, 15 women who had cases were interviewed and most of them belonged to the rural areas and the lower income groups and also castes like the SC and OBC. Again, the causes of separation were reported to be physical and mental torture due to dowry and some other reasons. In almost all the cases, women were being supported by their father after their separation, even though most of the fathers were themselves daily wage workers. They reported that their families had undergone severe financial strain and in some cases even sold off whatever land they had in order to give dowry. The amounts of dowry were completely disproportionate to the incomes of the family and included cash payments ranging from ₹30,000 to ₹100,000, jewellery, colour television, etc. The entire domestic work in the matrimonial home was done by the women. After separation, these women did less hours of domestic work. The Orissa report spoke of women belonging to the lower income groups imbibing the social attitude of middle-class women who do not want work outside the house. However, women who were working complained of facing the double or triple burden of household work, care work plus having to cope with their careers.

Darjeeling, North Bengal

The survey done in Siliguri and surrounding areas showed that 18 of the 20 women were unemployed prior to marriage. During marriage, all the 20 did only domestic work. All the women surveyed belonged to the lower income group or middle income group. Six out of the 20 had entered into a marriage of their own choice. Surprisingly, only eight cases had been filed. The main reasons for separation were domestic violence and dowry harassment and in some cases extra-marital relationships. After separation, these women had no means of sustenance so they had taken up paid work. Fourteen women were self-employed while the others were in regular employment. The women who were employed talked of their diminished capacity to work because of lack of experience. Sixteen women reported that during marriage they had to work 6 to 8 hours while the husbands did not do any domestic work. Most of them felt that the burden of work had decreased post separation. Surprisingly, none of the women knew what their husbands earned. Women reported a loss of assets after separation. The same complaints about lack of adequate maintenance, inability to prove husband's income and delays in the court procedures were given by the women who went to court.

Survey Reports in the Northern Region

Delhi

In Delhi, women belonging to all income groups were interviewed. It was found that dowry played a very important role and most of the 25 women who had been surveyed had been given huge amounts of dowry at the time of marriage. The dowry was usually beyond the economic capacity of their parents who had in many cases borrowed money for giving dowry. Yet these women had been harassed and subjected to physical and mental violence for more dowry. A critical issue for all these women was residence as, like in the rest of India, they were dependent on either their parents or some other relative and none could maintain themselves. Even if the women were educated and were working before marriage, most of them had stopped doing so during the marriage. Very few were able to go back to work and what they earned was completely insufficient to take care of their day-to-day needs. Most of the women complained of the great difficulties that they faced in the litigation process, the delays in the court and inadequate maintenance awards. The Delhi survey again highlighted the huge number of hours that women typically spent in doing domestic work. In the lower income group, women said that they spent 10–19 hours and in the high income group the minimum was around 10 hours. Most women said that the number of hours spent on domestic work had considerably lessened after they started living separately. After separation, these women complained of a huge loss in terms of income and most of their expenditure was being subsidised by their natal families. Some of the women detailed the various legal devices that their spouses had employed to delay the case and the award of maintenance by the courts.

Lucknow, Kanpur and Jaipur

In Lucknow and Kanpur, we interviewed 20 women who had approached women's organisations and groups. Most of these women belonged to the lower and middle income groups. The causes for separation were domestic violence on account of dowry, physical and mental violence after drinking alcohol, extra-marital relationships by the male spouse and contract of second marriage by the male spouse. The husbands' incomes ranged from around ₹5,000 to ₹35,000. All the women were engaged in domestic work ranging from 8–12 hours during marriage. Apart from 3 or 4 women, most said that their domestic work had decreased post separation. A lot of the women complained of trauma, stress and added responsibility after separation due to the manner in which they had been treated by their spouses and because they have to care for the children on their own. Most of the women said that marriage had affected their work life and career and they found it difficult to take up jobs post separation. Almost all the women said that their husbands had benefited by their domestic work. A lot of them said that their household expenditure was being borne mostly by their parents. Interestingly, most women felt that their spouses' lifestyle had not changed or had become better post separation while their lifestyle had been affected adversely post separation and that most of the assets are owned by or are in the possession of the husband. Women complained that their cases had been pending in the courts for a long time and they had either not yet been awarded the maintenance or had not received it despite the award by the court. The women also complained that most of the dowry items, barring a few, remained with their spouses. Except one, all the women complained about the police not helping them to recover their *stridhan* or register their complaint of domestic violence.

In Jaipur, we interviewed 34 women, mostly in a short-stay home called Shakti Stambh run by the Rajasthan University Women's Association and Mahila Suraksha Avam Sulah Kendra (Women's Protection and Advice Centre), which is an umbrella organisation of several women's groups and functions in a police station. Out of the 34 separated women who were interviewed, 23 women were staying with their parents or in a couple of cases with relatives. Eight women were staying alone and two were staying in the short-stay home. Most of the women belonged to the lower- and middle-income groups. Again, the causes of separation were physical and mental cruelty, harassment over dowry demands and extra-marital relationships. Dowry harassment and demands for money occurred in 15 of the cases while violence associated with alcohol occurred in about eight cases and in one case the separation was due to a a drug problem of the husband. Four cases of separation were related to extra-marital affairs. Prior to their marriage, eight women had been working of which four had stopped working during marriage. Post separation, nine women were working. Almost all the women were dependant to varying degrees on the natal family. Two of the women had been given maintenance by their spouses through mediation by the Shakti Stambh and by the Mahila Suraksha Kendra. Four women had been awarded maintenance by the court but they were not satisfied with the quantum and complained that they got the payment irregularly.

Survey in the Western Region

The survey was carried out in Ahmedabad and Bhavnagar in Gujarat by the project researchers. Similarly, in Bhopal (MP) and Goa, project researchers carried out the survey with the help of an advocate. In Pune, Mumbai, Bhandup and Raigad in Maharashtra the survey was carried out with the help of advocates.

Bhopal, Madhya Pradesh

Thirty women were interviewed in Bhopal with the help of a women's organisation[2] which worked amongst poor women. These women lived in *jhuggi jhopdi* colonies or *bastis*.[3] Half of these women were Muslim women. Almost all the women, barring two, belonged to the lower income group. Half of these women lived with their parents. Three women were separated along with their children. The major reasons for separation were extra-marital relationships and second marriage of the husband, husband's addiction to alcohol and physical and mental harassment by the husband. Most of these women (25) had been forced to work after separation though during marriage only eight of them were working. Only three women had managed to get maintenance orders against their husbands and none had actually got the maintenance amount. Almost two-thirds of these women reported that their *stridhan* and dowry articles were still with their husbands and in-laws and 17 women reported that their parents had borrowed money to give them dowry and other gifts. Interestingly, only nine of these women had initiated legal proceedings and most of the women complained of delays in court on frivolous grounds.

The survey from Bhopal showed that though the separated women approached the family counselling centre, they were afraid of going to the police station as the behaviour of the police was bad. The women also complained that they could not afford legal fees and, therefore, most of them did not go to court. In a case in which a Muslim woman had lost her husband in a railway accident, the compensation was given in the name of her father-in-law and the children were made nominees with her as guardian. Muslim women tended to approach the *maulvi* and take the *maulvi*'s advice but were

---

[2] The All India Democratic Womens Association (AIDWA), Bhopal office.

[3] Slum clusters.

often ill-treated in front of the *maulvis*. They were told that they were women and should follow their tradition. It was reported that women not only did domestic chores in the house but often helped with other work also. Muslim women did painstaking embroidery work at home, often for long hours. A number of women hardly got any monetary support even during their marriage or after from their husbands. In Bhopal, there were several girls who were married during the course of their education and they reported how it had affected their career. There were cases of three women doctors whose in-laws did not allow them to practise after marriage.

Gujarat

Twenty-nine women from Ahmedabad and 17 women from Bhavnagar were interviewed. Thirty-six women belonged to the lower income group while six belonged to the middle and two to the high income group. All these women had been in touch with a women's group. Out of the 56 women, 34 women lived with their parents while five lived with siblings and other relatives. A number of women were separated along with their children. The major reasons for separation were harassment on account of dowry, cruelty, alcoholism and not having a son during marriage. Nineteen women started working post separation. Only five women had managed to get maintenance orders against their husbands. Almost 30 of these women reported that their *stridhan* and dowry articles were still with their husbands and in-laws and quite a few women reported that their parents had borrowed money to give them dowry and other gifts. Twenty-four women had initiated legal proceedings.

Goa

Most of the women who were interviewed in Goa were educated and belonged to the middle- and higher-income groups. The majority of them said that marriage had affected their careers while the rest said that they could not say one way or the other. However, most said that their economic situation was worse off than their colleagues' and almost all said that their work had benefited their husbands. Almost all women did between 3 and 9 hours of domestic work while their husbands hardly did any. While some did not know about the lifestyle of their husband post separation, about half the women interviewed said that their husband's lifestyle improved. Diviya Kapoor, who helped with the research in Goa said that the interviews were from different sources. She reported that in almost all the cases the men did not do any housework. She further reported that post separation or divorce, the women's workload increased. The women, she said, had to give up promotions and travel opportunities because they had to be at home during the marriage to look after the children. She also reported that most of the educated women who were surveyed somehow felt ashamed and guilty of asking for maintenance. They felt that they had not contributed equally. She further said that women had complained about harassment that they face with the police and that their complaints had not been registered. Most women wanted a one-time settlement and said that their husbands should be subjected to penal action if they did not pay.

Maharashtra

The survey in Maharashtra was carried out in Pune, Bhandup and Raigarh. A total of 23 women were interviewed who came from diverse backgrounds. In Pune, only one person was living alone with her children while the rest were living with their parents and others. Most of the women in Pune had to work post separation and only 20 per cent had managed to get maintenance from their husband. Sixty per cent reported that their *stridhan* and dowry items were with their husband and in-laws. The Pune women also reported that extremely low amounts of maintenance had been awarded. In one case where the husband earned ₹45,000, a monthly maintenance of ₹5,000 had been ordered while in another case where the husband earned ₹7,000, a monthly maintenance of ₹500 for the wife and ₹750 to each of the two children had been awarded. Most of the women did not have any house and barely any assets after separation.

In Bhandup, most of the women interviewed belonged to the lower income group. The reasons for separation were again dowry, extra-marital affairs of the husband, etc. Only 30 per cent of the women received maintenance and the quantum was meagre. Sixty per cent of the women lived with their parents or siblings. From Raigarh, it was reported that the husbands held the land and other assets after separation.

Survey Findings in the Southern Region

In Tamil Nadu, the survey was carried out with the help of a well-known women's rights lawyer in Chennai and with the help of members of AIDWA in north and south Chennai, District Kancheepuram, Tiruvallur and Thenni. In Hyderabad, Andhra Pradesh, and in Bangalore, Karnataka, project researchers did the survey with the help of advocates in the Hyderabad Family Courts and with the help of a women's organisation and the Alternate Law Forum, Bangalore. In Kerala, advocates from the Family Court in Thiruvananthapuram helped project researchers with the survey with the cooperation of a judge of the Family Court who provided the researchers with a room for conducting interviews.

The survey findings in the south were more or less similar to those in the west, except for a few regional variations. The main reasons for women being forced to leave the marital home were again domestic violence including harassment for dowry, extra-marital affairs of the husband and alcoholism. While the women did most of the domestic work, the men hardly did any. The women were also the primary care givers for their children. Hardly any women got maintenance and most women were relatively asset-less.

Advocates who were helping with the survey pointed out that in Andhra Pradesh there was a ceiling of ₹3000 per month as the sum that could be awarded as maintenance under Section 125 CrPC. It is pertinent to point out that no such ceiling exists in the central Act. Andhra Pradesh, thus, has to change its laws to bring them in tandem with the central law.

Hyderabad, Andhra Pradesh

A total number of 14 women were interviewed in Hyderabad. Five belonged to the lower income group while five belonged to the middle income group and four came from a high income group. Ten out of the 14 were staying with their parents post separation. In three cases, the woman was living alone post separation and in one case the woman was living with her brother. In most of the cases, domestic violence and cruelty were the main reasons for separation and in three cases the husband was involved in extra-marital affairs. Most of the women did domestic work for 8–15 hours a day and only four worked for 4–6 hours and one woman had domestic help. In four cases, the women were assetless and only 3 of the 14 women were awarded maintenance. In 10 out of 14 cases, the women's *stridhan* or dowry was with the husband or in-laws. In one case the woman was allowed ₹15,000 for herself and the child but the male spouse was not paying it and had appealed against the quantum awarded by terming the amount as huge. In another case, the woman got ₹1,500 for herself and ₹1,000 for the child. She said that she was satisfied with the quantum of maintenance as she knew that the husband would not give more than this amount. In another case, the woman got ₹1,500 per month but she said that even her house rent was ₹5,000 per month. A lawyer from Andhra Pradesh reported cases of Muslim women in the old city of Hyderabad whose marriages were increasingly breaking up due to dowry and other reasons. She talked of the role of the *kazi*s and how they are not enforcing payments of *mehr* while divorces take place in front of them. She said that the government should set up a women's welfare fund and single women's children should be given proper facilities as far as health, education and shelter are concerned.

Bangalore, Karnataka

The problems faced by separated and divorced women in Bangalore were similar to the problems faced by women in the rest of the country. Dowry was reported to be a big issue and torture by mothers-in-law and sisters-in-law were common. Quite a few surveyees complained of the legal fees that lawyers demand from women and the fact that nothing happens in courts except adjournments. Some of the women complained that a woman needs maintenance as soon as a divorce petition is filed or separation takes place, but this does not happen. All the women who had been interviewed said that they wanted a share in marital property. Some women who had faced severe domestic violence did not want to approach the court for maintenance but said that they should get property automatically.

The total number of women interviewed in Bangalore was 27. More than half of them were living alone and 12 were living with parents. Most of them had an arranged marriage. Only 6 out of 27 had an inter-religion or inter-caste marriage. In six cases, the women filed for divorce and in 2 of the 6 cases, they got it. Cruelty—physical or mental—was the main reason for separation. The second marriage of the husband was also a cause of separation. In most of the cases, the women interviewed belonged to the lower income group and 20 were working post separation. In 12 out of 27 cases, the women did not have any clue about their husband's salary. Post separation, seven women had jewellery, five had access to a TV and four to a fridge while seven had no property (movable or immovable) at all. In seven cases, women had no idea about the financial assets of their husband. Fifteen out of 27 women did not file a case. Only three women had been awarded maintenance for their children. In two cases, the child support awarded was ₹2,000 per month and in the third case, ₹1,500 per month.

As many as 24 of the 27 women reported that they faced hostility on account of their separation.

Thiruvananthapuram, Kerala

Advocate Geena Kumari, a family lawyer from Kerala discussed[4] how women in Kerala suffered domestic violence and dowry-related harassment. She said that a lot of deserted women in Kerala do not want to actually say that they are single and wear the *mangalsutra* and put *sindhur* (jewellery and red vermilion on the forehead worn by married woman) so that they are socially accepted. She said that the courts were not accessible to everyone because family courts were only located in district headquarters and low income women could not spend the money to reach them or hire a lawyer. She said that the procedure also took a long time and that was why people normally went to the court as a last resort. She pointed out that to get maintenance women had to prove not only the income of the husband but also that they were living separately for some valid reason. She said that the courts are gender biased and women are frequently told to reconcile and live with their husbands. She said that the maintenance that is awarded is often not even 5 per cent of their spouses' income, particularly in cases where the male spouse has a high income. She also commented on how difficult it was to execute maintenance orders. According to her, in Kerala the dowry system was pervasive and people gave huge amounts and even property as dowry.

The total number of women interviewed in Thiruvanthapuram was 22. Out of these, 20 were separated while two were divorced. The reasons for separation were mainly extra-marital relationships of the husband, physical and mental cruelty, alcoholism and the suspicious nature of the husband. Fifteen out of 22 women were working post separation/divorce. The average number of hours put in by the women in doing the domestic chores was 10 hours during marriage and 6 hours post separation/divorce. Women complained that the burden of work increased after separation because they did not have any help from their husband. About 80 per cent of the women stated that marriage had affected their careers and that they had wanted to work during their marriage but their husbands had stopped them. They also said that their husbands benefited from their household work. A woman constable stated that not only did her husband benefit from her household

[4] Economic Research Foundation, *Economic Rights and Entitlements of Separated and Divorced Women,* Report of Regional Seminar Proceedings (2008–2009) (New Delhi: ERF, 2010), 219.

work but he also took her entire salary at the beginning of the month. Women complained that after separation their lifestyle had plummeted and even their parents did not want to help them. Most respondents had some of the jewellery given to them by their parents and some electronic goods which they had mostly bought themselves. Out of the 22 women interviewed, only four were awarded maintenance. One woman had fought her case for 27 years and only got ₹7,000 as ad hoc payment! The maintenance awarded varied from ₹500 per month to ₹3,000 monthly. Around half the women stated that they faced discrimination from neighbours and co-villagers who blamed them for the separation.

Chennai, Tamil Nadu

One difference that was noticed in some places in the south was that more women lived alone after separation. For instance, in Tamil Nadu out of 57 cases, 27 women were living alone. In 28 cases they were living with their parents and in 2 cases they lived with adult children. Out of these 57 cases 20 were from the lower income group, 17 were from the middle income group and 20 were from the high income group. In 21 cases, cruelty was the main reason for separation, in 10 cases another marriage or an extra-marital affair was the reason. In nine cases it was dowry harassment while in other cases, the husband's alcoholism or his suspicious nature were the main reasons. In 32 out of 57 cases, the woman did not have any assets with her. In other cases whatever she had been gifted by her parents or acquired by her own earnings was with her. Only in one or two cases the woman had got what had been gifted by her husband or in-laws. Legal proceedings for maintenance had been initiated in 26 cases. In four out of these cases payment was made as a lump sum amount, ranging between ₹60,000 and ₹300,000. In 10 cases monthly maintenance was allowed by the court and in seven of these, the amounts were less than ₹5,000 per month. In one case, it was ₹5,000 per month and in another case it was ₹35,000 per month. In 27 cases, the *stridhan* or dowry could not be recovered and was left with the husband or in-laws.

9

Conclusion and Recommendations

> To recognize that each spouse is an equal economic and social partner in marriage, regardless of function, is a monumental revision of assumptions. It means, among other things, that caring for children is just as valuable as paying for their food and clothing. It means that organizing a household is just as important as the career that subsidizes this domestic enterprise. It means that the economics of marriage must be viewed qualitatively rather than quantitatively.[1]

The survey on the economic status of separated and divorced women threw up a host of complicated issues for which no simple solutions are possible or perhaps even desirable. Many women who were surveyed felt that their husbands and society had ill-treated them and they had a deep sense of being wronged and betrayed. They wanted solutions to the problems they were posing to the researchers or action to address their vulnerable, at times miserable, financial position. They were disillusioned with the legal system and the police. A lot of the women also said that they should have studied further and been economically independent. One of the effects of the questionnaire was that they could articulate the extent to which they had contributed to the building up of the household and the fact that this contribution had not been accounted for or acknowledged anywhere. Thus, the survey helped them to formulate their feelings. They wanted the survey to lead to a change in their lives. Almost all wanted an equal share in the Marital Property and strong, enforceable and easily accessible maintenance laws.

The survey showed that women of all communities, castes and classes are severely disadvantaged when their marriage breaks down. Most women, and the children with them, experience a plunge in their lifestyle on separation and divorce. They lose their residence and experience a drastic fall in lifestyle,

---

[1] Justice Claire L' Heureux-Dube, 'Economic Consequences of Divorce: A View from Canada', *31 Hous. L. Rev. 451.*

living standards and social status. Poor women struggle to survive while the middle class can be plunged into poverty. They are forced to return to their natal homes as they have no place to live in. In their natal homes, they are often less than welcome and live as unwanted guests forever obliged to their parents, and male siblings and their families. The findings seem to suggest that in some ways women in north India suffer more heavily because of patriarchal attitudes and have less agency and freedom. Their age at marriage is lower, they have the least control over their assets, as evidenced from the fact that they were less able to retain assets on separation, and they suffer more hostility from relatives, friends and neighbours when they have to return to their natal homes than women in the other three regions surveyed. However, dowries in south India are higher than in the north.

Maintenance

The survey showed how limited the right to maintenance was for Indian women of all communities. It highlighted the difficulties that women face in trying to access even this limited right. It showed that when maintenance was eventually awarded, it was more symbolic in nature than a substantial amount on which they can live. In a large number of cases even this symbolic amount was never paid.

Many of the surveyees complained that they did not even have knowledge about how much their husbands earned. Though they were, in law, supposed to prove the income of their husbands they had no documents in their possession of either their husbands' incomes or their assets. Another issue that compounds this problem is the fact that many self-employed men including rich businessmen and others do not disclose their correct income to evade tax. Some courts have recognised this fact and refuse to rely on only the income-tax return of the husband.[2] Instead, they try to assess the income of the husband by looking at the style of living of the parties when they were married, the assets owned by the husband and the expenditure normally incurred by him through credit cards, etc. Some positive cases also exist in which an adverse inference is drawn against the husband if, after being directed, the husband does not produce papers relating to his income and status in court.[3] However, such cases are in a minority and maintenance,

---

[2] *Gaurav Nagpal v Sumedha Nagpal* I (2008) DMC 166.

[3] *Radhika v Vineet Rungta* AIR 2004 Del 324; *Rishi Kumar v Suman* I (2008) DMC 355.

throughout the country continues to be awarded in a haphazard manner and husbands continue to use various devices not to disclose their income and assets and to somehow evade the payment of maintenance. Another problem with the law of maintenance is that it is sometimes linked to the conduct of the wife. In a recent case,[4] the Supreme Court of India observed that a wife who has deserted the marital home does not deserve maintenance. Also, under Section 125 of the CrPC, which was meant to be a common, speedy law for maintenance to need/destitute women of all communities, an archaic and discriminatory Sub-section exists. This Sub-section stipulates that a wife will not be entitled to maintenance 'if she is living in adultery, or if, without any sufficient reason, she refuses to live with her husband'.[5] Maintenance is, thus, made dependant on the conduct of the wife and is not seen as a right which has accrued to a woman because of her past contribution to the marital home. This reliance on conduct to defeat the maintenance claim of the wife has been done away with in the laws of many countries. The Canadian Divorce Act 1983, in its Section on spousal support, specifically states that the court 'shall not take into consideration any misconduct of a spouse in relation to the marriage' in an application for support.[6] Justice Claire L'Heureux-Dube of the Canadian Supreme Court has noted that in Canada 'before 1968 women could be denied spousal support if they were "guilty" of marital misconduct regardless of whether their husband had committed a matrimonial offence'.[7] Canadian courts also recognised that spousal support had to be determined by recognising that the wife had suffered economic disadvantage because of the marriage.[8] She points out that many women give up their own career opportunities and advancements and contribute to the well-being of the family through child rearing and home-making and this allows the men to work outside.[9]

We did a survey of the reported cases[10] to see whether the amounts of maintenance and the time taken for the cases had any similarity to the findings of the survey in these areas.

---

[4] Deccan Herald News Service, 'No Alimony for Woman Who Desert Husband', *The Deccan Herald*, New Delhi edition, 18 November 2010. Available at http://www.deccanherald.com/content/36709/no-alimony-woman-desert-husband.html (last accessed on 2 May 2012.

[5] Sub-section (4) of Section 125, CrPC.

[6] Section 15(6), Canadian Divorce Act, 1985.

[7] Justice Claire L' Heureux-Dube, 'Economic Consequences of Divorce: A View from Canada', *31 Hous. L. Rev. 451.*

[8] Ibid.

[9] Ibid.

[10] We analysed cases from 1998 till 2010 from a popular Indian legal journal known as *Divorce and Matrimonial Cases.*

In the years 1998–2010, husbands, who were fairly well-off paid maintenance to their wives ranging between 1.2 per cent and 57 per cent of their income and the time taken ranged between 1 and 12 years. In one case in which 1.2 per cent of the husband's income was awarded as maintenance, the husband was earning ₹125,000 per month. The fact that the wife was earning ₹4,250 per month in this case seems to have persuaded the judge that there was no need to give more than ₹1,500 per month as maintenance to the child. However, in a positive case where the award of maintenance was 57 per cent the amount of award was ₹75,000 per month for the wife and their two children whereas the husband's income was ₹130,000 per month. When the husbands were in the income group of ₹10,000 to ₹20,000 per month, the maintenance awarded ranged between 2 per cent and 45 per cent of the husbands' income and the time taken ranged between 1 and 14 years. In one case, where the wife could not prove the income of her husband, maintenance of only ₹250 per month was awarded for the child. The wife had alleged that the income of the husband was ₹10,833 per month. In cases in which the husbands earned less than ₹10,000 per month, the wife was awarded maintenance ranging between 5 per cent and 66 per cent of their husband's income and the time taken ranged between 1 and 20 years. In a case where the amount awarded was 5 per cent of the husband's income the husband earned ₹4,000 per month.

In 121 of the 192 cases from the years 1998–2003, where the wife could not provide information about the husband's income, the maintenance awarded ranged between ₹75 and ₹1,000 per month in 75 cases, in seven cases it ranged between ₹1,000 and ₹2,000 per month and in five cases it ranged from ₹3,500 per month to ₹7,500 per month. The time taken in these cases ranged between 1 and 23 years. These cases showed that the present law on maintenance is unjust and the wife is disadvantaged for no fault of hers in the courts. In one case only medical expenses of ₹35,000 was allowed, and in another three cases one-time settlements were awarded ranging between ₹75,000 and ₹500,000. However, during the years 2006–2008 a somewhat higher maintenance amount was awarded at the rate of ₹20,000 per month in a case in which the wife could not prove the income of her husband. It is pertinent to point out that no maintenance was allowed to the petitioner wives in 22 of these 192 cases. However, even these cases took a long time to decide and the time ranged between 1 and 9 years.

In all, in 43 of 566 cases, no maintenance was granted to the wife and/or child(ren). Also, in eight of these cases, there was very little information about the husband's income.

Thus, some of the main issues that remain to be tackled are the length of time that such cases take to give relief, the inability of the Indian judiciary to view maintenance as a substantive relief which will allow a wife and any children with her to live in a manner similar to which they have been used to so that separation and divorce does not disadvantage them. Apart from this, divorce procedures have to be made more sensitive to women by shifting of onus of proof and by simplifying the procedures. A special enforcement machinery/agency also needs to be put in place to recover maintenance from erring husbands and partners. Activists and lawyers have suggested that a special fund needs to be set up to disperse maintenance amounts and it should not be the woman's responsibility to recover the maintenance once it has been ordered by the courts. One of the main challenges which remain is how to make the courts and justice more accessible. Family courts were instituted in several states to simplify legal procedures and enable quicker settlements of cases and to create a woman- and child-sensitive environment. In practice, however, apart from other problems that beset these courts, there are far too few family courts and these are clogged with cases, leading to inordinate delays even in the grant of interim maintenance. Crimes Against Women Cells established by the police too have proved inadequate, if not a hurdle, in the prevention of domestic violence against women, the settlement of disputes and the retrieval of the woman's dowry and *stridhan* when she is thrown out of the marital home.

Marital Property

Maintenance awards need to be supplemented by ensuring that a wife or partner has a right to immovable assets like house, land, etc., and movable assets like other household items, savings, etc., that the parties may have accumulated during the period they stayed together, regardless of whose name the property is bought in. The basic assumption of sharing of assets is that the assets have been acquired through the monetary or non-monetary contribution of both the parties to the household. However, apart from getting a token maintenance, married and separated women in India have no ownership rights to the home and assets accumulated during the marriage.

Indian women are governed by various personal or family laws. However, none of these laws give women a right to marital property, that is, property acquired by either or both spouses during the subsistence of marriage.

The legal regime of Community of Property is therefore non-existent as far as Indian women are concerned. More than 60 years after Independence these women have no ownership rights in the property acquired in their home. The law does not recognise their contribution to the household or the productive nature of the work that these women do in the household.

Apart from this highly unjust situation which treats women as second-class citizens and treats housework as work of no value, the subordinate position of women in the household is a major reason why they are subjected to domestic violence and why such a large number of women have very little say in household decisions. The NFHS-III figures show that 37 per cent of ever married women have experienced spousal physical or sexual violence and 16 per cent have experienced spousal emotional violence. Not surprisingly, 19.3 per cent of divorced, separated and deserted women faced emotional violence and 16.3 per cent of these women faced physical and sexual violence, often from their spouses and former spouses according to the NFHS-III. A total of 17.9 per cent of these women faced emotional violence and 18 per cent of these women faced physical and sexual violence, sometimes from their spouses and former spouses.

Even after several years of marriage, when a marriage breaks down or a woman is deserted and has to live separately, she becomes asset-less. This is so because, by and large, most of the property that is acquired in the household is in the man's name. The woman's work for and in the household and her contribution in building up the household are not accounted for in any way while the benefits remain with the male spouse. It has been said that the right to divorce without a right to equal division of marital property is violative of a woman's right to equality and results in further oppressing her.

Even working women, because of their vulnerable and subordinate position in the household, often let their spouses and in-laws dictate how their salaries should be spent or spend their salaries on day-to-day household expenses. NFHS-III points out that only about 20 per cent to 25 per cent of wives mainly make decision about the use of their own earnings. Capital assets like houses or other immovable properties are often acquired by and in the name of the male spouse in the Indian family.

The survey that we have carried shows that in most parts of the country women are forced to leave their marital homes, often with their children, with just a few of their personal belongings and if they can, and live with and are dependent on their natal families. It is, therefore, important to discuss the kind of Community of Property legislation that is required in India.

In several countries what is largely practised is what is known as a Deferred Community of Property regime. This system means that while the couple are married they individually own and manage the property they have bought. However, when they separate the entire property—movable and immovable—becomes common property and can be divided in various ways. It would, therefore, have to be decided whether the Community of Property Regime should come into being as soon as the parties start living together or whether we should have a Deferred Community of Property Regime which becomes effective the moment the couple separate. In the Community of Property Regime, 'the husband and wife are regarded as partners with respect to the marital assets'.[11] Indeed, in several Western and other countries where the law for division of marital property exists, marriage has been compared to a partnership with each of the spouses contributing in whichever way they can and need to. It does not matter which party has bought the asset or paid for it. However, in some countries—Australia and England—the way in which the property should be divided is left to the discretion of the judge while in other countries—Canada and USA—there is an equal division of assets between the spouses with a minimal discretion left with the judge to act in favour of a disadvantaged party or to give the house to the party who is the custodial parent. This is normally the mother.

The proposal to introduce a new law on equal division of marital property will also involve a discussion on the nature of the assets that will form a part of the Community of Property; for example, whether inherited property or only property acquired during the period that the parties lived together would form a part of the Community of Property; whether gifts, or whether pension benefits and life insurance should form a part of Community of Property, etc. The discussion will also have to take into account whether a spouse who is caring for the child/children needs to be given exclusive rights to certain assets like the marital home. It would also be important to discuss how women can be compensated for the loss of earning capacity and career opportunities due to the time spent by them in household chores and in caring for the children and the elderly. Other components in the proposed legislation would include discussions on whether just spouses or persons in relationships in the nature of marriage should have a right under this law, how long the parties should have lived together before the law applies to them, etc.

---

[11] B. Sivaramaya, *Matrimonial Property Law in India* (Oxford University Press, New Delhi, 1999), 1.

Government Policy and Social Security/Welfare Schemes

A discussion on Community of Property assumes that there is property to distribute. However, in a country like India where there is such large-scale poverty, often spouses may not have been able to accumulate any property. Any discussion on securing the economic rights of women and children would, therefore, be incomplete without discussing how women living in poverty need to be secured by the state. Officially, there are 34.3 million widows and 2.34 million divorced/separated women in the country. Some 6.9 per cent of women in India are widows, while 0.5 per cent are divorced or separated.[12] This figure, however, seems to be inaccurate as other studies point to a much higher percentage of separated women.[13] The NFHS-III found that 1.4 per cent women were divorced/separated and deserted.[14] Another 1.4 per cent above age of 30 were unmarried. In total, at least 7.5 per cent of women are single according to the Census. A total of 10.4 per cent of households are headed by women, one-third of these by married women, the rest by widows and some by deserted women.

While there has been some recognition of the social, cultural and economic problems of widows, there is no recognition of the other categories of single women. Practically, no government schemes exist to support these women. Yet, separated/divorced women and households headed by women tend to be among the poorest of the poor and perpetuate the cycle of poverty in the next generation. Our survey has also shown that in-laws rarely support the abandoned family. The woman's natal family may take her in but usually treat her as an outsider and a burden.

Having been primarily involved with household work and with the care of children and elderly, their capacity and capability to work outside the home gets vastly reduced. The economic deprivation that these women face is often compounded by illiteracy and the traditional and patriarchal gender division of labour in the market. This gender bias ensures that women's skills

---

[12] Census Data 2001, India, see http://censusindia.gov.in/Census_Data_2001/Census_Data_Online/Social_and_cultural/Age_and_Marital_Status.aspx (last accessed on 16 November 2012).

[13] Bina Agarwal, 'The Idea of Gender Equality: From Legislative Vision to Everyday Family Practice', in Romila Thapar (ed.), *India: Another Millennium?* (New Delhi: Penguin Books, 2001), 48.

[14] 'Table 3.1: Background Characteristics of Respondents', *National Family Health Survey (NFHS-3), 2005-06, India* Vol. I, p. 54, see http://www.nfhsindia.org/NFHS-3%20Data/VOL-1/India_volume_I_corrected_17oct08.pdf (last accessed on 26 May 2010).

are undervalued; they are permitted to do only certain forms of labour and are invariably paid lower wages than men.

There is clearly a great need for government intervention and affirmative action for single women and their families. The country's Eleventh Five Plan for the years 2007–2012[15] did recognise this by specifying that single women should get priority in housing and food and they as well as women in vulnerable situations, etc., should be included in the criteria for persons who live below the poverty line.[16]

However, as acknowledged by the Mid-term Appraisal for the Eleventh Plan,[17] in practice, several of the plan goals had not been met.

Also, no specific schemes of social assistance for women and families plunged into an economic crisis because of adverse domestic circumstances are envisaged.

The central and state governments have, over the years, introduced a plethora of social welfare and poverty alleviation programmes and schemes, including schemes for women and children. Yet, as the appraisal document admits, 'there has been little visible change in the living realities of women and children'.

The issue of how many people remain below the poverty line is a highly contentious one, with different government and non-government estimates of the number living below the poverty line. While there is little data to back this assertion, the multiple discriminations and disabilities that single women face inevitably push them to the bottom of the socio-economic ladder, particularly if they are burdened with young children. The dearth of data and lack of priority to these issues leads to a neglect of these women in government policies, programmes and schemes.

---

[15] Planning Commission of India, 'Part II: Social Sector, Chapter 11: Women's Agency and Child Rights', *Eleventh Five Year Plan 2007–2012* (2010).

[16] Ibid., 6.41: 'All housing provided by the government during the Eleventh Plan should either be half in the name of the woman in the household or in the single name of the woman. Single women, widows, and women in difficult circumstances will be given priority.'

6.42: 'During the Eleventh Plan attempts will be made to strengthen the PDS system and revise BPL census norms to ensure that women in vulnerable situations, particularly widows, single women, internally displaced women, and women in conflict situations are covered.'

6.71: 'There will be special measures for compensation, financial assistance, and support to widows and female headed households in conflict areas.' It said, for instance that:

6.63: 'In addition to the categories of vulnerable and marginalized women discussed above, the Eleventh Plan will also have to pay special attention to other categories including migrant women, urban poor women, and single women to fulfil its commitment of equality and gender justice.'

[17] Ibid.

With the introduction of the National Rural Employment Guarantee Act (NREGA), the government recognised the need for employment in the rural sector. Activists hoped that women would get a substantial share of such employment. However, single women have repeatedly been refused employment at sites on the specious grounds that people are required to work in pairs. Sometimes women are refused employment if they come to work in a *burqa*. Worse, single women living with their natal families are not treated as an independent unit when it comes to entitlement for the job card.[18]

Some anti-poverty government schemes exist but almost none are targeted specifically to single women. Only three central schemes are targeted to protect some interests of widows, divorced and deserted women. The first is the Swadhar and Short Stay Homes scheme meant for 'relief and rehabilitation of women in difficult circumstances'. The second is the Support for Training and Employment Programme (STEP) and skill upgradation which provides training to assetless and Below Poverty Line women. Finally, the third is the Indira Gandhi National Widow Pension Scheme (IGNWPS) which gives widows aged 40–64 years and living below the poverty line ₹200 per month—a sum that is obviously inadequate to lift anyone out of poverty.[19] The budgets and achievements of these schemes make it evident that they are token gestures rather than a serious attempt to tackle the problem. STEP, for instance, benefited only 231,000 women during the Tenth Five Year Plan period. As for the Swadhar scheme, it benefited only 21,464 women.[20] A field-level investigation of the state of implementation of the short stay homes and Swadhar scheme conducted in Karnataka by the Hengasar Hakkina Sangha, Bangalore, highlighted inadequate budgets, poor infrastructure, and lack of training for staff and inmates as well as inadequate monitoring as reasons for the poor functioning of these schemes.[21] The majority of deserted women do not, in any case, benefit from these schemes.

Access to food and housing are the foremost problems of the overwhelming number of single women. The Right to Food Campaign has ably

---

[18] U. Vasuki, National Secretary, AIDWA, Speech on 'State Entitlements in Tamil Nadu and the Experiences of Single Women', Economic Rights and Entitlements of Separated and Divorced Women, Report of Regional Seminar Proceedings, 2008–09, p. 226, (ERF, New Delhi, 2010).

[19] 'Schemes for Welfare of Women including Widows', statement to Lok Sabha by Smt. Krishna Tirath, Minister for Women and Child Development, issued by the Press Information Bureau on 14 March 2011. Available at http://pib.nic.in/newsite/erelease.aspx (last accessed on 16 November 2012).

[20] Planning Commission of India, *supra* note 15.

[21] Indu Subramaniam and B.N. Usha, *State Services for Women in Crisis in Karnataka* (Bangalore: Hengasara Hakkina Sangha, 2010).

documented the plight of many deserted women living in acute poverty, unable to afford two square meals a day.[22] Yet single women are often unable to get a ration card or a BPL card[23] and therefore are also denied the other benefits that could accrue from these, such as access to other state schemes. Some state governments such as the Government of West Bengal are issuing ration cards in individual names rather than per household and this move will certainly benefit single women.

The arbitrary and selective nature of BPL lists in most states works to exclude rather than include the most marginalised people such as single women. Kerala is perhaps the only state to have included all female-headed households in the BPL list, besides including marginalised groups such as the fishing community and all SC and ST households.[24]

A Supreme Court order of May 2003 specified that among others 'widows and other single women with no regular support' should be made eligible for the Antyodaya Anna Yojana scheme of subsidised food grain, but this laudable order remains largely unimplemented.

Government social security schemes may include some concessions and quotas for single women such as widows and the aged but there are practically no provisions for the deserted or divorced woman. In any case what passes for social security is usually a token 'pension' of a couple of hundred rupees. Data referred by the Ministry of Rural Development, Government of India,[25] in its agenda note on performance review, which lists pension rates by states out of their own funds, shows that monthly widow pensions are as low as ₹120 in Kerala, for widows who were from BPL families, and ₹200 in some states like Andhra Pradesh, Bihar, Chhattisgarh, Jammu and Kashmir, MP and Orissa for widows in general, with some conditions in certain states. Few states like Delhi and Goa are more generous. The coverage in all these schemes is low with only 18.5 per cent and 24.4 per cent of eligible women being covered in Maharashtra and Delhi respectively, according to calculations

---

[22] Harsh Mander and Archana Rai, 'Living with Hunger' in V. Manikandan (ed.), *Chronic Food Deprivation among Aged People, Single Women and People with Disability: A Study of Rural Destitution and Hunger* (New Delhi: CES, 2008), 13.

[23] Vasuki, *supra* note 18, p. 226.

[24] Mridul Eapen, Economist, Honorary Fellow, Centre for Development Studies, Thiruvananthapuram, Kerela, Speech on State Entitlements in Kerela and Comments on Presentation, Economic Rights and Entitlements of Separated and Divorced Women, Report of Regional Seminar Proceedings, 2008–09, p. 228, (ERF, New Delhi, 2010).

[25] Government of India, Agenda Note: Performance Review Committee, Ministry of Rural Development, 12–13 May 2008. Available at http://www.silverinnings.com/docs/Finance/Pension/PRC_AGENDANOTE.pdf (last accessed on 22 October 2010).

made by the Office of the Commissioners to the Supreme Court.[26] Again, a study by the Budget Analysis Rajasthan Centre has found that almost 50 per cent of BPL widows did not get pensions.[27] Although some states are beginning to include divorced and separated women in the category of pensioners, proof of their single status is difficult to provide, particularly in the case of the separated.

Though Kerala has the lowest widow pension per month, it is among the first state governments to have introduced an innovative Single Women Benefit Scheme.[28] This scheme is to meant to empower destitute and marginalised women such as widows, divorcees, separated, unwed mothers and unmarried women belonging to the BPL category, by enabling them to set up small enterprises. A one-time grant-in-aid of ₹10,000 is provided. The scheme is administered by the Social Welfare Department but draws upon the expertise of the Kerala State Women's Development Corporation (KSWDC). Selection is based on recommendation of a functionary of the local Panchayat or Director of KSWDC. The scheme was introduced on 1 April 2002 and runs up to 31 March 2015.

The Government of Goa's Dayanand Social Security Scheme offers a somewhat decent monthly pension of ₹1,000 to the aged, the disabled and to single women.[29] The scheme provides monthly pension to senior citizens of 60 years and above, disabled persons and single women. The pension is transferred by a transparent electronic clearance system into individual accounts.

Himachal Pradesh has an innovative education scheme for children from deprived homes. The Mother Teresa Matri Sabal Yojana provides 'poor and weak mothers having children below 14 years of age' a sum of ₹2,000 per annum per child for education.[30] It is available to all divorced, widowed,

[26] Dr N.C. Saxena, Commissioner, and Harsh Mander, Special Commissioner of the Supreme Court in the case PUCL v UOI and Ors. Writ Petition (Civil) No. 196 of 2001, Eighth Report of the Commissioners of the Supreme Court: *A Special Report on Most Vulnerable Social Groups and Their Access to Food, Commissioners of the Supreme Court* (New Delhi: Supreme Court of India, 2008). Available at http://sccommissioners.org/Reports/Reports/SCC8_0908.pdf (last accessed on 22 December 2010).

[27] Budget Analysis Rajasthan Centre, *The Destitution of Widows in Rajasthan: What Role Has the State Played?* Working Paper No. 4 (Jaipur: BARC, 2007).

[28] See http://www.india.gov.in/govt/viewscheme.php?schemeid=1729 (last accessed on 16 November 2012).

[29] See www.goasocialwelfare.com/dayanandsssheme.htm (last accessed on 3 October 2007).

[30] Ekal Nari Shakti Sangthan, *The Mother Teresa Scheme: An Analysis of the Scheme and the Application Procedure* (Jagjit Nagar: ENSS, 2007). This analysis has documented the practical problems that women in Himachal Pradesh face in applying for the Mother Teresa scheme (illiteracy, lack of proof of residence and income certificates, death certificates, etc.) including the inability to pay for repeated travel to distant offices to obtain documents and pay corrupt officials.

separated and deserted women who live below poverty line and have children aged 5–14 years.

Also activists from various women's groups like that of the Ekal Nari Shakti Sangathan, say the benefits of numerous schemes available in theory to single women do not reach them. 'The procedural wrangles prove to be a major bottleneck in single women getting benefit of the nine welfare schemes under which they can derive benefit', she points out.[31]

Many single women work in *anganwadis*, as these are among the few job options available to village women. However, the meagre 'honorarium' paid to these workers barely enables them to survive. Further, the woman who cooks or serves a school mid-day meal is not eligible for any government schemes even if she is earning much less than the minimum wage.

When the Maharashtra State Policy for Women was being formulated, NGOs working with women had made a number of recommendations including the suggestions that women be given preference in allotment of the Zunka Bhakar Kendras. According to their recommendations, this scheme can be used to give women's cooperatives a preference in running ration shops and government canteens so that these places can be used to sell their products and services. These recommendations have, however, not been translated into practice and no government resolutions have been passed to implement them. There needs to be political and bureaucratic will to execute such pro-women programmes.[32]

Recommendations

The Survey and the Regional Seminars[33] provided detailed grass roots reporting on the status of separated single women in different states, regions and communities. Women's extremely limited social and economic rights within families, the frequent and repeated harassment for dowry, domestic violence,

[31] Tribune News Service, 'Single Women Being Denied Welfare Benefits', *Tribune News Service*, Shimla edition , 23 July 2010.

[32] Kiran Moghe, AIDWA Secretariat member, Maharastra, in her speech in a seminar in New Delhi on 20 December 2010 on the economic rights and entitlements of separated and divorced women.

[33] Four regional seminars were held in Kolkata, Delhi, Mumbai and Chennai. In these seminars grass roots level workers and women related their experience of working with separated women and many separated women themselves spoke of the obstacles they had faced. Lawyers, judges and social scientists working in this area also participated and spoke. See, *supra* note 19.

the appropriation of their *stridhan* and other assets, the curbs on their freedom and mobility within marriage, the non-recognition of their household work and care work, and their plight when they are thrown out of the marital home with nothing but the clothes on their back was a constant refrain at the seminars. The role of the administrative and legal systems in redressing women's grievances and the numerous shortfalls therein came in for scrutiny. Women often felt that they were doubly harassed, first by husbands and their families and then by the police and lawyers who they approached for help. Frequently, women did not know that they were entitled to maintenance, had no idea how much the husband earned and were unable to provide proof of his income in order to ask for maintenance. Many lawyers in turn reported how difficult it is to get the women some financial relief, given the complex legal procedures and huge delays in the courts, the unrestricted discretionary power of the courts to grant maintenance, the problem of proving income and the linking of maintenance with custody and morality issues. The special problems of women from minorities such as Muslim and Christian women and women from tribal communities, who are governed by patriarchal customary laws, were spotlighted. Goa's unique Uniform Civil Code was discussed to understand whether it provided a more equitable legal regime for women. In each of the seminars, numerous suggestions and recommendations were made for reform of the legal system and revision and formulation of state policy.

A primary recommendation that emerged from the survey and the seminars is that all separated, deserted and divorced Indian women must be entitled to, at least, a half share of the assets of the marital home or assets acquired by a couple during the period that they have lived together regardless of whose name the asset is in. Women belonging to all communities must be entitled to this share on separation. This law must recognise them as equal partners in marriage and accordingly this must be reflected by state policy also. Thus, a recommendation was made for urgent reform of the laws to bring in a Deferred Community of Property Regime which will operate from the date of separation, in place of the present Separation of Property Regime that exists in Indian law today.

A call was also given for urgent legal reform of the law and procedures regarding maintenance—spousal and child support—which must be recognised as a right and not a dole. State policy and law need to recognise the work and effort put in by the woman in building up the household and primarily in looking after the children and the elderly. The right to maintenance also recognises and compensates to some extent the loss of earning capacity that a woman has suffered while performing and supervising various tasks at home.

It further recognises that while the woman's earning capacity is lessened, her husband or partner's capacity is strengthened precisely because of the work put in by the woman. Some of the reforms that were suggested included shifting of the onus of proof on the man to prove his income and assets, amendments in law to curb the discretion of the judiciary while awarding maintenance amounts, introduction of new enforcement mechanisms to ensure that the maintenance that is awarded is actually paid to the woman and creation of a special fund for immediate payment of maintenance to a woman. Many speakers in the seminars suggested that the state should perform the duty of recovering maintenance amounts and a woman should not be forced to fight another round of litigation to get the maintenance awarded to her.

It is a long-standing recommendation of various women's organisation and groups that the right to make a will should be restricted to stop disinheritance and discrimination against girls and women. The law needs to be amended to restrict women from relinquishing their rights in parental property in favour of their male siblings. One way could be by only allowing a sister to give up her share if she has been adequately compensated by payment of money.

Another demand that emerged from the survey is that of single women's entitlements from the state. In certain families, who live below the poverty line, there may be no property or income to divide. In situations where the woman is deserted by a man who disappears or who becomes an alcoholic or is chronically unemployed, it becomes impossible to obtain maintenance from him. Often the woman belongs to a poor family with no property to fall back upon and may be left destitute. In such situations, the single woman and her children must be entitled to financial support from the state. Adequate, comprehensive social security needs to be provided for single women and their families, to enable them to survive with dignity. The existing schemes for single women were examined and found completely inadequate to meet the needs of the majority of the women.

A demand that was repeatedly made was a demand that all land/plots distributed by the state should be in the name of both the man and the woman living together.

While law on its own cannot bring about reform, it is indeed a necessary first step to enable women to fight for their rights. The economic rights of women on separation need to written into the Indian law so that women can access these rights and persons who deny them these rights should know that they are violating the law of the land.

Appendix

Tables from Chapter 3

Table 3A.1 Percentage Distribution of the Surveyees in Different Regions by the Age Groups of the Surveyees

Regions	*18–22*	*23–27*	*28–32*	*33–37*	*38–42*	*43–47*	*48–52*	*> 52*	*Total (excluding the 3 missing cases)*
North	4.8	23.8	31.0	11.9	11.9	14.3	0.0	2.4	100.0
South	6.0	10.4	23.9	22.4	17.9	9.7	7.5	2.2	100.0
East	11.3	26.3	23.8	11.3	16.3	3.8	2.5	5.0	100.0
West	11.0	26.7	24.7	15.8	11.0	5.5	2.7	2.7	100.0
Total	8.7	20.9	24.9	16.7	14.4	7.5	4.0	3.0	100.0

Table 3A.2 The Current Residential Status of the Divorced and Separated Women (Surveyees) in Different Regions

Regions	*Alone*	*With Natal Family*	*With Others*	*Total (excluding the missing cases)*
North	15.9	77.3	6.8	100.0
South	36.6	51.5	11.9	100.0
East	16.3	73.8	10.0	100.0
West	21.9	63.7	14.4	100.0
Total	25.0	63.1	11.9	100.0

Table 3A.3.1(a) The Distribution of the Surveyees and Their Spouses by Their Current Employment Status after Divorce or Separation in Different Regions (Percentage)

	Surveyees		*Male Spouses of the Surveyees*		
Regions	*Working*	*Not Working*	*Working*	*Not Working*	*Surveyees Not Aware of the Working Status of Their Male Spouses*
North	38.6	61.4	93.2	2.3	4.5
South	65.7	34.3	86.6	5.2	8.2
East	47.5	52.5	82.5	1.3	16.3
West	63.9	36.1	85.0	10.2	4.8
Total	58.5	41.5	85.9	5.9	8.1

Table 3A.3.1(b) Percentage Distribution of the Surveyees Belonging to Different Caste Groups by Current Work Status

	No. of Surveyees			*Percentage Distribution across Social Caste Groups*		
	Non-Working	*Working*	*Total*	*Non-Working*	*Working*	
SC–ST	26.0	38.0	64.0	40.6	59.4	100.0
OBC	43.0	63.0	106.0	40.6	59.4	100.0
General	95.0	132.0	227.0	41.9	58.1	100.0

Table 3A.3.2 Distribution of Surveyees by Their Current Occupation

	Number of the Surveyees	*Percentage*
Engineer/Professional/Executive/Manager/Having Big Business/Consultant	11	2.7
Having Medium Business/Goldsmith/Tiffin Services/Handling Accounts or Clerical Work	13	3.2
Seller/Shop	8	2.0
Self-Employed	29	7.2
Domestic Workers	57	14.1
In Service	21	5.2
Advocate/Teacher/Doctor	20	4.9
Employed	72	17.8
Labourer	6	1.5
Student	6	1.5
Housewife	162	40.0
Total	405	100.0
Working	237	58.5
Not Working	168	41.5
Total	405	100.0

Table 3A.3.3 Distribution of the Spouses of the Surveyees by Their Current Occupation in Different Regions

	Number of the Spouses of the Surveyees					*Distribution within the Region*				
Region	*North*	*South*	*East*	*West*	*Total*	*North*	*South*	*East*	*West*	*Total*
Engineer/Professional/ Executive/ Manager/Having Big Business/ Consultant	3	19	11	13	46	6.8	14.2	13.8	8.8	11.4
Having Medium Business/Goldsmith/ Tiffin Services/Handling Accounts or Clerical Work	6	12	14	15	47	13.6	9.0	17.5	10.2	11.6
Seller/Shop	5	4	1	6	16	11.4	3.0	1.3	4.1	4.0
Self-Employed	0	2	2	7	11	0.0	1.5	2.5	4.8	2.7
Household Work Outside Home	6	19	11	24	60	13.6	14.2	13.8	16.3	14.8
In Service	8	29	9	15	61	18.2	21.6	11.3	10.2	15.1
Advocate/Teacher/Doctor	3	9	2	5	19	6.8	6.7	2.5	3.4	4.7
Employed	10	20	16	38	84	22.7	14.9	20.0	25.9	20.7
Student	0	0	0	1	1	0.0	0.0	0.0	0.7	0.2
Unemployed	1	7	1	14	23	2.3	5.2	1.3	9.5	5.7
Labourer	0	2	0	2	4	0.0	1.5	0.0	1.4	1.0
Non-Response/Not Aware	2	11	13	7	33	4.5	8.2	16.3	4.8	8.1
Total	44	134	80	147	405	100.0	100.0	100.0	100.0	100.0

Table 3A.3.4 Percentage Distribution of the Male Spouses of the 405 Surveyees by Their Current Monthly Income in Different Income Levels in Different Regions (in ₹ Thousand)

Region	*No Income*	*< 1*	*1–2*	*2–6*	*6–10*	*10–15*	*> 15*	*Not Aware*	*Total*
North	2.3	0.0	2.3	15.9	2.3	11.4	36.4	29.5	100.0
South	3.7	0.0	1.5	7.5	9.7	10.4	35.8	31.3	100.0
East	0.0	1.3	0.0	10.0	15.0	20.0	26.3	27.5	100.0
West	8.8	1.4	3.4	22.4	12.2	6.8	21.8	23.1	100.0
Total	4.7	0.7	2.0	14.3	10.9	11.1	28.9	27.4	100.0

Table 3A.3.6 Basic Table: Current Monthly Income of Self

		< 0.5	0.5–1	1–2	2–4	4–6	6–8	8–10	10–12	12–15	15–20	20 –25	25–30	30–35	> 35	Nil	No Response
Present Occupation of Self	Engineer/Professional/ Executive/Manager/ Having Big Business/ Consultant	0	0	0	0	2	0	0	0	0	1	4	0	1	3	0	0
	Having Medium Business/ Goldsmith/Tiffin Services/ Handling Accounts or Clerical Work	0	2	4	2	0	0	1	0	1	2	0	1	0	0	0	0
	Seller/Shop	0	2	2	1	3	0	0	0	0	0	0	0	0	0	0	0
	Self-Employed	1	4	9	6	2	1	1	3	0	0	0	0	1	1	0	0
	Household Work Outside Home	4	16	22	11	3	0	1	0	0	0	0	0	0	0	0	0
	In Service	0	0	3	5	1	1	1	1	3	1	2	2	0	1	0	0
	Advocate/Teacher/ Doctor	0	1	1	4	3	3	2	0	1	2	0	0	1	2	0	0
	Employed	3	14	20	19	4	3	1	2	0	0	2	2	1	0	0	1
	Student	0	0	0	0	0	0	0	0	0	0	0	0	0	0	6	0
	Housewife	0	0	0	0	0	0	0	0	0	0	0	0	0	0	162	0
	Labourer	1	1	1	1	0	1	0	0	0	0	0	0	0	0	0	1
	Total	9	40	62	49	18	9	7	6	5	6	8	5	4	7	168	2
	Working	9	40	62	49	18	9	7	6	5	6	8	5	4	7	0	2
	Not Working	0	0	0	0	0	0	0	0	0	0	0	0	0	0	168	0
	Total	9	40	62	49	18	9	7	6	5	6	8	5	4	7	168	2

Table 3A.4 Distribution of the Respondents by Their Religion in Different Regions

Regions	*Hindu*	*Muslim*	*Christian*	*Buddhist*	*Others*	*Total*
North	81.8	15.9	0.0	0.0	2.3	100.0
South	80.6	9.7	9.0	0.0	0.7	100.0
East	92.5	7.5	0.0	0.0	0.0	100.0
West	58.5	35.4	4.1	0.7	1.4	100.0
Total	75.1	19.3	4.4	0.2	1.0	100.0

Table 3A.5 Distribution of the 397 Surveyees by Their Caste in Different Regions

States	*SC–ST*	*OBC*	*General and Others*	*Total (excluding the missing cases)*
North	13.6	13.6	72.7	100.0
South	11.7	45.3	43.0	100.0
East	17.5	17.5	65.0	100.0
West	20.0	19.3	60.7	100.0
Total	16.1	26.7	57.2	100.0

Table 3A.6.1 Distribution of the 404 Surveyees by the Educational Level Attained by Them in Different Regions

Region	*Illiterate*	*Primary*	*Secondary*	*Higher Secondary*	*Graduate*	*Postgraduate and Professional*	*Others*	*Total*
North	9.1	11.4	20.5	6.8	20.5	31.8	0.0	100.0
South	9.0	16.5	16.5	12.8	19.5	24.1	1.5	100.0
East	11.3	16.3	23.8	22.5	11.3	12.5	2.5	100.0
West	29.9	19.7	28.6	6.8	6.8	6.8	1.4	100.0
Total	17.1	17.1	22.8	11.9	13.4	16.3	1.5	100.0

Table 3A.6.2 Distribution of the 396 Surveyees Belonging to Different Caste Groups by Their Educational Status

	Number				*Percentage Distribution*			
Educational Levels	*SC/ST*	*OBC*	*General*	*Total*	*SC/ST*	*OBC*	*General*	*Total*
Up to Primary	17	17	33	67	26.6	16.0	14.5	16.9
Up to Higher Secondary	26	36	76	138	40.6	34.0	33.5	34.8
Graduate and Above	9	37	78	124	14.1	34.9	34.4	31.2
Illiterate	12	16	39	67	18.8	15.1	17.2	16.9
Missing/NR	0	0	1	1	0.0	0.0	0.4	0.3
Total	64	106	227	397	100.0	100.0	100.0	100.0

Table 3A.7.1 Distribution of 405 Surveyees by the Number of Children They Have in Different Regions

Region	*No Child*	*1–2 Children*	*3–4 Children*	*> 4 Children*	*Total*
North	29.5	56.8	13.6	0.0	100.0
South	21.6	71.6	6.7	0.0	100.0
East	33.8	58.8	6.3	1.3	100.0
West	29.3	53.1	15.0	2.7	100.0
Total	27.7	60.7	10.4	1.2	100.0

Table 3A.7.2 Percentage Distribution of the 405 Surveyees by Age and Number of Children

Age of the Surveyees	*Percentage Distribution of Surveyees by the Number of Children They Had*							
	Number of Children							
	0	*1*	*2*	*3*	*4*	*5*	*6*	*Total*
18–22	51.4	37.1	11.4	0.0	0.0	0.0	0.0	100.0
23–32	35.9	37.5	19.0	4.9	2.2	0.5	0.0	100.0
33–42	13.6	39.2	33.6	6.4	5.6	0.8	0.8	100.0
43–52	15.2	26.1	30.4	15.2	8.7	4.3	0.0	100.0
> 52	16.7	16.7	41.7	16.7	8.3	0.0	0.0	100.0
Total	27.4	36.1	24.9	6.5	4.0	1.0	0.2	100.0

Table 3A.7.3 Parents with Whom Children of the 405 Surveyees Are Staying

Region	*Surveyee*	*Her Male-spouse*	*Both of them*	*Others*	*Total*
North	78.95	14.04	7.02	0.00	100.00
South	85.19	9.26	0.00	5.56	100.00
East	84.81	6.33	3.80	5.06	100.00
West	88.18	5.91	2.46	3.45	100.00
Total	85.63	7.98	2.40	3.99	100.00

Table 3A.8 Percentage Distribution of the 399 Surveyees by the Age at Marriage in Different Regions

State	*< 18*	*18–22*	*23–32*	*> 33*	*Total (excluding the missing cases)*
North	10.0	50.0	32.5	7.5	100.0
South	2.3	7.5	62.4	27.8	100.0
East	17.7	39.2	41.8	1.3	100.0
West	8.8	21.1	56.5	13.6	100.0
Total	8.5	23.1	53.1	15.3	100.0

Table 3A.9.1 Percentage Distribution of 405 Surveyees by the Type of Marriage They Had in Different Regions

Regions	*Arranged*	*Own Choice*	*Others*	*Total*
North	93.2	6.8	0.0	100.0
South	84.3	14.9	0.7	100.0
East	78.8	20.0	1.3	100.0
West	88.4	10.9	0.7	100.0
Total	85.7	13.6	0.7	100.0

Table 3A.9.2 Distribution of Surveyees by the Type of Arrangement of Marriage by Type of Marriage—Inter-caste or Interfaith

	Inter-caste	*Inter-religion*	*Same Caste, Same Religion Marriages*	*Total*
North	13	3	28	44
South	16	8	110	134
East	9	8	63	80
West	5	3	139	147
Total	43	22	340	405

Table 3A.10.1 Distribution of Surveyees by the Law under Which They Married in Different States

Regions	*Hindu Law*	*Muslim Law*	*Christian Law*	*Special Marriage Act*	*Others*	*Total (excluding the missing cases)*
North	81.8	15.9	0.0	2.3	0.0	100.0
South	82.0	8.3	6.8	2.3	0.8	100.0
East	86.3	3.8	0.0	10.0	0.0	100.0
West	53.1	37.4	0.0	3.4	6.1	100.0
Total	72.3	18.8	2.2	4.2	2.5	100.0

Table 3A.10.2 Distribution of Surveyees by the Law under Which They Married by the Type of Marriage They Had

Type of Marriage	*Hindu Law*	*Muslim Law*	*Christian Law*	*Special Marriage Act*	*Others*	*Total (excluding the missing cases)*
Arranged	74.1	19.9	2.3	2.6	1.2	100.0
Own Choice	61.1	13.0	0.0	14.8	11.1	100.0
Others	66.7	0.0	33.3	0.0	0.0	100.0
Total	72.3	18.8	2.2	4.2	2.5	100.0

Table 3A.11 Distribution of Surveyees by the Type of the Marital House in Different Regions

Frequency and Percentage	*Joint/ Extended*	*Nuclear*	*Total Per Cent*	*Joint/ Extended*	*Nuclear*	*Total*
North	87.5	12.5	100.0	28	4	32
South	81.25	18.75	100.0	104	24	128
East	96.43	3.57	100.0	54	2	56
West	90.71	9.29	100.0	127	13	140
Total	87.92	12.08	100.0	313	43	356

Table 3A.12 Distribution of Surveyees by the Time Duration of Marriage in Different Regions (Years)

Region	*< 1*	*1–2*	*2–6*	*6–10*	*> 10*	*Total*
North	20.9	7.0	37.2	2.3	32.6	100.0
South	11.9	14.3	27.0	17.5	29.4	100.0
East	23.4	15.6	28.6	16.9	15.6	100.0
West	11.8	13.9	31.3	16.0	27.1	100.0
Total	15.1	13.6	30.0	15.1	26.2	100.0

Table 3A.13 Percentage Distribution of the Surveyees by Their Status of Separation

Region	*Divorced*	*Separated*	*Widow*	*Total*
North	20.0	77.8	2.2	100.0
South	11.9	88.1	0.0	100.0
East	13.8	86.3	0.0	100.0
West	25.3	74.7	0.0	100.0
Total	18.0	81.7	0.2	100.0

Table 3A.14 Percentage Distribution of Surveyees by Reasons for Separation

Particulars	*North*	*South*	*East*	*West*	*Total*
Cruelty/Domestic Violence	85.4	72.7	81.0	67.8	74.0
Desertion	0.0	5.0	5.1	6.3	4.9
Both Desertion and Cruelty/ Domestic Violence	9.8	5.0	6.3	12.6	8.6
Cruelty/Domestic Violence and Impotency	0.0	0.8	0.0	0.7	0.5
Other Reasons	4.9	16.5	7.6	12.6	12.0
Total (Excluding NA, Missing, NR)	100.0	100.0	100.0	100.0	100.0

Tables from Chapter 4

Table 4A.1 Difference of Hours Spent on Housework by the Surveyees/Their Spouses during Marriage and after Separation (in Numbers)

	Wife					
	During Marriage		*After Separation*		*Male-Spouse*	
Hours of Work	*During Weekdays*	*Sundays or Off Days*	*During Weekdays*	*Sundays or Off Days*	*During Marriage*	*After Separation*
No Work	7	19	35	52	334	152
≤ 4 hrs	16	20	73	63	33	14
4–8 hrs	96	82	154	139	6	4
8–12 hrs	135	132	67	70	1	1
12–16 hrs	94	95	27	31	2	2
> 16 hrs	32	32	8	8		
No Response/Missing	25	25	41	42	29	232
Total	405	405	405	405	405	405
Total (excluding missing and no response cases)	380	380	364	363	376	173

Table 4A.2 Difference of Hours Spent on Housework by the Surveyees/Their Spouses during Marriage and after Separation (in Per Cent)

	Wife (in per cent)				*Male-Spouse (in per cent)*	
	During Marriage		*After Separation*			
Hours of Work	*During Weekdays*	*Sundays or Off Days*	*During Weekdays*	*Sundays or Off Days*	*During Marriage*	*After Separation*
No Work	1.8	5.0	9.6	14.3	82.5	37.5
≤ 4 hrs	4.2	5.3	20.1	17.4	8.1	3.5
4–8 hrs	25.3	21.6	42.3	38.3	1.5	1.0
8–12 hrs	35.5	34.7	18.4	19.3	0.2	0.2
12–16 hrs	24.7	25.0	7.4	8.5	0.5	0.5
> 16 hrs	8.4	8.4	2.2	2.2	0.0	0.0
No Response/Missing					7.2	57.3
Total					100.0	100.0
Total (excluding missing and no response cases)	100.0	100.0	100.0	100.0		

Table 4A.3 Whether the Burden of the Surveyees' Work Increased or Decreased Post Separation/Divorce

	Number of Surveyees				*Percentage Distribution within Regions*			
Regions	*Increased*	*Decreased*	*No Change*	*Total (Excluding Non-Responses)*	*Increased*	*Decreased*	*No Change*	*Total (Excluding Non-Response)*
North	11	14	6	31	35.5	45.2	19.4	100.0
South	60	51	20	131	45.8	38.9	15.3	100.0
East	17	31	7	55	30.9	56.4	12.7	100.0
West	63	47	33	143	44.1	32.9	23.1	100.0
Total	151	143	66	360	41.9	39.7	18.3	100.0

Table 4A.4 Pressures Experienced after Separation by Surveyees in Different Regions

	Number of Surveyees					*Percentage Distribution within Regions*			
Regions	*Anxiety/Stress/ Responsibility*	*Responsibility*	*Burden*	*Feel Free*	*Total*	*Anxiety/Stress/ Responsibility*	*Responsibility*	*Burden*	*Feel Free*
North	21	15	14	3	31	67.7	48.4	45.2	9.7
South	72	66	27	16	131	55.0	50.4	20.6	12.2
East	33	30	25	2	55	60.0	54.5	45.5	3.6
West	93	84	58	13	145	64.1	57.9	40.0	9.0
Total	219	195	124	34	362	60.5	53.9	34.3	9.4

Note: As this question brought out multiple responses from the surveyees, the sum of percentage for each region is greater than 100 per cent.

Table 4A.5 Impact of Marriage on the Earning Capacity of the Surveyees in Different Regions

	Number of Surveyees				*Percentage Distribution*			
Region	*Yes*	*No*	*Can't Say*	*Total*	*Yes*	*No*	*Can't Say*	*Total (Excluding Non-Responses)*
North	31	9	1	41	75.6	22.0	2.4	100.0
South	81	37	2	120	67.5	30.8	1.7	100.0
East	35	23	1	59	59.3	39.0	1.7	100.0
West	67	53	2	122	54.9	43.4	1.6	100.0
Total	214	122	6	342	62.6	35.7	1.8	100.0

Table 4A.6 Distribution of Surveyees Who Had to Give Up Work or Aspirations to Work because of Their Marriage in Different Regions

	Number of Surveyees			*Percentage Distribution*		
Region	*Yes*	*No*	*Total (Excluding NA and Missing cases)*	*Yes*	*No*	*Total (Excluding NA and Missing cases)*
North	6	6	12	50.0	50.0	100.0
South	45	36	81	55.6	44.4	100.0
East	11	12	23	47.8	52.2	100.0
West	24	42	66	36.4	63.6	100.0
Total	86	96	182	47.3	52.7	100.0

Table 4A.7 Comparison of Work Status of Surveyees with Other Colleagues of Same Age in Different Regions

	Number of Surveyees				
Region	*Worse*	*Good*	*Same*	*No Comparison*	*Total (Excluding Non-Responses*
North	17	6	4	12	39
South	53	9	13	23	98
East	46	11	6	9	72
West	43	12	11	58	124
Total	159	38	34	102	333
	Percentage Distribution within the Regions				
North	43.6	15.4	10.3	30.8	100.0
South	54.1	9.2	13.3	23.5	100.0
East	63.9	15.3	8.3	12.5	100.0
West	34.7	9.7	8.9	46.8	100.0
Total	47.7	11.4	10.2	30.6	100.0

Note: The distribution has been normalised to the applicable cases only.

Table 4A.8 Did Your Male Spouse Benefit by the Household Work or Talents and Skills of the Wife

Regions	*Yes*	*No*	*Can't Say*	*Total (Excluding the Non-Response Cases)*	*No. of Reporting Cases (Total Sample)*
North	90.5	9.5	0.0	100.0	42 (44)
South	70.5	14.4	15.2	100.0	132 (134)
East	85.5	9.2	5.3	100.0	76 (80)
West	82.8	7.6	9.7	100.0	145 (147)
Total	80.0	10.4	9.6	100.0	395 (405)

Tables from Chapter 5

Table 5A.1 Distribution of Surveyees in Different Regions by the Type of Marital Home

	Number of Surveyees					
	FIL–MIL House	*Your or Your Husband's House*	*Parents' House*	*Others*	*Non-Response*	*Total*
North	23	2	0	5	14	44
South	74	30	3	25	2	134
East	42	9	1	4	24	80
West	103	21	0	22	1	147
Total	242	62	4	56	41	405
	Percentage Distribution within Regions					
	FIL–MIL House	*Your or Your Husband's House*	*Parents' House*	*Others*	*Non-Response*	*Total*
North	52.3	4.5	0.0	11.4	31.8	100.0
South	55.2	22.4	2.2	18.7	1.5	100.0
East	52.5	11.3	1.3	5.0	30.0	100.0
West	70.1	14.3	0.0	15.0	0.7	100.0
Total	59.8	15.3	1.0	13.8	10.1	100.0

Table 5A.2 Change in the Husband's Lifestyle Post Separation or Divorce

	Number of Surveyees				
	Change Better	*Change Worse*	*No Change*	*Not Known/ Non-Response*	*Total*
North	11	0	4	29	44
South	47	12	29	46	134
East	27	2	7	44	80
West	33	14	45	55	147
Total	118	28	85	174	405
	Percentage Distribution within Each Region				
North	25.0	0.0	9.1	65.9	100.0
South	35.1	9.0	21.6	34.3	100.0
East	33.8	2.5	8.8	55.0	100.0
West	22.4	9.5	30.6	37.4	100.0
Total	29.1	6.9	21.0	43.0	100.0

Table 5A.3 In Whose Possession Were the Assets after Separation?

	In Whose Possession Were the Following Assets after Separation (Numbers)					*In Whose Possession Were the Following Assets after Separation (per cent)*			
	In-Laws	*Wife*	*Both*	*Others*	*Total*	*In-Laws*	*Wife*	*Both*	*Others*
House	170	41	5	6	222	76.6	18.5	2.3	2.7
Land	47	19	0	2	68	69.1	27.9	0.0	2.9
Other Immovable Property	13	4	0	0	17	76.5	23.5	0.0	0.0
Vehicle	105	30	1	0	136	77.2	22.1	0.7	0.0
Jewellery	102	65	1	1	169	60.4	38.5	0.6	0.6
Television	102	60	0	4	166	61.4	36.1	0.0	2.4
Fridge	75	30	0	7	112	67.0	26.8	0.0	6.3
Other Electronic Goods	47	21	0	2	70	67.1	30.0	0.0	2.9
Cash in Bank or Other Sources	23	45	0	0	68	33.8	66.2	0.0	0.0
Deposits	4	9	1	2	16	25.0	56.3	6.3	12.5
Mutual Funds and Shares	2	8	0	0	10	20.0	80.0	0.0	0.0
Insurance	10	14	0	0	24	41.7	58.3	0.0	0.0
Other Savings	3	4	0	1	8	37.5	50.0	0.0	12.5

Table 5A.4 Whether the Surveyee Was Getting Any Further Support from Her Male-spouse or In-laws

	Yes	*No*	*Not Applicable*	*Total (excluding missing cases)*	*No of Respondents (excluding the missing cases)*
North	4.5	93.2	2.3	100.0	44
South	2.9	95.1	1.9	100.0	103
East	5.0	92.5	2.5	100.0	80
West	3.9	90.6	5.5	100.0	127
Total	4.0	92.7	3.4	100.0	354

Table 5A.5 Opinion of the Surveyees in Different Regions on the Rights of the Spouses to Receive Maintenance

	Yes, They Should	*No, They Should Not*	*Can't Say*	*Total*	*Total*
North	9.5	90.5	0.0	100.0	42
South	8.9	84.8	6.3	100.0	112
East	1.9	98.1	0.0	100.0	52
West	12.1	87.2	0.7	100.0	141
Total	9.2	88.5	2.3	100.0	347

Table 5A.6 Opinion of the Surveyees in Different Regions on the Subject of Sharing of Household Assets Equally with Husband

	Yes	*No*	*Can't Say*	*Total*	*No. of Responses*
North	93.2	6.8	0.0	100.0	44
South	77.0	15.0	8.0	100.0	113
East	80.6	19.4	0.0	100.0	72
West	76.2	22.4	1.4	100.0	143
Total	79.3	17.7	3.0	100.0	372

Table 5A.7 Percentage of Surveyees Who Could and Who Could Not Prove Their Husbands' Income in Court or Outside in Different Regions (as Percentage of the Responding Cases in Each Region)

	Yes, Could Prove	*No, Could Not Prove*	*Total*	*No. of Responses (excluding the non-response and missing cases)*
North	40.0	60.0	100.0	25
South	40.8	59.2	100.0	71
East	40.6	59.4	100.0	32
West	41.4	58.6	100.0	58
Total	40.9	59.1	100.0	186

Table 5A.8 Percentage of Surveyees Whose Spouses Tried to Conceal Their Income in Different Regions (as Percentage of the Responding Cases in Each Region)

	Yes	*No*	*Do Not Know*	*Total*	*No. of Responses (excluding the non-response and missing cases)*
North	75.0	21.4	3.6	100.0	28
South	46.5	52.1	1.4	100.0	71
East	78.1	21.9	0.0	100.0	32
West	51.8	48.2	0.0	100.0	56
Total	57.8	41.2	1.1	100.0	187

Table 5A.9 Percentage of Surveyees Whose Spouses Transferred Assets to Others during Court Proceedings in Different Regions (as Percentage of the Responding Cases in Each Region)

	Yes	*No*	*Do Not Know*	*Total*	*No. of Responses (excluding the non-response and missing cases)*
North	23.3	16.7	60.0	100.0	30
South	19.4	55.6	25.0	100.0	72
East	23.5	47.1	29.4	100.0	34
West	8.8	73.7	17.5	100.0	57
Total	17.6	53.4	29.0	100.0	193

Table 5A.10 Percentage of Surveyees Who Wanted Their Spouses to Disclose Their Income instead of Proving It, in Different Regions (as Percentage of the Responding Cases in Each Region)

	Yes	*No/NA*	*Do Not Know*	*Total*	*No. of Responses (excluding the non-response and missing cases)*
North	97.7	2.3	0.0	100.0	43
South	94.8	5.2	0.0	100.0	96
East	81.8	9.1	9.1	100.0	33
West	86.5	11.5	1.9	100.0	104
Total	90.6	7.6	1.8	100.0	276

Table 5A.11.1 Total Value of *Stridhan* including Jewellery (Number of Responses and the Percentage Distribution)

	Number of Surveyees								
*Stridhan**	*0–5*	*5–10*	*10–20*	*20–50*	*50–100*	*100–500*	*> 500*	*Jewellery and Things*	*Total No. of Responses*
North	2	1	3	2	5	6	4	9	32
South	1	1	3	1	13	23	16	36	94
East	1	0	1	2	6	9	1	12	32
West	7	1	14	27	16	24	5	12	106
Total	11	3	21	32	40	62	26	69	264

	Percentage Distribution within Each Region								
*Stridhan**	*0–5*	*5–10*	*10–20*	*20–50*	*50–100*	*100–500*	*> 500*	*Jewellery and Things*	*Total*
North	6.3	3.1	9.4	6.3	15.6	18.8	12.5	28.1	100.0
South	1.1	1.1	3.2	1.1	13.8	24.5	17.0	38.3	100.0
East	3.1	0.0	3.1	6.3	18.8	28.1	3.1	37.5	100.0
West	6.6	0.9	13.2	25.5	15.1	22.6	4.7	11.3	100.0
Total	4.2	1.1	8.0	12.1	15.2	23.5	9.8	26.1	100.0

Note: **Stridhan* is the total value of *stridhan* including jewellery (in ₹ thousand).

Table 5A.11.2 Total Value of Dowry from Parents in Terms of Rupees

	Number of Surveyees								
*Dowry**	*0–5*	*5–10*	*10–20*	*20–50*	*50–100*	*100–500*	*> 500*	*Jewellery and Things*	*Total*
North	1	0	1	2	9	20	1	1	35
South	3	6	5	6	8	26	19	2	75
East	0	1	1	7	10	15	1	0	35
West	3	4	8	15	18	22	5	2	77
Total	7	11	15	30	45	83	26	5	222

	Percentage Distribution within Each Region								
*Dowry**	*0–5*	*5–10*	*10–20*	*20–50*	*50–100*	*100–500*	*> 500*	*Jewellery and Things*	*Total*
North	2.9	0.0	2.9	5.7	25.7	57.1	2.9	2.9	100.0
South	4.0	8.0	6.7	8.0	10.7	34.7	25.3	2.7	100.0
East	0.0	2.9	2.9	20.0	28.6	42.9	2.9	0.0	100.0
West	3.9	5.2	10.4	19.5	23.4	28.6	6.5	2.6	100.0
Total	3.2	5.0	6.8	13.5	20.3	37.4	11.7	2.3	100.0

Note: *Dowry is the total value of dowry the parents of the surveyees gave during marriage (in ₹ thousand).

Table 5A.11.3 Co-relation between Parents' Income and Dowry Given at the Time of Marriage of the Surveyees by Their Parents, as Distributed between Caste-Groups

		Total Dowry Given at Time of Marriage						
	Parents' Income	*< 10,000*	*10,000 to 50,000*	*50,000 to 100,000*	*100,000 to 500,000*	*> 500,000*	*Jewellery and Other Things*	*Total*
SC/ST	< 5,000	19.0	19.0	23.8	38.1	0.0	0.0	21
	5,000–20,000	0.0	40.0	20.0	40.0	0.0	0.0	5
	20,000–100,000	0.0	0.0	0.0	0.0	100.0	0.0	1
	Total	14.8	22.2	22.2	37.0	3.7	0.0	27
OBC	< 5,000	5.9	35.3	23.5	17.6	11.8	5.9	17
	5,000–20,000	0.0	25.0	8.3	33.3	33.3	0.0	12
	20,000–100,000	0.0	0.0	0.0	0.0	100.0	0.0	1
	> 100,000	50.0	50.0	0.0	0.0	0.0	0.0	2
	Total	6.3	31.3	15.6	21.9	21.9	3.1	32
General	< 5,000	6.8	20.5	29.5	36.4	4.5	2.3	44
	5,000–20,000	2.6	15.8	15.8	50.0	13.2	2.6	38
	20,000–100,000	0.0	0.0	11.1	77.8	11.1	0.0	9
	> 100,000	0.0	0.0	0.0	0.0	100.0	0.0	1
	Total	4.3	16.3	21.7	45.7	9.8	2.2	92
Total	< 5,000	9.8	23.2	26.8	32.9	4.9	2.4	82
	5,000–20,000	1.8	20.0	14.5	45.5	16.4	1.8	55
	20,000–100,000	0.0	0.0	9.1	63.6	27.3	0.0	11
	> 100,000	33.3	33.3	0.0	0.0	33.3	0.0	3
	Total	6.6	20.5	20.5	39.1	11.3	2.0	151

Note: Three persons did not state the value of jewellery and other items given as dowry.

Table 5A.12 Percentage Distribution of the Surveyees in Different Regions as Per Incomes of Their Parents (in Terms of ₹ Thousand)

	Number of Surveyees									
	Surveyees' Parents' Income									
Region	*No income*	*< 1,000*	*1,000–5,000*	*5,000–10,000*	*10,000–20,000*	*20,000–50,000*	*50,000–100,000*	*>100,000*	*Total (excluding NR)*	*Total*
North	3	1	16	7	4	1	1	1	34	44
South	14	3	24	13	17	3	1	3	78	134
East	8	2	11	12	3	3	0	0	39	80
West	14	6	60	19	3	6	0	1	109	147
Total	39	12	111	51	27	13	2	5	260	405
	Percentage Distribution of the Surveyees within the Region									*Per cent of Responses*
North	8.8	2.9	47.1	20.6	11.8	2.9	2.9	2.9	100.0	77.3
South	17.9	3.8	30.8	16.7	21.8	3.8	1.3	3.8	100.0	58.2
East	20.5	5.1	28.2	30.8	7.7	7.7	0.0	0.0	100.0	48.8
West	12.8	5.5	55.0	17.4	2.8	5.5	0.0	0.9	100.0	74.1
Total	15.0	4.6	42.7	19.6	10.4	5.0	0.8	1.9	100.0	64.2

Table 5A.13.1 Dowry as a Financial Burden on the Parents

	Number of Surveyees										
	Did your parents/family borrow money to acquire the dowry, stridhan *or gifts?*			*Was your marriage a great financial burden on your family?*			*With whom are these dowry,* stridhan *or gift items now?*				
	Yes	*No*	*Total*	*Yes*	*No*	*Total*	*Wife*	*In-laws and male spouse (1 + 2)*	*FIL/MIL (1)*	*Male spouse (2)*	*Total*
North	23	19	42	19	11	30	11	33	17	16	44
South	68	45	113	79	46	125	28	69	20	49	97
East	18	34	52	11	20	31	23	21	5	16	44
West	73	58	131	61	80	141	33	91	60	31	124
Total	182	156	338	170	157	327	95	214	102	112	309

Table 5A.13.2 Whether the Dowry, *Stridhan*, Gift Items Post Separation or Divorce Are with Surveyees (This Table Is Derived from Table 5A.13.1)

Percentage	*Wife*	*FIL/MIL*	*Husband*	*Total (excluding NA and missing cases)*
North	25.0	38.6	36.4	100.0
South	28.9	20.6	50.5	100.0
East	52.3	11.4	36.4	100.0
West	26.6	48.4	25.0	100.0
Total	30.7	33.0	36.2	100.0

Table 5A.13.3 Whether the Dowry, *Stridhan*, Gift Items Post Separation or Divorce Are with Surveyees (This Table Is Derived from Table 5A.13.1)

Regions	*Wife*	*FIL/MIL*	*Male Spouse/ Husband*	*Total*	*Regions*	*Wife*	*In-laws (male spouse/ husband and FIL/MIL)*
North	11	17	16	44	North	11	33
South	28	20	49	97	South	28	69
East	23	5	16	44	East	23	21
West	33	60	31	124	West	33	91
Total	95	102	112	309	Total	95	214

Table 5A.14 Surveyees Who Had to Approach the Police to Get Back the *Stridhan*/ Dowry/Gift Items and Other Personal Items

	In Numbers				*In Percentage*		
	Yes	*No*	*Total*		*Yes*	*No*	*Total*
North	29	15	44	North	65.9	34.1	100.0
South	48	76	124	South	38.7	61.3	100.0
East	22	34	56	East	39.3	60.7	100.0
West	48	95	143	West	33.6	66.4	100.0
Total	147	220	367	Total	40.1	59.9	100.0

Tables from Chapter 6

Table 6A.1 List of the Average Maintenance Awarded to the Surveyees

State/Place	Salary of Wife	Salary of Husband	Maintenance as Percentage of Husband's Income	Total Monthly Maintenance Paid to Wife and Child	Time Taken	Process
Kolkata	500	25,000	16.0	4,000		Family Settlement
UP	500	25,000	4.0	1,000	6 years	Court
UP	1,000	5,000	20.0	1,000	6 months	Court
Jaipur	1,000	15,000	13.3	2000	4 years	Court
Orissa	1,000	50,000	0.6	300	3 years	Court
Kerala	1,000	56,000	1.6	900	17 years	Court
Kolkata	1,000	7,000	21.4	1,500	8 months	Court
Pune	1,500	7,000	28.6	2,000	NR	Conciliation
Bhandup	1,500	10,000	13.0	1,300	4 months	Court
Chennai	2,000	7,500	13.3	1,000	1 year	Court
Bangalore	2,000	14,000	14.3	2,000		Court
Jaipur	2,500	5,000	24.0	1,200	3 years	Court
Chennai	2,500	15,000	33.3	5,000	NR	Court
UP	2,500	15,000	13.3	2,000	6 months	Court
Bhavnagar	3,000	8,000	43.8	3,500	2 years	Court
Jaipur	3,000	15,000	20.0	3,000	4 months	Court
Darjeeling	3,000	15,000	13.3	2,000		Court
Jaipur	3,500	10,000	5.0	500	5 months	Court
Goa	3,900	15,000	23.3	3,500	3 years	Court
UP	4,000	15,000	5.3	800	7 years	Court
Kolkata	4,500	100,000	12.0	12,000	4 months	Court
Guwahati	5,000	15,000	6.0	900	3 years	Court
Goa	5,000	20,000	1.8	350	1 year	Court
Darjeeling	8,000	40,000	5.0	2,000		Family Conciliation
Goa	10,000	100,000	10.0	10,000	NR	Other
Delhi	25,000	250,000	4.0	10,000	4 months	Court
Goa	30,000	100,000	5.0	5,000	NR	Court
Orissa	Nil	6,000	16.7	1,000	2 years	Court
Hyderabad	Nil	8,000	31.3	2,500	1.5 year	Court
Chennai	Nil	8,000	12.5	1,000	7 years	Court
Orissa	Nil	9,000	14.4	1,300	3 years	Court
Orissa	Nil	10,000	25.0	2,500	2 years	Court
Guwahati	Nil	10,000	15.0	1,500	2 years	Court
Kolkata	Nil	10,000	4.0	400	2 years	Court
Bhavnagar	Nil	12,000	12.5	1,500	0.2 year	Court
Chennai	Nil	12,500	24.4	3,050	3 years	Court

(Continued)

(Continued)

State/Place	Salary of Wife	Salary of Husband	Maintenance as Percentage of Husband's Income	Total Monthly Maintenance Paid to Wife and Child	Time Taken	Process
Guwahati	Nil	13,000	16.5	2,140	9 years	Court
Kerala	Nil	13,486	22.2	3,000	4 years	Court
Kerala	Nil	14,000	17.9	2,500	3 months	Court
Kolkata	Nil	15,000	16.7	2,500	8 months	Court
Chennai	Nil	15,000	6.7	1,000	NR	Court
Chennai	Nil	20,000	25.0	5,000	NR	Court
Orissa	Nil	20,000	1.5	300	2 years	Court
Bhandup	Nil	22,000	3.4	750	1 year	Court
Delhi	Nil	25,000	8.0	2,000	7 months	Court
Kolkata	Nil	25,000	6.0	1,500	4.5 months	Court
Orissa	Nil	25,000	2.0	500	7 years	Court
Kolkata	Nil	30,000	13.3	4,000	4 months	Court
UP	Nil	30,000	1.7	500	7 years	Court
Pune	Nil	45,000	11.1	5,000	NR	Court
Hyderabad	Nil	50,000	3.0	1,500	3 years	Court
Goa	Nil	60,000	16.7	10,000	NR	Other
Hyderabad	Nil	62,000	24.2	15,000	More than 1 year	Court
Chennai	Nil	100,000	35.0	35,000	NR	Court
Jaipur	Nil	100,000	10.0	10,000	2 years	Reconciliation Centre
Delhi	Nil	500,000	9.0	45,000	3 years	Court
Delhi	Nil	500,000	2.0	10,000	2 years	Court
Delhi	Nil	700,000	5.7	40,000	4 years	Court
Kolkata	Nil	10,000	13.0	1,300	2 years	Court
Kolkata	Nil	35,000	3.4	1,200	1 year	Court

Table 6A.2 How Long Did the Court or Other Process Take in Different Regions (in Years)?

	Regions	*< 1 year*	*1–3 years*	*3–5 years*	*5–10 years*	*> 10 years*	*Total*	*Total*
From Court	North	**42.9**	28.6	14.3	14.3	0.0	100.0	7
	South	**37.8**	27.0	18.9	5.4	**10.8**	100.0	37
	East	16.7	**38.9**	27.8	16.7	0.0	100.0	18
	West	**44.0**	36.0	4.0	16.0	0.0	100.0	25
Through	North	**100.0**	0.0	0.0	0.0	0.0	100.0	1
Conciliation/	South	**25.0**	**25.0**	**25.0**	**25.0**	0.0	100.0	4
Family	East	**100.0**	0.0	0.0	0.0	0.0	100.0	3
Discussion	West	**50.0**	40.0	0.0	10.0	0.0	100.0	10
Other Process	North							0
	South							0
	East							0
	West	0.0	**100.0**	0.0	0.0	0.0	100.0	2
Case Pending	North	**52.2**	8.7	21.7	17.4	0.0	100.0	23
	South	**64.3**	21.4	14.3	0.0	0.0	100.0	14
	East	38.5	**48.7**	7.7	5.1	0.0	100.0	39
	West	**45.5**	36.4	9.1	9.1	0.0	100.0	22

Tables for Chapter 7

Table 7A.1 Frequency/Percentage of Surveyees Who Had to Face Hostility or Prejudice on Account of Their Separation

	Number of Surveyees				*Percentage Distribution within the Regions*		
Regions	*Yes*	*No*	*Total*	*Regions*	*Yes*	*No*	*Total*
North	31	12	43	North	72.1	27.9	100.0
South	73	55	128	South	57.0	43.0	100.0
East	24	32	56	East	42.9	57.1	100.0
West	73	70	143	West	51.0	49.0	100.0
Total	201	169	370	Total	54.3	45.7	100.0

Table 7A.2 Percentage of Surveyees Whose Interaction with Others Got Affected due to Their Separation

Regions	*Relatives*	*Landlords*	*School Authorities*	*Employers*	*Other Authorities*	*Other Persons*	*No Effect*	*No Response*	*Total*
North	22	9	0	9	8	17	12	1	44
South	59	28	0	32	32	45	41	12	134
East	16	4	0	4	4	8	36	24	56
West	37	17	1	19	17	47	72	6	147
Total	134	58	1	64	61	117	161	43	381

Table 7A.3 Who Were the Decision-makers during Marriage, in the Marital Home regarding Various Tasks?

	Frequency Distribution of the Decision-makers during Marriage					
Nature of tasks	*Both*	*Wife*	*Husband*	*FIL/MIL*	*Others*	*Total*
Education of child	14	44	56	27	5	146
Expenditure in house	23	45	136	112	16	332
Expenditure outside the house	21	37	139	106	16	319
Expenditure on investment	6	22	92	38	6	164
Applying for loans	8	21	92	31	5	157
Applying for jobs	7	31	87	26	5	156
Buying jewellery	8	23	85	55	9	180
Choosing place of residence	15	33	124	61	55	288
Health-related decisions	22	50	123	87	18	300
Children's marriage	2	2	19	25	1	49
Entertainment	27	24	66	25	49	191
Holidays	16	22	79	23	5	145
Whom to meet	22	49	150	81	11	313
Where to go	23	46	149	87	11	316
What to cook	23	73	118	102	14	330
What to wear	11	133	111	69	9	333

Table 7A.4 Who Is the Decision-maker regarding Various Tasks after Separation?

	Frequency Distribution of the Decision-makers after Separation					
Nature of Tasks	*Jointly with Parents*	*Wife*	*Daughter/ Son*	*Parents*	*Others*	*Total*
Education of child	4	122	7	32	1	166
Expenditure in house	15	181	3	120	15	334
Expenditure outside the house	14	173	1	110	13	311
Expenditure on investment	4	98	2	45	3	152
Applying for loans	6	90	2	36	2	136
Applying for jobs	6	126	2	35	3	172
Buying jewellery	6	111	2	59	4	182
Choosing place of residence	7	139	2	86	6	240
Health-related decisions	13	185	2	102	10	312
Children's marriage	1	37	2	14		54
Entertainment	7	117	2	31	3	160
Holidays	6	111	2	31	2	152
Whom to meet	11	229	2	80		322
Where to go	11	237	2	76		326
What to cook	17	238	8	73		336
What to wear	3	289	2	39	2	335

Table 7A.5.1 Correlation between Education and the Identity Cards Held by the Surveyees

	Ration Card	*Voter ID Card*	*Driving License*	*Passport*	*Total (number)*
Primary	65.2	66.7	2.9	2.9	69
Secondary	68.5	69.6	1.1	4.3	92
Higher Secondary	75.0	83.3	8.3	8.3	48
Graduate	48.1	68.5	31.5	25.9	54
Postgraduate	65.6	81.3	28.1	21.9	32
Professional	47.1	61.8	52.9	50.0	34
Others	83.3	66.7	66.7	50.0	6
Illiterate	66.7	65.2	2.9	0.0	69
Total	63.9	70.0	14.1	12.6	404

Table 7A.5.2 Correlation between Income and the Identity Cards Held by the Surveyees

	Ration Card	*Voter ID Card*	*Driving License*	*Passport*	*Total*
No Income	101	104	17	19	168
< 1,000	31	35	0	1	49
1,000–2,000	43	45	4	5	62
2,000–6,000	45	54	6	5	67
6,000–10,000	11	13	3	1	16
10,000–15,000	8	8	6	4	11
> 15,000	17	22	21	16	30
Total	256	281	57	51	403

Questionnaire

IDRC Project on Financial Status of Divorced and Separated Women

Section I

General Information

Personal Information

1. Name:
2. Age: Date of Birth:
3. Address of Present Residence:
4. Mother's/Father's (Name and address):
5. Husband's name/address:
6. Residential Status: Living Alone With Parents
   With Brother/Sister With Others
   Present Occupation: Self: Husband:
7. Income: (a) Present Monthly Household Income: Self:
   Others (Specify):
   (b) Husband's Income:
8. Religion: Hindu Muslim Christian
   Other (Specify)
9. Caste/Biradari: SC ST OBC Other (Specify)
10. Educational Qualification: Nil Primary
    Secondary Higher Secondary BA/BSc
    MA/MSc Professional Other (Specify)

11. Children

Name of Children	Sex	Age	Staying with Whom		
			Mother	Father	Other (Specify)

Marital Status

12. Date of Marriage: Age at Marriage:

13. Type of Marriage: (a) Arranged Own Choice
Other (specify)
(b) Inter Caste (c) Inter religion

14. Under what law were you married:

15. How many persons and who all were living in your marital home? (Specify relationship)

16. Date of Separation/Divorce:

17. Status of Separation: Divorced Separated Pending Case

18. Nature of Pending Case: Divorce Separation Restitution
Maintenance Recovery of dowry/personal property
DVA 498-A 406 IPC others (specify)

19. Cases Filed by Whom and under What Law: (give description and reasons, if required on a separate sheet)

Cases	Husband	Wife	Others
Divorce/Separation/ Restitution			
Maintenance/ Compensation			

For Residence			
Recovery of Dowry 406,IPC/DPA			
Dowry Harassment(Crl) 498A/DPA			
Cruelty/Domestic Violence(Civil)DVA			
Cruelty/Domestic Violence(Crl)498-A			
Custody			
Others			

20. Reasons for Separation/Divorce: (These can be detailed in a separate sheet and also give case details if any.)

Section II

Work Status and Earning Capacity

21. (a) Employment and Work of Wife

Marital Status	**Type of Work**			
	Employed/ Salaried	**Home-based**	**Self Employed**	**Professional/ Other (Specify)**
Before Marriage				
During Marriage				

Presently After Separation				

(b) Employment and Work of Husband

Marital Status	Type of Work			
	Employed/ Salaried	Home-based	Self Employed	Professional/ Other (Specify)
Before Marriage				
During Marriage				
Presently After Separation				

22. (a) Domestic Work by Wife

Number of Hours	During Marriage		After Separation	
	Weekdays	Sunday/ Off Day	Weekdays	Sunday/ Off Day
4 am–6 am				
6 am–8 am				
8 am–10 am				
10 am–12 pm				
12 pm–2 pm				
2 pm–4 pm				
4 pm–6 pm				

6 pm–8 pm				
8 pm–10 pm				
10 pm–12 am				
> 12 am				

(b) Domestic Work by Husband

Number of Hours	During Marriage		After Separation	
	Weekdays	Sunday/ Off Day	Weekdays	Sunday/ Off Day
4 am–6 am				
6 am–8 am				
8 am–10 am				
10 am–12 pm				
12 pm–2 pm				
2 pm–4 pm				
4 pm–6 pm				
6 pm–8 pm				
8 pm–10 pm				
10 pm–12 am				
> 12 am				

23. Has the burden of your work increased or decreased post separation/ divorce? Give details and reasons.

24. What do you feel about your work in terms of (a) anxiety or stress (b) responsibility (c) burden?

25. (a) Details of Wife's Monthly Income

Marital Status	From Employment	From Assets and Savings	Income from Other Sources	Total
Before Marriage				
During Marriage				
Presently After Separation				

(b) Details of Husband's Monthly Income

Marital Status	From Employment	From Assets and Savings	Income from Other Sources	Total
Before Marriage				
During Marriage				
Presently After Separation				

26. Loss of earning capacity:
    Did your marriage affect your career? If so, how?

27. Did you have to give up work?

28. Did your separation/divorce affect your career? If so how?

29. How does your work status and income compare with other colleagues (married or unmarried men/unmarried women) of your age group and comparative experience?

30. Did your husband benefit because of your household work or talents and skills in terms of his money, career, saving, assets?

Section III

Family Status and Lifestyle

31. Was your marital home a joint family house
father-in-law's/mother-in-law's house your/your husband's house
your mother's or father's house other's (specify)

32. Household expenditure during marriage of both the spouses and children and after separation of the wife and the children if any

Items	Amount		Source	
	During Marriage	After Separation	During Marriage	After Separation
Residence				
• Food				
• Education				
• Medical expenses				
• Travelling expenses				
• Entertainment				

• Clothing and toiletries				
• Electricity and water				
• Telephone/ mobile				

33. Is there any change in your husband's lifestyle post separation/divorce? Has it improved? If so, in what ways?

34. (a) Information on Household Assets (Movable and Immovable)

Assets	**During Marriage**	**After Separation (wife)**	**Source of Acquisition**	**In Whose Possession Now**
Immovable assets • House • Land • Any other immovable property				
Movable assets • Vehicle • Jewellery (attach list) • TV • Fridge • Other electronic goods				

Financial assets • Cash in bank/ other • Deposits • Mutual funds/ shares • Insurance • Other savings				

(b) Husband's Household Assets Now (Movable and Immovable)

Assets	**Description**	**Source of Acquisition**	**Time of Acquisition During Marriage or after Separation**
Immovable assets • House • Land • Any other immovable property			
Movable assets • Vehicle • Jewellery • TV • Fridge • Other electronic goods			

Financial assets • Cash in bank/ other • Deposits • Mutual funds/ shares • Insurance • Other savings			

Section IV

Spousal and Child Support

35. Did you get any spousal support/maintenance for yourself and how much?

36. Did you get any support/maintenance for the child and how much?

37. Are you satisfied with the quantum of maintenance?

38. Process and length of time taken to get maintenance for spouse and child:

    - from court (if so, nature of proceeding Interim Final and Execution)
    - through conciliation/family discussion
    - Or any other process (Specify)

39. How long did the court or other process take (specify time period) and why (please give details)?

40. Was any appeal/s filed against the maintenance order? If so, by whom (give details)?

41. Process and time taken for the appeal.

42. Do you get any other/further support from your husband/in-laws or anyone else apart from court order/informal settlement? If yes, how much and why?

43. Did you get a lump sum payment or monthly maintenance payment?

44. Do you get these payments? yes no

    - If you get your monthly payments do you get them regularly?
    - What were the main reasons, according to you, for the delay in getting the payments (give details)?

45. Did you have to file an execution application?

46. How long did this execution application take? What was the result (give details)?

47. Do you feel you are entitled to share the house-hold assets equally with your husband? yes no
    - If yes why (give details of reasons)

48. Do you feel that your husband should also have a right to maintenance? yes no
    - If not, why?

49. Proof of income:

    - Could you prove the income of your husband in the court or outside? yes no
    - What were the difficulties that you encountered?

- Did your spouse try to conceal his income? yes no
  a. If yes specify?

- Did your husband transfer any assets during the court proceedings or after you were separated? yes no
  b. If yes specify what assets?

- In whose name did he transfer the assets?

50. Should your husband be asked to disclose his income instead of you proving it?

51. Dowry and *stridhan* (attach list in separate sheet):

By Whom	Before Marriage	During Marriage	After Marriage	Remarks
Parents				
Brothers/Sisters				
Relatives				
In-laws				
Others				

52. Total value of *stridhan* including jewellery:
    (a) From Parents
    (b) Other Relatives
    (c) In-laws

- Total Value of Dowry from Parents (in Rupees)

(a) From Parents
(b) Brother/Sister
(c) From Others (Specify)

53. What is the income of your parents?

54. Did your parents/family borrow money to acquire the dowry, *stridhan*/ gifts? If so, how much?

    - Was your marriage a great financial burden on your family?
      Yes No

55. With whom are these dowry *stridhan*/gift items now?

56. What items were given to your husband and in-laws during marriage and after? (Attach sheet if necessary.)

57. Did you have to go to the police/file a criminal complaint/go to court to get your dowry and other personal belongings including *stridhan*/ gifts given to you by your relatives and friends and *stridhan* from your in-laws?
    Yes No

    - If yes, what happened during the proceedings and how long did it take? (Attach a sheet if necessary.)

Section V

Social Status, Mobility, Skills and Decision-making

58. Did you face hostility or prejudice on account of your separation?

59. Did it affect you in terms of interaction with:

    - relatives landlords school authorities employers other authorities other persons (specify)?

    - If so, describe the nature of discrimination.

60. Who makes decisions regarding:

Nature of Tasks	During Marriage	After Separation	Remarks
Education of child			
Expenditure in house			
Expenditure outside the house			
Expenditure on Investments			
Applying for loans			
Applying for jobs			
Buying jewellery			
Choosing place of residence			
Health-related decisions			
Children's marriage			
Entertainment			
Holidays			
Whom to meet			
Where to go			
What to cook			
What to wear			

61. Did you learn any new skills or did you have to perform any new tasks after your separation?

Nature of Tasks	During Marriage	After Separation	Remarks
Paying bills			
Shopping for household goods			
Keeping household accounts			
Operating bank account			
Repairing household items			
Going to children's school			
Driving a car/two wheeler			
Acquiring assets			
Travelling inside the city			
Travelling out of town for work or other purposes			
Booking rail and air tickets			
Meeting/socialising with own friends			

Meeting/socialising with common friends			
Meeting/socialising with own relatives			
Meeting/socialising with husband's relatives			
Acquiring new friends			
Daily hours of leisure time/time for yourself			
Do you read newspapers			
Additional technical/ educational skills			
Operating Computer/ Accessing Internet			
Others			

62. Do you have: ration card voter ID card driving license passport?

Consent Form

I consent to being interviewed through this questionnaire. The purpose and objectives have been explained to me. I want/do not want my name to be mentioned during any discussions of the questionnaire.

....
Signature

Bibliography

List of Books and Journals

Agarwal, Bina. 'The Idea of Gender Equality: From Legislative Vision to Everyday Family Practice', in RomilaThapar (ed.), *India: Another Millennium?* p. 48. New Delhi: Penguin Books, 2001.

B., Sivaramaya. *Matrimonial Property Law in India*, p. 1. New Delhi: Oxford University Press, 1999.

Budget Analysis Rajasthan Centre. *The Destitution of Widows in Rajasthan: What Role has the State Played?* Working Paper No. 4. Jaipur: BARC, 2007.

Central Statistical Organisation. *Report of the Time Use Survey*. New Delhi: Central Statistical Organisation, 2009.

Cossman, Brenda. 'Contesting Conservatisms, Family Feuds and the Privatization of Dependency', *American Journal of Gender, Social Policy and Law* 13, p. 415.

Deccan Herald News Service, 'No Alimony for Woman Who Desert Husband', *The Deccan Herald*. New Delhi, 18 November 2010.

Desai, Satyajeet. *Mulla's Hindu Law*. Nagpur: LexisNexis-Butterworths Wardha, 2010, 21st edition.

Economic Research Foundation. *Economic Rights and Entitlements of Separated and Divorced Women,* Report of Regional Seminar Proceedings 2008–2009. New Delhi: ERF, 2010.

Eggebeen, David J. and Daniel T. Lichter. 'Race, Family Structure, and Changing Poverty among American Children', *American Sociological Review* 56, p. 801.

Ekal Nari Shakti Sangthan.*The Mother Teresa Scheme: An Analysis of the Scheme and the Application Procedure*. Jagjit Nagar: ENSS, 2007.

Eveneet Singh v Prashant Chaudhri and Ors. MANU/DE/3497/2010.

Frantz, Carolyn J. and Hanoch Dagan. 'Properties of Marriage', *Columbia Law Review*104, p. 75 and p. 99.

Gaurav Nagpal v Sumedha Nagpal I (2008) DMC 166.

González, Libertad and Tarja K. Viitanen. 'The Effect of Divorce Laws on Divorce Rates in Europe', *Sheffield Economic Research Paper Series,* No. 2006003. Sheffield: Department of Economics, The University of Sheffield, March 2006.

Government of India. *Census of India 2001*. New Delhi: Ministry of Health and Family Welfare, 2001.

Government of India.Report: *A Handbook of Statistical Indicators on Indian Women*. New Delhi: Ministry of Women and Child Development, 2007.

Government of India. *Agenda Note: Performance Review Committee*, 12–13 May. New Delhi: Ministry of Rural Development, 2008.

Government of India. Report: *Gendering Human Development Indices—Recasting the Gender Development Index and Gender Empowerment Measure for India*, Part III, 47. New Delhi: Ministry of Women and Child Development, 2009.

Government of India. *Provisional Census of India 2011*. New Delhi: Ministry of Health and Family Welfare, 2011.

Hirway, Indira. *Estimating Work Force Using Time Use Statistics in India and Its Implications for Employment Policy*. Ahmedabad: Centre for Development Alternatives, 1999.

International Clinical Epidemiologists Network (INCLEN).*Domestic Violence in India 3: A Summary Report of a Multi-Site Household Survey*. Washington, DC: International Center for Research on Women and the Centre for Development and Population Activities, 2000.

International Institute for Population Sciences (IIPS) and Macro International. *Summary of Findings, National Family Health Survey (NFHS-3), 2005–06, India*. Mumbai: IIPS, 2007. Available at www.measuredhs.com/pubs/pdf/FRIND3/00FrontMatter00.pdf (last accessed on 16 November 2012).

———. *National Family Health Survey (NFHS-3), 2005-06, India*, Vol. 1. Mumbai: IIPS, 2007.

Jeffery, Patricia. 'A "Uniform Customary Code"? Marital Breakdown and Women's Economic Entitlements in Rural Bijnor', in Imtiaz Ahmed (ed.), *Divorce and Remarriage among Muslims in India*, p. 101. Delhi: Manohar Publications, 2003.

Joginder Singh v NCT of Delhi MANU/DE/2448/2010.

L' Heureux-Dube, Justice Claire. 'Economic Consequences of Divorce: A View from Canada', 31 *Houston Law Review* 451.

Mander, Harsh and Archana Rai. 'Living with Hunger' in V. Manikandan (ed.), *Chronic Food Deprivation among Aged People, Single Women and People with Disability: A Study of Rural Destitution and Hunger*, p. 13. Delhi: CES, 2008. Available at http://sccommissioners.org/Starvation/Articles/livingwithhunger.pdf (last accessed on 15 July 2010).

Mayne, John D. *Hindu Law and Usage*.New Delhi: Bharat Law House, 2006, 15th edition.

Komalam Amma v Kumara Pillai, Raghavan Pillai and Ors. AIR 2009 SC 636.

Lok Sabha. Report: *Joint Committee of the Houses to examine the Question of the Working of the Dowry Prohibition Act, 1961*., p. 24. New Delhi: Lok Sabha, 1982.

Mangat Mal (Dead) and Anr. v Smt. Punni Devi (Dead) and Ors. AIR 1996 SC 172.

Mukhopadhyay, Maitrayee.*Legally Dispossessed, Gender Identity and the Process of Law*. Calcutta: Stree, 1998.

Mulla. *Principles of Hindu Law*, Vol. 1. Nagpur: Butterworths India, 2001, 18th edition.

———. *Principles of Hindu Law*, Vol 2. Nagpur: Butterworths India, 2001, 18th edition.

N., Neetha and Rajni Palriwala. 'Unpaid Care Work: Analysis of the Indian Time Use Data', in Debbie Budlender (ed.), *Time Use Studies and Unpaid Care Work*, p. 92. London: Taylor and Francis, 2010.

National Commission on Children. *Beyond Rhetoric: A New American Agenda for Children and Families*. Washington, DC: National Commission on Children, 1992.

National Crime Records Bureau (NCRB). *Crime in India 2008*. New Delhi: Ministry of Home Affairs, 2010.

Nirmala and Ors. v Government of NCT of Delhi and Ors. MANU/DE/2717/2010.

Omprakash v Radhacharan 2009 (15) SCC 66.

Patnaik, Utsa. *Poverty and Neo-Liberalism in India*. New Delhi: Centre for Economic Studies and Planning, Jawaharlal Nehru University, 2006.

Planning Commission of India. 'Part II: Social Sector, Chapter 11: Women's Agency and Child Rights', *Eleventh Five Year Plan 2007–2012*. New Delhi: Planning Commission of India, 2010.

Pratibha Rani v Suraj Kumar AIR 1986 SC 628.

PUCL v UOI and Ors. Writ Petition (Civil) No. 196 of 2001.

Radhika v Vineet Rungta AIR 2004 Del 324.

Radhika Narang and Ors. v Karun Raj Narang and Anr. 159 (2009) DLT 158.

Raheja, Devinder. *Who Is Maintaining Whom: An Analysis of the Working of Maintenance Provisions under Section 125 of the Criminal Procedure Code, 1973*, Occasional Papers on Perspectives in Indian Development, No. XLIV (for private circulation only) New Delhi: Centre for Contemporary Studies, Nehru Memorial Museum and Library, September 1994.

Rishi Kumar v Suman I (2008) DMC 355.

Sagade, Jaya. *Law of Maintenance: An Empirical Study*. Mumbai: N.M. Tripathi Pvt. Ltd., 1996.

Saxena, N.C., Commissioner and Harsh Mander. Eighth Report of the Commissioners of the Supreme Court: *A Special Report on Most Vulnerable Social Groups and Their Access to Food, Commissioners of the Supreme Court*. New Delhi: Supreme Court of India, 2008, in *PUCL v UOI and Ors.* Writ Petition (Civil) No. 196 of 2001.

Shrinivasan, Rukmini. '55% of India's Population Poor: Report', TNN, 15 July 2010.

SOPPECOM. *Hindola, Assessing the Extent and Nature of Desertion in Daundtaluka and Ghole Road Ward of Pune City*. Pune: SOPPECOM, 2008.

Subramaniam, Indu and B.N. Usha. *State Services for Women in Crisis in Karnataka*. Bangalore: Hengasara Hakkina Sangha, 2010.

Swaminathan, Hema, Suchitra J.Y. and Rahul Lahoti. *KHAS: Measuring the Gender Asset Gap*. Bangalore: Indian Institute of Management, 2011.

S.R. Batra v Taruna Batra MANU/SC/0007/2007: 2007 (3) SCC 169.

Tahir Mahmood.*Civil Marriage Law; Perspectives and Prospects*. Bombay: N.M. Tripathi Private Ltd., 1978.

Tribune News Service. 'Single Women Being Denied Welfare Benefits', *TNS*, Shimla, 23 July 2010.

United Nations Development Programme (UNDP). Human Development Report 2009, *Overcoming barriers: Human Mobility and Development*. New York: UNDP, 2009.

Vatuk, Sylvia. 'Muslim Women in the Indian Family Courts: A Report from Chennai', in Imtiaz Ahmed (ed.), *Divorce and Remarriage among Muslims in India*, p. 137. Delhi: Manohar Publications, 2003.

V.D. Bhanot v Savita Bhanot (2007) 3 SCC 169.

Willigen, John Van, 'Social Ageing in India and America', *Seminar*, No. 488 (April 2000).

List of Weblinks

http://censusindia.gov.in
http://ncrb.nic.in
http://sccommissioners.org

http://timesofindia.indiatimes.com
http://hdr.undp.org
www.deccanherald.com
www.goasocialwelfare.com
www.india-seminar.com
www.kswdc.org
www.mospi.gov.in
www.networkideas.org
www.nfhsindia.org
www.pib.nic.in
www.righttofoodindia.org
www.shef.ac.uk
www.silverlinnings.com
www.unescap.org
www.wcd.nic.in

Index

About the Author

Kirti Singh is a noted lawyer working and practising on women's issues in Delhi. As a part-time member of the 18th Law Commission of India, she worked on the reports on laws related to child marriage and acid attacks.

She has recently drafted a bill on crimes and killings in the name of 'honour' on behalf of All India Democratic Women's Association (AIDWA), of which she is the legal convenor. This draft law has been adopted with some changes by the National Commission for Women (NCW). She is also working on other issues with NCW and is on their expert committee on laws. In the past she has worked on amendments to laws relating to sexual assault and sexual harassment in the Indian Penal Code, 1860 for AIDWA and NCW. She has also worked for reform in the laws related to 'maintenance' under Section 125, Code of Criminal Procedure. During the early 1980s, she was involved in suggesting reforms to laws related to dowry and rape.

Currently she is working on an extensive study of laws which promote son preference and discrimination against the daughter for the United Nations Population Fund (UNFPA).